Redemptions:
Contemporary Chassidic Essays on
the Parsha and the Festivals

לכבוד אלישע יניר יח׳

לברכה ולשמח אזכי׳ אלש

אודה ל׳ כל ה׳ חמ״ך.

ננ׳ גל׳ לקם

Redemptions:
Contemporary Chassidic Essays on the Parsha and the Festivals

Rabbi Zvi Leshem

Southern Hills Press

southern hills PRESS

Redemptions:
Contemporary Chassidic Essays
on the Parsha and the Festivals

This book may be ordered through booksellers or by contacting:

Southern Hills Press
POB 7074, Jerusalem, 91070, Israel
www.southernhillspress.com

ISBN: 1-933882-03-4

INTRODUCTION

ACKNOWLEDGEMENTS

Redemptions: Contemporary Chassidic Essays on the Parsha and the Festivals

INTRODUCTION

"A voice arouses consciousness, leading to the revelation of divine consciousness, which is the essence of redemption."

Rebbe Nachman of Breslov

The genre of Chassidic Biblical commentary that informs this work can be distinguished by two main characteristics. These are a nearly complete disinterest in *pshat*, the simple contextual meaning of the text, and an acute focus on practical lessons to help us in our *Avodat Hashem* in its broadest context. This includes fortifying our faith, love, and fear of God, as well as encouraging us to perform mitzvot with more passion and deeper intent. The *drashot* in this book represent an attempt to continue this tradition in a language that makes Chassidic ideas relevant to our times.

The Piaseczner Rebbe wrote some seventy years ago of the need to compose Chassidic books that speak in contemporary language and explain Chassidic concepts to the modern Jew. While the present work is hardly a systematic exposition of those concepts, it does attempt to guide the reader through that which is most familiar, the weekly Torah readings and the Holidays. Week after week, Yom Tov after Yom Tov, we are taught by the great Rebbes that the holy Torah, in addition to its simple and allegorical meanings, also points the way to its Author, Hashem. In the Chassidic view, articulated in the *Tanya*, *Torah Lishmah*, Torah for its own sake, refers to that study which leads to *deveikut*, cleaving to Hashem. The Baal Shem Tov teaches us that the primordial light of creation was hidden in the Torah itself. When we study with proper intent we are able to touch that light, internalize its secrets, and connect with the Divine. For a Jew there is no need to travel to India to seek spiritual meaning. Joyous prayer, mitzvot and Torah study hold all of the answers to our questions and provide the real framework for a vibrant life of spiritual depth and satisfaction.

There is a great thirst today for *Pnimiyut haTorah*, the inner dimension of the Torah. In Israel and elsewhere, thousands of Jews, especially young people, have turned to the study of Kabbalah and Chassidut and to ecstatic Chassidic prayer as an authentic avenue in serving the Creator. This spiritual avenue serves as the true alternative to the false and foreign "spiritualities" that unfortunately also compete for the hearts of those who seek deeper meaning in a superficial world all too focused upon materialism. It is also crucial for us to provide faithful renditions of these holy ideas as a viable alternative to the "pop-Kabbalah" that is unfortunately able to prey upon the thirsty souls of so many unsuspecting and sincerely seeking Jews.

Not every *drasha* in this book quotes Chassidic or Kabalistic sources. Many are based upon traditional Midrash and medieval exegesis. Often I have based myself upon the words of non-Chassidic commentators as well. Yet in all cases it is the Chassidic worldview, stressing joy, intense emotions, powerful prayer, deep intention, and communal service in *Avodat Hashem* that informs my understanding. This is apparent in both the *drashot* for Shabbat and for the Holidays (some of which overlap, just as they do in traditional Chassidic commentary). Chassidic Torah is also personally redemptive in a profound and powerful way, hence the title of this volume. I pray that all of my words find favor in the eyes of God and of my readers, and will inspire those readers to greater service of Hashem.

Most of these *drashot* were written during difficult times in the 1990s and early 2000s. In the background were the second Intifada, with unprecedented terrorism in Israel, and the disengagement from Gaza and the Northern Shomron, which left thousands of our brethren homeless as parts of our Holy Land were given to terrorists. Throughout this period Israel also suffered from disunity and poverty. On the world scene 9/11 occurred, as well as horrific natural disasters, such as the tsunami. Disease, racism, genocidal wars, and anti-Semitism continued to plague humanity. Thus the discerning reader will detect echoes of all of the above in this work. Yet despite everything, Chassidut remains a dramatically optimistic worldview. We may not understand what is happening around us, but we know that ultimately all is in Hashem's hands, and that in the last analysis the world is heading for the Final Redemption. We are reminded of Rebbe Nachman's dramatic proclamation, "There is no despair in the world at all."

ACKNOWLEDGEMENTS

This book is the result of years of learning, teaching, giving *drashot*, and writing. In a sense it reflects the influence of all I have had contact with and who have influenced my Torah outlook, learning, and teaching. As *Chazal* teach us, we learn from our teachers, even more from our colleagues, and most of all from our students. All of you deserve to receive honor as my *rebbe* in some sense. While it is impossible to name everyone, nonetheless I must mention certain individuals to whom I owe special thanks. I pray that Hashem will bless them all with only goodness in the spiritual and physical realms.

To the *Ribbono Shel Olam*, for everything. The Piaseczner Rebbe writes that whenever we learn Torah it is actually Hashem who is teaching us. I know that all of my Torah has been a gift from You, a *chessed* that I don't deserve. So many times You even let me know that it was a gift, with moments of inspiration and clarity that certainly were beyond the vessels that I was capable of creating on my own. I feel so inadequate to express my thanksgiving. May the fact that I try my best to spread Your holy Torah throughout the world be the thanks that I can put into print. May I be *zocheh* to continue to sit in the Tents of Torah, to study, teach, and write. Rav Hutner writes that the Land of Israel is the greatest teacher of all. Thank You Hashem for the unbelievable merit of spending most of my years surrounded by the intense holiness of *Eretz Yisrael*, where no doubt, if I have merited any wisdom, it is because of the holy air of *Eretz Yisrael* that makes one wise. I pray that my Torah be worthy of the name *Torat Eretz Yisrael*. I pray to Hashem to protect the Land and her inhabitants from all harm.

To the holy Rebbes who have taught me all I know, even though I know you only through your printed words. I love all of you, but for the sake of brevity will mention only the holy Baal Shem Tov, *zt"l*, the holy Rebbe Nachman of Breslov, *zt"l*, the holy Rebbe Mordechai Yosef of Ishbitz, *zt"l*, and the holy Rebbe Kalonymos Kalmish of Piaseczna, *zt"l*, *Hy"d*. Lastly, although not a Chassidic Rebbe, I would also like to include the holy Rav Avraham Yitzchak Hakohen Kook, *zt"l*.

iv

ACKNOWLEDGEMENTS

To my congregants at Shirat Shlomo Congregation in Efrat, I give special thanks. Many of these *drashot* were originally given at the shul. You are a very special congregation and it is my great honor to serve in such a remarkable community that truly strives to fulfill the Chassidic ideal of communal service of the Divine. Special thanks to the members of the board and to Doug Goldstein for your support in general and for this project in particular. Thanks to Rav Shlomo Riskin, Chief Rabbi of Efrat, for your ongoing encouragement and advice. Much thanks to my editor, Naomi Grossman, for the difficult task of transforming what was essentially Oral Torah (in written form) into Written Torah, and to Stuart Schnee, the project coordinator.

Much of the Torah in these pages was developed during the many years that I have been *zocheh* to teach Torah to the outstanding students of Nishmat, the Jerusalem Center for Higher Torah Study for Women. At Nishmat I have served as both associate dean and director of the Alisa Flatow Overseas Program, and grown immeasurably from the experience. At this unique institution of Torah study I am challenged daily to delve deeper and deeper into the Torah that I study and teach. I wish to thank Dean Rabbanit Chana Henkin and *Posek* Rav Yehuda Herzl Henkin for creating and maintaining a very special school, where neither sincere spiritual striving nor intellectual excellence are ever compromised. To all of my fellow faculty members, my deepest thanks for the thousands of learned interactions that have helped to make me who I am. To my students throughout the years, you are truly my spiritual daughters, and have enriched my life in a way that I don't think you will ever be able to comprehend.

To my teachers and *chevrutot*, I owe more than I can possibly express. I would be nothing were it not for the Torah you taught me and studied with me. Although I cannot begin to mention everyone, I must give very special thanks to my *Rebbeim*, Rav Mendel Blachman, Rav Shlomo Carlebach, *z"l*, Rav Professor David Weiss Halivni, Rav Yaakov Moshe Poupko, Rav Shabbtai Rappaport, Rav Yehoshua Reich and Rav Shagar. Thanks as well to my *chevrutot* Rav Chaim Kornberg and Rav Natan Siegel, and to my colleague, Mrs. Biti Roi, for all the time that we have spent analyzing Chassidic works together. Lastly, to my teachers at the university, Professor Moshe Halamish, Professor Moshe Idel, Professor Yehuda Leibes, and Professor Shalom Rosenberg, for giving me the tools to see Chassidut in its broader context within the entire realm of Jewish thought throughout the ages.

I wish to thank my parents, Michael and Sylvia Blain, for raising me with your intense dedication to the Jewish People, Jewish education, Jewish values and *chessed.* Thanks for your dedication to the State of Israel and to the rights of all downtrodden and suffering people in the world. Thanks to my brothers David and Daniel and their families for many years of special friendship and support. Thanks to my in-laws Professor Alan and Dr. Rita Kropf for the years in which you helped to support my learning, and much more.

To my relatives, the Blobstein and Mermelstein families of Brooklyn, New York, who introduced me to my Chassidic heritage. To my sons, Eliyahu Yosef (and Hadar), Zion Yitzchak (and Rivka and Chemda Rachel), and Maayan Zeev. To my daughters, Leora Simcha Chaya, Kinneret Bracha, and Shoshana Sophie (Shoshi). When you were little you would ask me, "Abba, when are you going to write a book?" As you grew up your questions got a lot harder, and you challenged and continue to challenge me and help me to grow. May you all continue to grow and develop and be blessed from Heaven with all good things.

I dedicate this book to my most special friend and helpmate, Julie (Yocheved), my wife and companion of almost thirty years. Words cannot possibly express the debt of gratitude that I owe you. You have always made raising our children with absolute love and devotion your top priority, and the results of your *mesirut nefesh* are evident in every one of them. Your beautiful art is a real fulfillment of *hiddur mitzvah* for people throughout the world. Your endless encouragement of me in my learning and your self-sacrifice in this regard are the true reason that this book, and so much more, really belong to you. This book, like all of my work, benefits greatly from your encouragement, constructive criticism, and uncompromisingly high standards. (See the *Mai Hashiloach* on the phrase *Ezer Kenegdo*). May Hashem grant us to see all of our children and grandchildren engaged in the study of Torah and the joyous performance of mitzvot here in *Eretz Yisrael*.

Zvi Anshil Halevi Leshem
17th Iyar 5766, Erev Lag Baomer, the Festival of *Penimiyut haTorah*,
May 15, 2006
Efrat, Gush Etzion, Israel

THE WEEKLY TORAH
PORTION

PARSHAT BEREISHIT

The Book of the Straight

When we begin a new year, we focus on the theme of renewal, and we look for new ways to serve our Creator. To help us realize this objective, we need to study basic morals and ethics. As the Ramchal writes in the introduction to *Mesilat Yesharim*, it is always necessary to review basic moral truths for, paradoxically, due to their obviousness we have a tendency to forget them.

The festival of Sukkot celebrates the topic of unity, as expressed through the *arba minim*, the four species, which represent every type of Jew, as well as through the sukkah itself. But where do we find this idea in the book of *Bereishit*, which we begin to read on Simchat Torah?

The Ramban writes that the patriarchal narratives provide us with the essence of our faith. The *Netivot Shalom* is more specific when he refers to *Bereishit* as *Sefer Hamiddot*, "The Book of Character Traits," because *Bereishit* teaches us that before we can keep the mitzvot properly, we need to refine our personality traits. The Netziv reinforces this theme when he writes in his introduction to *Haemek Davar* on *Bereishit* that *Sefer Bereishit* is also referred to as *Sefer Hayeshar*, "the Book of the Straight," because our Forefathers were ethically *yesharim*, meaning "straight," or honest people. This was expressed in their concern for others and for the general good of society, even in relation to their idolatrous Canaanite neighbors.

The Netziv contrasts this approach with the situation of the Jews at the time of the Second Temple, which was ultimately destroyed due to causeless hatred. He defines this as a situation of factionalism in which each group delegitimized the religious approach of the other groups, insisting that only they had the correct path to Hashem. This ultimately led to hatred, bloodshed, and the destruction of our holiest site. In the words of the Netziv, "God can't stand that kind of Tzaddikim!"

In *Sefer Bereishit*, we also learn the principle of *Maaseh Avot Siman L'Banim*, that the deeds of the Patriarchs are a lesson for the children. By looking at the actions of our Forefathers, as described in *Bereishit*, we are given a perfect example of unity. By respecting diversity while remaining faithful to our principles, we can only increase in unity as a nation. But we must first strengthen the unity within our own communities, after which we can focus our energies on wider circles of people. In this way, we will hopefully be granted the wisdom to successfully fulfill our own needs and principles while remaining as one with our fellow Jews.

PARSHAT BEREISHIT

Creation and the Nature of Love

The story of Adam and Eve in the Garden of Eden is more than a story of two individuals and their adventures at the beginning of human history. It is the *foundational narrative* of humanity. When we study the creation of the first man and woman, their relationships with Hashem and with each other, their temptations, failures, and punishment, we are really learning about ourselves.

In chapter two of *Bereishit*, Rashi quotes the *aggada* that Adam and Eve were originally created like Siamese twins, with two heads, but attached to each other at the back. The Ramban points out that this hermaphroditic being was capable of reproduction. Therefore, if the real purpose of humanity were to populate the world, this being was fully functional in its original state. So why did man and woman have to be divided?

In the Torah, Hashem states that "it is not good for man to be alone," and He decides that man needs an *ezer kenegdo*, literally, "a helper opposite him." He therefore separates Adam into two beings, man and woman, who now face each other. This is the opposite of their previous situation, in which they were connected at the back and faced away from each other. In the Ramban's words, "Hashem saw that it was good that the helper would stand across from him, so that he would see her, separate from her, and reconnect with her according to his will." (Here we should note that in this reading of *Chazal* on the creation of man, there is complete equality between man and woman. They are each created from equal halves of the same original being, and are equally meant to be helpers to each other.) Man and woman are therefore called *ish v'isha*, for they are taken from each other, and are in fact of the same "flesh and bone." In response to this new situation, we are told that people should leave their parents and cling to their spouses to be as "one flesh." Rashi explains that the expression "one flesh" refers to the child that they will bear, whereas Ramban interprets it as the loyalty that a married couple should have to their monogamous relationship.

Let us look more closely at the relationship between man and woman before and after this separation. It would seem that previously, Adam and Eve lived an ideal life, being constantly together, with no possibility of parting. And yet, surprisingly, in relation to this Hashem declares man to be in the evil state of existential loneliness. This is for several reasons: Firstly, the very fact that Adam and Eve were forced to be constantly together rendered their relationship largely meaningless. As the Baal Shem Tov taught, such a relationship would eventually cease to bring joy and pleasure to either side, because "constant pleasure ceases to be pleasurable."

Moreover, the relationship must have been severely inhibited because Adam and Eve could not gaze into each other's faces, the part of the body (*panim*) that expresses one's inner soulful dimension, (*penimiyut*). Paradoxically, as the Ramban writes, it is the ability to leave, and consequently the constant need to renew the bonds of love and commitment that makes the marriage relationship significant. And it is the yearning to reunite after periods of absence and longing (such as we re-enact through the laws of *taharat hamishpacha*, family purity) that makes pleasure powerful and significant. Lastly, it is the ability to gaze into the face of our beloved (the main purpose of the separation, according to *Meshech Chochma*) that takes our relationships beyond the physical, enabling human beings to achieve powerful and lasting relationships beyond those of the animals.

The Ramchal speaks of the separation of man and woman as an allegory for all of creation, for once there was only an endless sea of divinity until we were separated from Hashem and created in this world. Here, we also experience the pain of alienation and loneliness, and we long to reconnect with holiness after periods of perceived *hester panim*, the hiding of the Divine Face. Yet only here, in this world, can we build a relationship that is chosen and meaningful, thus bringing pleasure to Hashem and to ourselves.

At the beginning of a new year we stand again at the threshold of creation. It is a time to reestablish and renew our relationships with Hashem and with those closest to us. In this way, we will feel the light of real love in our lives.

PARSHAT NOACH

My Needs vs. Society's Needs

Parshat Noach describes two great calamities that befell the ancient world - the Flood and the Dispersion of the nations after the destruction of the Tower of Babel. God's reactions to the evil caused by both of these generations radically altered the nature of human existence. The world of Noach was built upon the destruction of the Flood, and that of Avraham upon the destruction caused by the Dispersion.

Numerous explanations have been given to define the evil of these two generations. Before the Flood, the world was in a state of anarchy, caused by extreme violence and theft combined with a total breakdown of sexual morality. In the generation of the Tower of Babel Rabbi Shimshon Rafael Hirsch sees the danger of a totalitarian regime, completely crushing individual rights for the needs of the collective. His frightening description is reminiscent of modern works such as Orwell's *1984*. In the words of Levinas, "'We' is not the plural of 'I.'"

The issue of the balance between societal and individual needs is a major topic in public discourse in Israel today. People feel the need for "self-fulfillment," but if this becomes all-pervasive there is a danger both of weakening the collective, and disregarding the needs of others. On the other hand, when one feels no room to express his sense of "self" he can reach a state of alienation from society, feeling lost and lonely.

There is a clear need to find the right balance. We must be careful not to become extreme regarding individual rights (as seen during the generation of the Flood), nor regarding the strength of the central authority (as happened during the generation of the Dispersion). These words are not only true on the national level, but also on the community level. According to the Piaseczner Rebbe, the community exists to help individuals maximize their spiritual potential. On the other hand, without dedication to the welfare of the community, there is also no chance for true personal growth.

Striking the right balance between providing for our own individual needs and our commitment to our community is one of the challenges of our age. However, by finding it, our community and each of us as individuals will only continue to grow.

PARSHAT NOACH

Warming Ourselves by the Light of the Torah

When God commands Noach to build the Ark (*taiva*), He tells him to "make a *tzohar* for the Ark." Rashi defines a *tzohar* as either a window or a luminous stone. Either way, it provides light for the Ark. According to the *Torah Temimah*, the main difference between both types of light is whether or not those inside can see the destruction of those outside.

The word *taiva* (translated here as "Ark") also means "word" in Hebrew, and there is a well-known Chassidic saying from the Maggid of Mezeritch, quoting the Baal Shem Tov, that one's *words* of Torah and prayer should shine. In the next generation, the *Noam Elimelech* expanded on this idea with another play on words. Through the words of Torah that we learn, we transform suffering into light *(tzara letzohar)*. Similarly, the *Sfat Emet* states that through our words of Torah and prayer we are saved from all our troubles.

In the Chassidic view, holy words are much more than mere symbols for linguistic communication. As the building blocks of creation, the Hebrew letters (and the words built from them) contain much divine light. By reciting them with the proper intent and the exact pronunciation, we are able to enter them and connect with that light. At the higher meditative levels practiced by holy Rebbes such as the Baal Shem Tov, this technique could be used to achieve "soul ascents" to the Heavens, and to reach a level close to prophecy, meaning the ability to tell the future or to be aware of events occurring in a different location. For us simple people, the words of prayer and Torah provide a spiritual refuge from the storm waters of the insane reality of the world around us, much in the same way that the Ark afforded refuge to Noach and his entourage from the Flood.

The *Zohar* states that the story of Noach alludes to the concept of rest (*menucha*), and hence of Shabbat. Rav Leibele Eiger points out that we always read *Parshat Noach* in the month of

Cheshvan, known as *Marcheshvan*, meaning, "Bitter Cheshvan." The bitterness of this month stems from the letdown we feel after all of the holidays of Tishrei are finally behind us. Nonetheless, Noach teaches us that in the same way that he was protected in the Ark, we can also be enveloped in a peaceful and restful Torah atmosphere. As the winter approaches at this time of the year, we all want to stay inside and be protected from the elements. This is also a time when we request rain. By enveloping ourselves in the warmth and light of the Torah, we can protect ourselves from harmful outside influences so that we can benefit from "the rains of blessing."

PARSHAT NOACH

Ridding the World of Anger

As the floodwaters subside, Noach (whom Rav Shimshon Rafael Hirsch describes as the "Second Adam") sends two very different birds out from the Ark - the raven and the dove. While a superficial reading may give the impression that both birds share the same mission, a closer look clearly reveals that this is actually not the case. The Torah tells us that forty days after the Ark comes to rest, Noach "opened the window he had made and sent forth the raven, which flew back and forth until the water dried up on the earth." There is no mention of any specific mission, nor does there appear to be any subsequent contact between Noach and the bird. This stands in stark contrast to the subsequent verses in which Noach "sent the dove *from himself* to see if the waters had dried." Since they hadn't, he "took her and brought her *to himself* in the Ark." Seven days later, Noach repeats the process, and this time the dove "returned in the evening with an olive branch grasped in her mouth, and Noach knew that the waters had subsided from the earth." Seven days later he again sends forth the dove, and this time she does not return.

This sets the stage for God's instruction to Noach to leave the Ark. Noach sent the raven forth after a forty-day period, whereas the dove was sent out three times, at intervals of seven days each. Whereas he simply *sent* the raven, he sends the dove *from himself*, later bringing her back *to himself*. Clearly Noach feels a bond with the dove, and besides entrusting her with this crucial mission is also concerned for her well-being and comfort. As our Sages state, "pure birds dwell with the righteous" (*Sanhedrin* 108b). The most obvious difference, however, is the mission itself. The dove is sent to "test the waters," but why does Noach send out the raven?

Rabbinic tradition deals harshly with the raven. He was one of three creatures who ignored the ban on sexual relations in the ark, and upon being sent away accused Noach of wishing to

19

destroy the species of ravens or even of desiring "Mrs. Raven" for himself! (*Sanhedrin* 108b). According to *Bereishit Rabbah* 33, Noach's rejoinder is that the raven is an animal that is "useless both for food and as a sacrifice." Of course the same could be said of any non-kosher beast, and Noach is informed that in the future the raven would be needed to bring food to Eliyahu the Prophet, hiding in the desert.

Who, then, is this mysterious raven? Unlike the white dove, the symbol of peace, who comes bearing olives from which oil is produced to illuminate the world, the black raven strikes fear into our hearts and perhaps into that of Noach as well. Similar to Edgar Allan Poe's terrifying raven, this one also refuses to leave, and hovers constantly nearby as a harbinger of seeming doom. The *Mai Hashiloach* tells us that "the raven hints at anger, and Noach desired that no anger be found in the world." This makes sense, since the fate of the generation of the Flood was sealed by their theft and violence toward each other. However, God showed Noach that anger is still sometimes needed in the world to counterbalance evil sensual desires.

This is related to the notion that the character traits of love (*chessed*) and power (*gevurah*) are often in danger of being dangerously distorted by their extremes, and need each other for balance. The generation of the Flood was also guilty of severe sexual immorality, and by totally removing the possibility of anger, this dangerous imbalance could return to the world. It is therefore fitting that Eliyahu, the angel of the covenant (also identified with Pinchas), would later be served by a raven when he dried up the world from rain. Someday, says the *Mai Hashiloach*, immorality (as symbolized by the floodwaters) will disappear from the world, and then anger will no longer need to exist, but we are not there yet.

Noach wanted to send anger away because he realized the propitious nature of the moment. The world had been purified by forty days of rain, signifying the 40 *saeh* of water in a mikvah [ritual bath] (*Torah Ohr*). Noach had just endured another forty days of waiting for the waters to recede, equal to the forty days of the formulation of the embryo (*Kli Yakar*). Later, after further purification, represented by a seven-day cycle, such as that which precedes the immersion in a mikvah, Noach would send the dove on her holy mission. But first the world had to be rid of its anger. The *Sod Yesharim* writes that the Ark is the womb, and the emergence of Noach and his family is nothing less than the rebirth of humanity. Noach longs for a world of only love, and tries desperately to dispose of all anger, but he is simply ahead of his time.

By learning to properly balance our love and power, we will soon merit to live in a world of pure love, where anger is no longer necessary.

PARSHAT LECH LECHA

Go... To Yourself

Although Avraham is already journeying toward the Holy Land at the end of the previous parsha, *Parshat Lech Lecha* opens with the enigmatic divine imperative, *Lech Lecha*, "Go to yourself." Early commentators, such as Rashi, discuss the seeming redundancy of this phrase, while the triple expression "from your land, your birthplace, and your father's home" also merits much attention. The martyred Rav Hillel Zeitlin writes in *Sifran shel Yichidim* (Warsaw, 1928) that God's call to Avraham is the eternal spiritual calling of each and every one of us: "God's voice calls to every person in every place and at every time, 'please leave human being, please leave... patriotism... your nationalistic feelings... and the special customs and opinions of your family... to the source of your higher soul.'"

The *Mai Hashiloach* gives three complementary explanations of the phrase *Lech Lecha*. His first explanation deals with the second word, *lecha*, which means "for" or "to yourself." Like many of us, Avraham was seeking meaning in the world. (This idea is all too familiar to us today as a theme that has become central to modern and post-modern literature depicting the alienation of the individual from society.) When Avraham finally reaches the stage where life seems meaningless, God intervenes and informs him that the most one can expect from worldly pleasures is to temporarily escape the existential pain of loneliness and alienation. Significant and positive life, however, can only be found deep within one's own soul by connecting with one's innate Godliness.

The *Mai Hashiloach* then elucidates the famous *Midrash* in which Avraham discovered God after seeing a burning building and realizing that someone must be in charge of it. The *Midrash* states that the Master of the Building glared at him. The *Mai Hashiloach* interprets this to mean that Avraham studied ancient history as a young man and learned of the cataclysmic events of history, the Flood and the Dispersion. God now tells him to leave this Gentile view of reality behind and to enter a Jewish "head space," where God is perceived in every moment in time and in every aspect of nature, and not only when there are dramatic supernatural miracles.

Thirdly, Avraham is told that he must abandon his habits and be willing to break new ground as a religious revolutionary. As long as one remains complacent and self-satisfied there is little chance of true religious growth.

So too, all of us who seek to grow in our divine service need to work on these three areas: inner contemplation, an authentic Jewish perspective on reality, and the ability to leave habit behind and move forward. The actualization of this process will ultimately take place in *Haaretz asher areka*, "the Land that I will show you." In the *Mai Hashiloach*'s reading this is the land where God constantly reveals more and more of Himself, and needless to say, that is only in *Eretz Yisrael*.

PARSHAT LECH LECHA

Times of Solitude and Community

In *Parshat Lech Lecha*, the personality of the multi-faceted Avraham Avinu, father of the Jewish People, really begins to develop. A true revolutionary, Avraham risks his life to rebel against the pagan society in which he was raised. In a world where monotheism had been forgotten for many generations, and only a few individuals were able to serve God underground, Avraham bursts upon the scene, physically and figuratively smashing idols, debating the religious-political establishment and, like the first great Rebbe, gathers a cadre of dedicated Chassidim. They, he, and his devoted Rebbetzin Sara, are willing to live on the edge of society in order to dedicate their lives to truth. We are reminded of the spiritual society described in Rebbe Nachman's story, "The Master of Prayer."

Avraham undergoes numerous trials, among them the abandonment of his ancestral homeland on a long trek to an unknown land, *Aretz asher areka*, "the land that I will show you," or, according to the *Mai Hashiloach*, "the land where I (Hashem) will reveal Myself to you." The command to go to this land begins with the words *lech lecha*, "you go." Rashi explains that this apparently redundant expression means, "for your good and benefit - there you will become a great nation; here you will not merit children." The Ramban responds that as this sentence is grammatically correct, there is no need for Rashi's explanation.

The Netziv compares the phrase *lech lecha* used at the beginning of the parsha with its appearance later on in the *Akeidah*, the commandment to sacrifice Yitzchak, which is described in *Parshat Vayera*. There, as well, Avraham is commanded *lech lecha*, to go and sacrifice Yitzchak. According to the Netziv, each *lech lecha* represents a different facet of the religious path. Sometimes, as here, when Avraham travels with his wife and their Chassidim, the companionship of the fellow traveler creates an experience of happiness and satisfaction. On the other hand, the religious path can sometimes be one of existential loneliness and alienation, as in Avraham's solitary path to the *Akeidah*.

This aspect of the religious experience is encapsulated in the title of Rav Soloveitchik's classic essay, *The Lonely Man of Faith*. Chassidism, on the other hand, places great emphasis upon community. In modern times, the martyred Piaseczner Rebbe revived the concept of the *chevriya kaddisha*, the holy society, for group spiritual fraternity and service. In his view, one can reach spiritual achievements more easily as part of a group of like-minded individuals dedicated to the same goals. With constant striving and true endeavor, we can hopefully strike the correct balance between the communal and personal in our divine service, helping us to achieve our true goals in life.

PARSHAT VAYERA

The Service of God and the Divine Will

This parsha opens with Hashem's visit to Avraham, who is recuperating from his circumcision. Avraham, the ultimate servant of Hashem, kept all the mitzvot before they were even given. In the words of the Sages, "his two kidneys were like two Rabbis," and he intuitively connected with the Divine will. Rav Kook writes in *Shabbat Haaretz* that in spite of the famous rabbinic view that "greater is the commanded who performs than the non-commanded who performs," Avraham represents the highest level of service born of love, with no ulterior motive whatsoever. It is therefore surprising to find that Avraham does not perform his brit milah until he is explicitly commanded to do so by God.

The *Meor Aynaim* and *Avodat Yisrael* both write that milah is such a crucial mitzvah that Avraham preferred to perform it as one commanded. They do not, however, explain why circumcision was singled out as the exception to Avraham's usual approach. The *Mai Hashiloach* explains that while all mitzvot come to perfect creation; only in the case of milah do we actually make a physical change to the human body. This very point later became the basis of a famous debate between the Rabbis and Hellenism. Avraham, the humble Jew, asked himself, "Who am I to mess with creation? If God created me a certain way, how can I be so presumptuous as to make changes?" He thus waited for the command before submitting to milah.

Later, God appears to Avraham in the land of his friend Mamre, who, according to Rashi, was the one friend who urged Avraham to perform the brit, while the others were opposed. The *Sfat Emet* explains that they were opposed since they understood that Hashem was choosing Avraham and they were being excluded. Mamre realized, however, that ultimately service is defined by the Divine will, and not by human preferences. He was willing to accept Avraham's chosenness, in spite of his own disappointment. God then revealed Himself in Mamre's land, (and according to Reb Simcha Bunim of Pshischah, to Mamre himself), and he who was willing to be far was brought close. The message is a powerful one for our generation, which stresses personal autonomy and spiritual fulfillment. Authentic spirituality is predicated upon the meticulous fulfillment of God's will, as revealed through the Torah and Halachah. Deviating from this may reflect ego and self-service instead of divine service. May we all learn to sublimate our own desires to those of Hashem. This *bittul*, self-annulment, is the key to a close relationship with Hashem.

PARSHAT VAYERA

The Ultimate Sanctification of the Divine Name

The ultimate culmination of Avraham's career is very definitely the *Akeidah*, the binding of Yitzchak, which is described at the end of *Parshat Vayera*. Almost no other topic has received so much attention in the Midrash, medieval commentaries, or modern religious philosophy. By examining certain trends in Chassidic commentary, we learn some very practical lessons in faith and divine service from this key episode in the Torah narrative.

The Baal Shem Tov taught us that *a person is tested in a state of unclear consciousness*. In the description of the *Akeidah* God is referred to as *Elokim*, which alludes to God's more hidden aspects, since Avraham was in a state of constricted consciousness. One of the most difficult features of the *Akeidah* for Avraham was its doubtful nature since it took place in constricted consciousness. When things in our lives are clear and we understand what we need to do, we have already passed much of the test. The biggest problem is that we often go through life wondering what exactly it is that God expects from us in various situations.

As with many topics in Chassidut, the words of the Baal Shem Tov set the tone for much of the subsequent literature. The *Mai Hashiloach* therefore writes that we can understand why the *Akeidah* was more of a test for Avraham than it was for Yitzchak. Avraham received an unclear command from *Elokim*, (rather than from Hashem, God's more revealed aspect). This command is further confused by its ambiguous language, such as *na* (meaning "please") and "raise him" (rather than "sacrifice him"). And with this information Avraham has to decide whether he should seemingly violate the severe prohibition of bloodshed, killing his beloved son, thus contradicting an earlier divine edict that his progeny would be descended from Yitzchak. In so doing, points out the *Sfat Emet*, Avraham is effectively committing genocide, wiping out the entire Jewish People from the very start. For Yitzchak, on the other hand, the test is not as great, for he heard an explicitly clear statement from Avraham.

The culmination of the test therefore arrives, according to the *Kedushat Levi*, when the angel commands Avraham not to slaughter Yitzchak, for at that moment it is revealed that Avraham was willing to follow God's dictate to fulfill what was, after all, a meaningless commandment. Since God never intended for Avraham to slaughter Yitzchak, Avraham was in effect unconsciously acting in a type of "theater of the absurd," without really understanding what was actually taking place

The *Sfat Emet* explains why Avraham saw Mount Moriah "from a distance." Avraham served God through love and normally felt complete internal identification with the commandments. Here, he feels existential alienation and distance from the command since the command itself did not actually reflect God's authentic will. Avraham intuitively connects with the dissonance between what God told him and what in God in fact desired, and walks towards Mt. Moriah as he is tossed back and forth between these two poles of consciousness.

After the *Akeidah*, Avraham is referred to as *yerei Elokim*, "the one who fears God." This test was especially difficult for Avraham, whose essential character trait was *chessed*, kindness and love, for this act completely negated his essential self. This was not the case for Yitzchak, whose service is defined by *gevurah*, fear of God combined with self-discipline. For Yitzchak, self-sacrifice is a natural component of serving Hashem. The *Akeidah* combines the two, adding the concept of *gevurah* to Avraham's repertoire while softening and sweetening the *gevurah* of Yitzchak, who is now bound by the *chessed* of Avraham.

Another fascinating insight is found in the *Maor V'shemesh* (in the name of the Ari) and in the *Imrei Elimelech*. Yitzchak is identified with *gevurah*, a feminine attribute, and is therefore not ready to marry and have children. Only after the *Akeidah*, when his *gevurah* is balanced by the masculine *chessed*, is he ready, and we are informed of the birth of his soulmate Rivka. Now he is able to marry her and give birth to Yaakov, representing the perfectly balanced concept of *tiferet*, beauty and truth.

In the *Aish Kodesh*, written in the Warsaw Ghetto, the Piaseczner Rebbe grapples with the question of martyrdom in the Holocaust in relation to the classic model of medieval times. Then, the Jews were given the choice to convert or be killed. In choosing death the Jew made a conscious religious decision to die as a martyr rather than betray his faith. During the *Shoah*, the situation was entirely different. All Jews were to be killed regardless of their religious convictions. There was no way to save one's life through conversion. What is the status of *Kiddush Hashem*, the sanctification of God's Name, when it occurs without a conscious religious decision? The Rebbe's answer is powerful and shocking. At the *Akeidah* there was self-sacrifice in thought only, as the act was ultimately prevented. During the Holocaust, on the other hand, self-sacrifice occurs in deed only, lacking forethought. Thus the death of the Jews in the Holocaust serves to complete the process begun at the *Akeidah*, and together these serve as a "complete sacrifice."

One could say the same regarding the martyrs of the last few years, who have perished in so many terror attacks. When people are (God forbid) killed in a sudden explosion they die as martyrs without having made a prior conscious decision. Nonetheless their souls ascend to Heaven as a perfect sacrifice with the intentions of Avraham and Yitzchak from the *Akeidah*.

Through our prayers and divine service, we hope that we will merit clarity in our service of Hashem, and that we may achieve the proper balance between *chessed* and *gevurah*. It is our hope that we will sanctify God's name through lives of Torah, prayer, and mitzvot, rather than through death or suffering.

PARSHAT VAYERA

Self-Sacrifice and Reaching out to Others

Parshat Vayera follows the spiritual development and activities of our ancestors Avraham and Sara. It begins with the visit of the angels to Avraham's tent. Here, the Midrash develops the theme of Avraham's love for the mitzvah of hospitality and his dedication to reaching out to others. As for Sara, she spends this time in her tent, becoming an early model for the innate modesty of the Jewish woman. Nonetheless, her modesty does not limit her public role for, as the Midrash tells us, "Just as Avraham converts the men, Sara converts the women." The Kozhnitzer Maggid writes in *Avodat Yisrael*, "It is the way of the tzaddik to bring the entire world close to Hashem, and it is certainly the way of Avraham." This is true, says the Maggid, despite the spiritual dangers inherent within close contact with the common people, a theme widespread in Chassidic literature dealing with the relationship between a Rebbe and his flock. The Rebbe must constantly involve himself with the people, even at the risk of "falling" from his own spiritual heights.

At the end of the parsha, Avraham undergoes the ultimate test - *Akeidat Yitzchak*, "the binding of Yitzchak." Here, Sara disappears entirely from the Torah narrative. *Chazal* and the commentators keenly feel her absence, and reintroduce her to the story in various ways. Even non-Jewish commentators such as Soren Kierkegaard in *Fear and Trembling* viewed the question of Sara's involvement in the decision regarding the *Akeidah* as a central moral issue.

According to the *midrash* quoted by Rashi, Sara died when the Satan told her about Yitzchak being bound upon the altar. The Piaseczner Rebbe in *Aish Kodesh* takes this a step further. He states that Sara died in order to demonstrate to Hashem that *Am Yisrael* is not capable of withstanding all suffering. Sometimes the suffering is just too much, and there is a limit to what we can be expected to endure. In his view, Sara died out of *mesirut nefesh* for *Am Yisrael.*

An outstanding example of these qualities was the late Rav Shlomo Carlebach, who passed away in the week of *Parshat Vayera.* He reached out to a great many people, drawing them closer to Yiddishkeit, and displayed great *mesirut nefesh* for *Am Yisrael.* His positive influence continues to guide so many people in their *Avodat Hashem.* These qualities of *kiruv* and *mesirut nefesh* should only continue to inspire all of us in our daily lives.

PARSHAT CHAYEI SARA

The Joy of Youth

In *Parshat Chayei Sara*, we bid farewell to our great and pious mother, Sara, who dies at the age of 127. Rav Yosef Bechor Shor (one of the Tosafists) writes, "It is not the way of the Torah to record the ages of women ... their years were not mentioned except for Sara, the most important of them all."

Rashi, relating to the seemingly extraneous language of the verse, informs us, "Each set of years is written separately to tell us that each can be understood separately. At the age of one hundred she was as free from sin as at the age of twenty, and at the age of twenty she was as beautiful as at the age of seven." Sara therefore manages to maintain youthful vitality all of her life.

Rav Kook, in *Maamarei Haraiya*, learns an amazing principle from Rashi's commentary, and his words have tremendous significance regarding the way in which we educate our children. We find two main attitudes toward childhood in the world: the "Western," and the "Torani." According to the modern Western approach, childhood has no inherent significance. The only purpose of this time period is to prepare the child to become an adult, i.e. a "productive" member of capitalistic society, capable of producing wealth. This approach, which has dominated the world since the Industrial Revolution, pushes for a shortened childhood, with all effort going into rushing the child onto the production line as quickly as possible.

The Torah perspective is diametrically opposed to the above approach. Human beings have a much longer childhood than animals do for a very good reason. There is so much to learn before we are ready to function as independent adults. But that is not all. Childhood has a crucial, independent status. We find that children have many precious and beautiful qualities, such as honesty, simplicity, curiosity, spontaneity, joy, generosity, and a natural relationship with Hashem.

The Piaseczner Rebbe writes in *Bnei Machshavah Tovah*, "One can learn a lot from children regarding the discovery of one's soul. [A child's] actions are not self-conscious, and his soul is naturally revealed." Thus, according to Rav Kook, the question is not how to speed up childhood, but the opposite - how to preserve the positive qualities of the child when we become adults! Sara was the greatest example. At the age of twenty, she was not a sophisticate, but rather still maintained the pure and innocent beauty of a seven year old. At the age of one hundred she still maintained the same fresh holiness she had exhibited at the age of twenty. The years, with all of their difficulties, had not jaded her.

This is a crucial message for us as parents and educators. We need to cultivate the youth of our children. While teaching proper character traits, ethics, and divine service, we must be careful not to turn our children into overly serious miniature adults. They will have plenty of opportunities for that later! Furthermore, we ourselves should try to remember some of those magic moments of our own childhood and integrate those happy memories into our current lives. By so doing, we will be able to preserve our youth, revealing more inner positive energy to help others and to serve Hashem with innocence and joy.

PARSHAT CHAYEI SARA

The Message of Hebron

Chayei Sara opens with the bitter news of Sara's death at the age of 127 in Kiryat Arba-Hebron. Rashi explains that the name *Kiryat Arba* ("the village of four") originates from the burial of four couples in the Cave of Machpelah: Adam and Chava, Avraham and Sara, Yitzchak and Rivka, and Yaakov and Leah. Avraham purchases the cave to bury Sara and thus formalizes the connection between the People of Israel and the Land of Israel.

In a rather shocking comment, the *Aish Kodesh* writes that Sara died after hearing about the *Akeidat Yitzchak* to tell Hashem that certain sufferings are simply too much to bear. After giving her life for the good of *Am Yisrael*, she was buried in Hebron. And what is so special about Hebron? The *Zohar* says that King David's reign began in Hebron in order to connect (*hibur*, meaning "connection," comes from the same root as the word *Hebron*) with our forefathers. The *Beit Yaakov* elaborates on this idea: "King David's reign begins in Hebron, the burial place of the Patriarchs... At the beginning of his reign he needed to connect with them so that the power of their divine service would influence him. Only in this manner could he merit to be king."

David's kingship begins in Hebron with his connection to the Patriarchs. Our forefathers' connection with Hebron began with Sara's death, when she died for the good of the Jewish People and to prevent their future suffering. David is unable to be a proper king until he internalizes the message of Hebron, the message of Sara. In this he is reminiscent of Calev, who goes to Hebron and prostrates himself upon the Patriarchs' graves, praying, "may God save me from the plan of the spies."

We are currently without the Davidic Dynasty and are ruled by the government of Israel, which is enjoined to work for the good of the Jewish People in the Land of Israel. We hope that our government will follow in the footsteps of our Mother Sara and King David to strengthen *Am Yisrael* and *Eretz Yisrael*, by putting the good of the Jewish People first. We pray that in the merit of those buried in Hebron, the place where Heaven and earth connect, we will soon witness the complete redemption, and that the kingdom that was founded in Hebron will return to Jerusalem with the Messiah and the Third Temple.

PARSHAT CHAYEI SARA

To Be Blessed *B'Kol*

Avraham is described at the end of his life as being *zaken, ba b'yamim,* "old, having come into his days," and we are told that Hashem blessed him with *b'kol,* with everything. According to Rashi, *b'kol* is Avraham's son, Yitzchak. The Gemara has several opinions. According to one, *B'kol* was his daughter (perhaps that was her name). Yet conversely, a different opinion states that *b'kol* refers to the fact that he did not have a daughter. The Ramban explains that in Avraham's situation not having a daughter was a blessing, for she would have had to marry an idolater. He also implies that *b'kol* may in fact hint at the *sefirah* of *yesod* that Avraham was now blessed with.

The Mezritcher Maggid explains our verse more deeply. What is the meaning of "come into his days"? There are two types of "days." Firstly, this refers to the concept of serving God by fulfilling the mitzvot. Secondly, it also means the idea of serving God through all of our worldly activities, when we elevate every aspect of our lives to the level of a sacramental act (*avodah b'gashmiut*). Avraham is called *zaken,* old, since he achieved wisdom and knew how to integrate both types of days into a unified life of holiness. The Sages teach us with a play on the words *bhibaram-b'Avraham,* that the world was created through Avraham's merit. This, says the Maggid, is Avraham's quality of *chessed,* loving-kindness. When his name is changed from *Avram* to *Avraham,* the additional letter *hey* represents the five types of verbalization, for the elevating of letters and words is central to our service of the Divine.

At the end of the trial of the *Akeidah,* God calls to Avraham twice, *Avraham Avraham.* For the Maggid, this signifies that the two facets of Avraham, the earthly and the sublime, have now been truly united. He has become *zaken,* beyond time, beyond *days.* Now that his essential (masculine) *chessed,* loving-kindness, has been balanced with the (feminine) *gevurah,* self-limitation, he is ready to become the father of a daughter, *B'kol, Bayit Shel Kol,* the House of Entirety, which refers to the woman. *B'kol's* narrative is not openly expressed in the Torah. It is left for the Sages to revive it. The Maharal explains that the name *B'Kol* means that woman is the completion of creation and of each individual man. Of course, for Avraham to fulfill the commandment of procreation he also needs to father a daughter, and *B'kol* finally brings entirety into her father's house. May we also be blessed *b'kol,* with everything we need in the physical and the spiritual realms.

PARSHAT TOLDOT

Educate a Youth According to His Way

In *Mishlei* 22:6, we read, "Educate a youth according to his way, and even when he is old he will not depart from it." Rashi emphasizes the aspect of youth; effective education begins when one is young. Malbim adds an additional point, generally seen as the verse's main thrust; that education must be individualized. Each child's unique talents, interests, and proclivities must be taken into account. These are determined by studying what interests the child. When we do so, education is effective and the child will follow in its path as an adult. (According to the *Pachad Yizchak*, he will continue the process of being educated).

Our story begins with the twins Yaakov and Esav. The first became a quiet Torah scholar, the second a violent hunter. How could twins end up so differently? According to the famous opinion of Rav Hirsch, Yitzchak and Rivka forgot the lesson of *Mishlei*, and gave both of their sons the same education.[1] "To try to bring up a Yaakov and an Esav in the same college ... and educate them in the same way for the studious, sedate, meditative life is the surest way to court disaster ... Had Yitzchak and Rivka studied Esav's nature and character ... and asked themselves how can even an Esav, how can all the strength and energy, agility and courage that lies slumbering in this child, be won over to ... the service of God ... then Yaakov and Esav, with their totally different natures, could still have remained twin brothers." He

---

[1] Rav Hirsch, here and in other places, along with the Netziv in *Haemek Devar*, for example at the end of *Chayei Sara*, when Yitzchak and Rivka first meet, can be seen as forerunners of the contemporary method of Bible study known in Israel as *Peshuto shel Mikra*, the simple explanation of the Torah. This approach unfortunately is often taken to extremes and must be balanced with traditional *midrash* and *parshanut*, and a strong dose of humility and reverence.

even implies that this might have changed history, sparing us from the persecutions of Esav's descendants, the Christians.

In modern terms we now understand that a child suffering from ADHD cannot be expected to sit all day in a regular yeshiva setting. These children are actually at a statistically higher risk of leaving *Yiddishkeit*. When I was younger I found this hard to believe; after all, what do learning disabilities have to do with faith and observance? Now older and hopefully wiser, it is obvious that a child who feels like a failure in school will develop a low self-image and look elsewhere for a situation in which he can feel successful and better about himself. According to Rav Hirsch, this was Esav's problem. Today, however, we are fortunately more aware of these issues, and alternative educational institutions are being created. This is not only true regarding learning disabilities, but also for music and the arts. Although this need for variety seems intuitively obvious, there is potentially a dark side as well. We need to avoid heavy-handed tracking that may sell some of our kids short, writing them off at a young age as underachievers and settling for a second-best education that may hinder them from reaching their full potential in the future.

Rav Kook writes in *Orot HaTorah* that one of the main reasons people leave Torah observance is that "their way of study and spiritual education betrayed their unique personal quality." He argues that while a basic Torah curriculum is essential for all, at a certain stage, one who has, for example, a strong leaning toward esoteric studies should be allowed to pursue that as their main curriculum, while continuing to review the basics. May Hashem guide us to see the unique essence of each child (and student) so that we can educate each properly "according to his or her way," enabling them to actualize their potential as educated and happy Jewish adults who serve Hashem and contribute to society as best they can.

Special thanks to my daughter Leora with whom I learned this sugya. She enriched me with her deep insights.

PARSHAT TOLDOT

Digging Wells and Bringing Divinity into the World

One of Yitzchak's main activities in *Parshat Toldot* is digging wells. Rav Ginsburgh points out in *Maayan Ganim* that of the ten specific wells mentioned in the Torah, six are connected with Yitzchak, and he dug four of them. What is the significance of digging a well?

According to Rebbe Nachman, digging wells represents revealing God's presence in the world. In *Likkutei Halachot,* he is quoted as saying, "The Patriarchs who began to reveal divinity in the world were always digging wells." This also explains the bizarre interference of the Philistines for, as Rav Shimshon Rafael Hirsch points out, everyone benefits from wells.

Rebbe Nachman continues, "Therefore, the Philistines opposed them and tried to stop up the wells... they wanted to destroy the corrections of God's presence in the world, which had been achieved by Avraham's digging of the wells and Yitzchak's reopening of them." According to the *Beit Aharon* (Karlin), before the Torah was given, our forefathers would perfect and unify cosmic reality in the world by digging wells. The *Mai Hashiloach* adds that each well symbolizes a different spiritual quality that Yitzchak wanted to utilize to deepen the difference between himself and the surrounding nations. This is part of the process of the separation within Avraham's family (Yitzchak from Yishmael, and Yaakov from Esav) which was necessary for the establishment of *Am Yisrael*, the Jewish nation.

Rav Ginsburgh also discusses the difference between a *bor* (pit of rainwater) and a *be'er* (well of spring water, like those of Yitzchak). A pit remains empty until it is filled with content such as rainwater. If it continues to stand empty, it becomes a dangerous vacuum, for with no water it will be filled with malign influences, such as snakes and scorpions. A well is different because it fills up right away with underground water, *mayim chayim* (living waters) flowing from below. This symbolizes the type of *Avodat Hashem* that is based upon *itoruta d'litata* (arousal from below), and according to Rebbe Nachman is related to the more powerful levels of purification that can be achieved in a *maayan* (wellspring) rather than in a mikvah of rainwater.

For the Ramban, each of the wells symbolizes one of the Temples. The first is named *Asek* ("Contention"), referring to the First Temple, which was destroyed by the contentiousness of the nations. The second is called *Sitna* ("Hatred"), an allusion to the Second Temple, which was destroyed by the hatred of the nations. Rabbeinu Bechaya sees a connection here with the name of the *Satan,* the guardian angel of Esav, who was the forefather of the Romans who destroyed it. We could also add that this could refer to the internal hatred among the Jews themselves that ultimately led to its destruction and our dispersal among the nations. The third well, *Rechovot* ("Expansiveness"), alludes to the Third Temple. This is, "the future Temple, to be built speedily in our days, that will be built without argument, for God will expand our borders and all of the nations will worship in it together."

By digging our own "wells" of divine service within our souls, we will help to perfect the world until we can ultimately worship Hashem in the Third and eternal Temple in the very near future.

PARSHAT TOLDOT

A Time for Blindness and
A Time for Clear Sight

Regarding the verse, "And it came to pass when Yitzchak was old, that his eyes became dim ..." (*Bereishit* 27:1), the Ishbitzer writes in the *Mai Hashiloach* (Part One), "The idea of Yitzchak is the opposite of the idea of Moshe. Yitzchak was not allowed to leave the Land of Israel and his eyesight was taken from him. Moshe, on the other hand, was not allowed to enter the Land of Israel and at the end of his life is told to gaze into the land (with his still powerful eyesight)." What does this enigmatic comment really mean?

Yitzchak's essential quality is *Gevurah*, constricted self-discipline, to the extent of being willing to undergo total self-annihilation and be sacrificed upon the altar. What was Yitzchak's role in world history? He serves as the transition from Avraham, who began to reveal Hashem's presence in the world, to Yaakov, who gave birth to the Twelve Tribes of Israel. Avraham served God through *Chessed*, the total expansiveness of love and holiness, even to the undeserving, such as Lot and Yishmael. In order to achieve the proper balance in divine service it was necessary to limit the realm in which this holiness could be spread. Yitzchak plays this crucial role, limiting Avraham's *Chessed* with his own *Gevurah*, paving the way for the birth of Yaakov, who serves Hashem with the beauty of *Tiferet*, the middle path. In order to do so, Yitzchak leads his family in an intense atmosphere of holiness, in self-imposed isolation in the desert. Due to his intense holiness, Yitzchak was not allowed to leave the Land of Israel even temporarily, in case he became spiritually tainted by the impurity of the Gentile lands.

Moshe Rabbeinu, on the other hand, had an entirely different role to play. Rather than heading a small family, he was the leader of an entire nation of millions. In addition to his spiritual leadership, he was also responsible in matters of politics, military and diplomatic affairs, and socioeconomic needs, all for the sake of Heaven. Moshe Rabbeinu was also a man of incredible holiness. He is the only prophet that Hashem spoke to "mouth to mouth," and as the prophet of "clear vision," he ascended Mount Sinai and brought the Written and the Oral Torah down into the world. Perhaps, due to his unique and powerful holiness, he alone among the Jewish People had no *need* to enter the Land of Israel, despite his yearning to fulfill the commandment of settling there and performing the special mitzvot of the Holy Land.

Paradoxically, while the special nature of Yitzchak's holiness interdicted his leaving the Land, it was the special nature of Moshe's holiness that prevented him from entering it!

Rashi, on our verse, quotes the *midrash* that when Yitzchak was bound upon the altar the angels began to cry in Heaven. Their tears trickled down into his eyes, and he began to go blind. At this moment of total self-abnegation, even Yitzchak's sight, the main way in which we connect with the outside world, began to diminish. Moshe Rabbeinu, on the other hand, was the prophet of clear vision, and he maintained his keen eyesight until the end of his life. Even though he was not able to enter *Eretz Yisrael* he was able to gaze upon it from afar, and absorb its holiness with his eyes.

There are times in our lives when we feel that we have clear vision and understanding about what is happening and how we should respond. At other times, we feel completely clueless and "blind." Sometimes our eyes may deceive us, and we would be better off allowing ourselves to be led by others, or better still directly by Hashem. We need to be more in touch with our innermost feelings and with the world around us in order to know when to use each of these important qualities.

PARSHAT VAYETZEI

Dealing with the Outside World

In *Parshat Toldot*, Yitzchak stated that Yaakov had "the voice of Yaakov but the hands of Esav." From this we can learn that even Yaakov, who naturally spent his time studying Torah and engaging in spiritual pursuits, occasionally had to use his hands to work in the physical arena. However, going against his intrinsic nature in this way was very difficult for Yaakov.

The *Mai Hashiloach* writes that when he fled to Lavan's home Yaakov became depressed because he was being forced to leave Israel, where his ancestors had spent most of their lives in pursuit of the spiritual, and enter the material Diaspora. Yaakov may have been unaware of the long-term significance of his journey, but, as the *Sfat Emet* states, "This trip was preparation and guidance for the future exile, that we will be able to correct ourselves even outside of Israel."

But exactly why did Yaakov have to leave Israel? According to Reb Simcha Bunim of Pshischah, "The main reason for Yaakov's sojourn at Lavan's [home] was to gather positive understandings and traits and bring them into holiness, for as long as a good trait is held by them, it is in exile." In this sentence, the word "them" refers primarily to Rachel and Leah, those holy sparks that had fallen into the evil domain of Lavan and awaited Yaakov to redeem them to holiness. Thus, the *Zohar* states that Rachel represents the Revealed World of *Malchut*, whereas Leah symbolizes the Hidden World of *Binah*. These are two different approaches to the service of God that Yaakov brings to *Am Yisrael*.

Before Yaakov left the Land of Israel, the accompanying angels of Israel returned to heaven, ascending the ladder of his dream. New angels of the Exile then descended to accompany him on the remainder of his journey. So, too, when he returns the angels of the Exile are replaced by those of *Eretz Yisrael*. In between, Yaakov lives with Lavan and deeply engages with general culture. Upon returning to the Holy Land he announces to his

45

family and servants, "Remove the foreign gods and purify your-selves...and we will ascend to Beit El." Sometimes, we are required to become involved with foreign culture so as to raise fallen sparks that await our redemption, to be used in the realm of the Holy. This, however, requires careful analysis of what is or is not appropriate to bring in. Certain aspects of foreign culture are invalid and irredeemable, as we learned from our encounter with Greek culture at the time of the Chanukah story.

Thus while some aspects of foreign (Western) culture have intrinsic value, and may enhance our *Avodat Hashem* if we use them carefully, others are either intrinsically evil or are fraught with grave danger if used unwisely. This is often an individual question. What may be appropriate for one person will not be for another. These issues require much study and careful guidance in our increasingly complex world. For those of us who choose not to try and hide, but rather to engage with the world around us, the challenge is even greater. We need to learn to view the world through the eyes of the Torah, and not the other way around. Only then will we be in a position to make the proper decisions.

PARSHAT VAYETZEI

Spiritual Ascent

Fleeing from Esav, Yaakov reaches Bet El, future home of the Temple, and davens Maariv. His prayer experience is called *pigia*, touching, and according to Rav Kook it represents the deepest kind of prayer, leading to a prophetic experience. Yaakov sleeps, prophetically dreaming of the ladder that stands on the ground but reaches to Heaven, with angels going up and down. Hashem stands over him and reiterates the promise of the Land and the People. Awakening, he proclaims, "Yes, the Lord is in this place and I didn't know it …how awesome is this place …the house of God and the gate of Heaven." (Rav Charlop quoted these words when he read Rav Kook's Kabbalistic treatise on the alphabet, *Raish Milin*). The *Midrash Rabbah* has various interpretations of the significance of the angels in the dream. One opinion (quoted in Rashi) is that they are the angels of Israel and the Diaspora, "changing the guard" for Yaakov. Another commentator (Rambam) sees them as the guardian angels of the nations that in the future would subjugate Israel, only to descend afterwards from their power.

Based upon the *Zohar*, the *Kuntres Ha'avodah* of Lubavitch and the *Beit Aharon* of Karlin see the ladder as a symbol of prayer. During morning prayers we ascend higher and higher from one world until the next, ultimately reaching *Atzilut* when we daven the *Amidah*. We are then able to descend back to our world, *Asiyah*, bringing with us the Divine influx. The *Beit Aharon* also views the ladder as representing man himself. One must be moderate, neither raising oneself too high nor lowering oneself too much. Clearly the ladder also represents our ability to reach spiritual heights, while remaining firmly rooted in earthly physicality.

Before sleeping Yaakov made a pillow out of stones that are later referred to as "the stone." According to Rashi, many stones competed to become Yaakov's pillow and Hashem united them

47

into one. The *Meor Aynaim* brings two explanations. Firstly, each stone is one of the Twelve Tribes, each offering its unique approach to *Avodat Hashem*. Hashem accepts them all, for "these and those are the words of the living God." Additionally they represent the 22 letters of the alphabet (*vayishkav*=*vayesh k"v*, "and he laid"="and there are 22"). These letters are the building blocks of the prayers that help us ascend the ladder to Heaven, to cleave to Hashem. Let us all ascend; mindful of the warning of the *Kuntress Ha'avodah*, that the higher one climbs the more dangerous it is to fall. Hold on tight!

PARSHAT VAYETZEI

The Power of An Unconscious *Bracha*

The following verses, which describe our ancestor Yaakov's marriage to Leah, appear in *Parshat Vayetzei*: "And it came to pass in the evening, that he took Leah his daughter, and brought her to him, and he went in to her ... And it came to pass that in the morning, behold it was Leah. And he said to Lavan, 'What is this thou hast done to me? Did I not serve thee for Rachel? Why then hast thou beguiled me?' And Lavan said, 'It must not be so done in our country, to give the younger before the firstborn.'" (*Bereishit* 29:23-25). If this shocking story sounds strangely familiar, it is worthwhile looking back at the previous parsha:

"And it came to pass, that when Yitzchak was old, and his eyes were dim, so that he could not see, he called Esav, his eldest son, and said to him, 'My son,' and he said to him, 'Here I am' ... And Rivka took the best clothes of her eldest son, Esav, which were with her in the house, and put them upon Yaakov, her younger son ... And he came to his father, and said, 'My father,' and he said, 'Here am I. Who are you, my son?' And Yaakov said to his father, 'I am Esav your firstborn ...'"

When we look at both of these episodes, we see a clear case of *middah kenegged middah*, measure for measure. Just as Yaakov posed as his older brother when his father was "in the dark," so too did Leah and Rachel swap places years later, when Yaakov was in the dark. The *Ohr Hachaim* goes so far as to say that as a result of Yaakov's being with Leah while thinking that she was Rachel, all the holiness that should have gone into the conception of Reuven, their oldest son, was diffused and scattered. Reuven, born of this union, loses all of the signs of leadership that should have been his. Levi receives the priesthood, Yehudah the kingship, and in a sense, Yosef acts as the oldest son. According to the Ari, this is even the reason why the tribe of Reuven was not able to enter the Land of Israel proper, and received its inheritance on the other side of the River Jordan. Of the many questions here, the simplest, and yet the most compelling is, why? Why does the nation of Israel begin its formation through deceit? Yaakov receives the *bracha* intended for Esav, and Leah bears a child intended for Rachel. Why did God's holy nation have to be born in such a manner?

The *Mai Hashiloach* states that Hashem specifically wanted Yitzchak to bless Yaakov unknowingly. A conscious *bracha* from Yitzchak could only be as strong as Yitzchak's own intent. As strange as this sounds, an "unconscious" *bracha* is even more powerful. It is as though Hashem is blessing Yaakov directly, with Yitzchak serving as the conduit through which the *bracha* passes, without being limited by a human element. From here there emerges a curious concept. Despite all of our (justified) emphasis on our intent in divine service, our unconscious actions may actually contain more spiritual potency than our conscious ones.

The Torah tells us that Leah's eyes were *rakot*, meaning "soft," or "weak." The Netziv explains that her eyes were super-sensitive, and therefore, unlike Rachel, she was not a shepherdess. She always remained indoors to avoid the hurtful rays of the sun. According to the *Zohar*, Rachel represents the *alma di'itgalya*, the revealed world, while Leah symbolizes the *alma di'itkasia*, the hidden world. This reading corroborates our initial perception of Leah: private, hidden, and inward.

The Midrash, in *Bereishit Rabbah* 68:3-4, distinguishes between two types of marriages. The first is the case of "one who goes to his intended," whereas the second is "one whose intended comes to him." The first model is that of Yaakov and Rachel, while the second refers to Yitzchak and Rivka. The Beit Yaakov writes that the second model represents divine intervention, above conscious human capabilities, and is therefore on a higher level. Leah's marriage to Yaakov was also of this type.

We know from Kabbalah that Yaakov represents the mediating *sefirah* of *Tiferet*, *Emet*, balance, truth, and completeness. Among the manifestations of this trait is a direct connection to and near-total identification with the divine will. This is an unconscious process that is not dependent upon self-awareness, conscious decision-making, and action. It is a state of being, not of doing. It is therefore appropriate that Yaakov received the blessing of his destiny as the forefather of *Am Yisrael* directly from Hashem, with Yitzchak merely acting as the conduit. Similarly, Yaakov's union with Leah, the mother of half of the future tribes (or of most of them, if we view Zilpah as an extension of Leah) and Dina, had to take place while Yaakov himself was unaware of what was really happening, as an unknowing actor in the great drama that only Hashem Himself can direct.

In the beginning of the parsha, when Yaakov goes to sleep in Beit El, the Torah states that Hashem stood over him. Both the *Beit Yaakov* and Rav Tzaddok Hakohen in *Pri Tzaddik* point out that even while Yaakov is in an unconscious state of sleep, he is constantly and totally attached to Hashem.

Aish Kodesh (Purim, 1942) speaks of two levels of salvation for *Am Yisrael* - that which is according to our merits and that which is above our merits. The latter is, of course greater.

When we connect fully with the depths of our innate Jewish identity, we are following in the footsteps of Yaakov Avinu. Even in our sleep, we should be totally in touch with Hashem and His will. Finally, even if we have not merited it through our own actions, we should still pray that Hashem will bestow upon us the ultimate salvation that we, as His children, deserve.

PARSHAT VAYISHLACH

Different Names, Different Roles

When the names of Avram and Sarai were changed to Avraham and Sara, the old names fell into disuse and we are enjoined not to use them. Yaakov, on the other hand, receives the new name of Yisrael, yet throughout the Biblical narrative both names are used, seemingly interchangeably. The Netziv writes that *Yaakov* represents nature and physicality, whereas *Yisrael* is the name of miracles and spirituality. The Jewish People have inherited both names, representing different facets of our collective persona, just as Yaakov, a complex individual, requires two names to portray his multifaceted being. He is *Tiferet*, beauty, representing the balance between *Chessed*, loving-kindness and *Gevurah*, self-restraint. Thus he is also *Emet*, truth. It is perhaps fitting that such a complex man would need two wives.

The *Zohar* has a very rich portrayal of Leah and Rachel. Leah is *Alma d'itkasia,* the hidden world of *Binah,* whereas Rachel is *Alma d'itgalia,* the revealed world of *Malchut.* While it is normally forbidden to marry two sisters, Yaakov must unite with both of them to serve as the meeting grounds for these two profoundly different spiritual forces. The fact that he is the patriarch whose "bed is perfect," for all of his children are righteous, is a result of this marriage and the cause of *Am Yisrael's* future holiness.

Yaakov's marriage to Leah and Rachel was not always easy. He had to balance himself between their differing needs and have the flexibility to move between them without confusing each one's unique style and approach. He needed to switch back and forth between the Leah mode (Yisrael?) and the Rachel mode (Yaakov?) day in and day out.

Nowadays, we only have one spouse and we often find that a difficult balancing act, as we contend with changing needs and unexpected mood shifts. We, too, are complex personalities and our relationships are very dynamic. Within each man are aspects of Yaakov and Yisrael, and within each woman are aspects of

Leah and Rachel. In a sense, Yaakov had it easy. He knew which wife he was speaking to at any given moment. We, on the other hand, are not always sure with which spouse we are speaking. May we merit clear self awareness and awareness of our closest Other in order to properly balance our roles. May our work in this microcosm help us and all of *Am Yisrael* lead balanced lives of *Avodat Hashem.*

PARSHAT VAYISHLACH

Protection from Domestic Violence

As Yaakov prepared to finally confront Esav, he engaged in numerous preparations, including prayer, appeasement, and war. With all of this going on, he took the time for one last crucial act. Rashi tells us that Yaakov hid his daughter Dina in a box so that the evil and violent Esav would not lay eyes upon her. While it is true that Rashi criticizes Yaakov for preventing a match that might have led Esav to repent, Yaakov's actions should come as no surprise. In the previous parsha, Rashi teaches us that Dina's mother Leah had weak eyes due to her excessive crying because she thought that she was destined to marry the coarse hunter Esav. When Yitzchak blessed Esav, he summed up his essence with the statement, "You will live by the sword." No responsible parents would ever knowingly allow a daughter to marry a man with a reputation for violence, and Yaakov and Leah took all possible precautions to protect Dina from such a horrible fate. In fact, although the *midrash* upon which this Rashi is based suggests that marriage to Esav might have protected Dina from being abducted and raped by Shechem, this is hardly a good reason to marry Esav.

In more modern times, as with numerous other afflictions of today's society, such as substance abuse and the sexual abuse of children, the Orthodox community used to cover up and deny the existence of domestic violence in its midst for fear of creating a *chillul Hashem* (disgracing God's name). Fortunately, this is no longer the case and these issues are now out in the open, where they can hopefully be dealt with more effectively. Regarding domestic violence, Rav Dr. Abraham J. Twerski has written, "It is not my intent to disrupt marriages. To the contrary, ignoring and denying spouse abuse is what will ultimately result not only in the dissolution of marriages, but also in an impact on the children that will cause them to be dysfunctional spouses and parents when they mature and marry."

Another related problem, which is equally serious, is that of the *agunah,* a woman prevented from marrying due to her husband's refusal to grant her a *get,* a religious divorce. Rav Twerski writes, "Every case of a husband's refusal to give a *get* will reveal a history of a woman's having been abused during the marriage. This last and perhaps greatest abuse of power, refusal to give a *get,* occurs only in individuals who were abusers." Our goal should be to identify mistreatment in its earliest stages, when it is still at the level of emotional or verbal abuse, and to intervene before it escalates into physical violence. Of course, young women can and should be taught to identify potential abusers while dating, thus sparing themselves much future agony. As a community we need to send a loud and clear message of zero tolerance toward spouse abuse of any sort.

Unfortunately, with all of Yaakov's and Leah's best efforts they were not able to protect Dina from sexual assault. The Torah demands that we all take a clear stand to safeguard the safety and dignity of every woman. As parents and educators, rabbis and community leaders, we all have a role to play in combating this horrific plague. If we all work together, then we will be successful, eradicating the evil of domestic abuse from our society.

PARSHAT VAYISHLACH

"A Lot" or "Everything"?

In *Parshat Vayetzei*, Yaakov fled *Eretz Yisrael* to escape from Esav. According to Rav Ginsburgh, this was a case of "going down in order to go up," as Yaakov would return when he was sufficiently strong to conquer the land from Esav. Here, in *Parshat Vayishlach*, Yaakov finally returns, battling both Esav and Esav's angel, and is victorious.

In the eyes of *Chazal*, Yaakov and Esav respectively symbolize the forces of goodness and spirituality in their struggle with the evil and material aspects of the world. This battle is fought on several levels, including a physical battle against an angel, and a spiritual battle against a man. In relation to the first, Rav Zalman Sorotzkin wrote, "The spirit of the flesh and blood defeated the physicality of the angel!"

While battling the angel, Yaakov also advances towards his meeting with Esav. Not relying upon miracles, he prepares his gifts and military tactics in addition to his prayers. When they do finally meet, it is readily apparent that Esav is no match for Yaakov's finely honed spiritual powers. This point is expressed also in a seemingly banal conversation between the two, as Yaakov insists that Esav accept his gifts. "And Esav said, 'I have a lot' (*rov*)… and Yaakov said … 'I have everything' (*kol*), and he insisted and he [Esav] took." What is the difference between Esav's "*a lot*" and Yaakov's "*everything*"? Rashi explains that Yaakov meant, "I have everything: Whatever I need." But Esav spoke arrogantly - "I have a lot - much more than I need."

Looking at this in broader terms, Esav thinks in quantitative terms of acquisition, competition, and materialism. On the one hand, he has more than he needs, but on the other he is always ready to acquire more. Yaakov, in contrast, expresses *Chazal's* dictum in *Pirkei Avot*, "Who is wealthy, he who is content with what he has." Yaakov has everything, a qualitative assessment expressing a spiritually centered view of reality. Who has "everything"- one who feels connected with Hashem, and therefore lacks interest in worldly materialism. The brothers take leave of each other with Esav desiring a continued relationship, while Yaakov, ignoring him, travels to "Sukkot," where he builds sukkot, spiritual homes.

Parshat Vayishlach is read during the month of Kislev, the month of Chanukah. In the Chanukah story, we see how Esav's materialism, found among the Greeks, was opposed by the spirit of the Hasmonean High Priests. The light of Chanukah represents Yaakov's *"everything,"* and this is the message we are broadcasting with our miracle-publicizing candles.

By internalizing the light of the spiritual *"everything"* of Yaakov, we are able to push aside the darkness of the Esav's material *"a lot."* In so doing, we are happy with the life that Hashem has given us, and reach a state of true joy.

PARSHAT VAYESHEV

The Master of Dreams

With the story of Yosef, we enter into a new phase in the early history of the Jewish People. The *Mai Hashiloach* writes that until now the Torah has dealt with the clarifications between the Jews and the other nations. Avraham separates from his Mesopotamian family, Yitzchak from Yishmael and Yaakov from Esav. Once Yaakov has achieved such a high level of purity that all of his children are holy, it is time for *birurim* within *Am Yisrael*, as each brother-tribe receives his designated role within the broader framework.

It first appears that Reuven, the firstborn, would receive the mantle of leadership, but this is not to be. The holy *Ohr Hachaim* writes that since he was conceived at a time when Yaakov was actually with Leah but thought he was with Rachel, his *kavanot*, mystical intentions, were confused. This caused a diffusion of the holiness that otherwise would have gone to Reuven. The result is that Yehudah becomes the king, Levi the priest, and Yosef, in a sense, the firstborn.

Yosef is the paradigmatic tzaddik, the master of sexual purity who is able to sustain the world with the divine influx he draws down. He achieved this distinction when he managed to extricate himself from the ultimate test of the obscene temptation of the wife of his employer, Potifar. He applied it in his role in Egypt, where he sustained everyone during the great famine. According to the Midrash, Yosef even had all of the Egyptians undergo circumcision.

Part of the secret of Yosef's success is that he sees Hashem's hand in everything that happens and constantly praises Him. Additionally, he is a *Baal Hachalomot*, a master of dreams. This gives him the perspective needed to weather the many storms that threaten him every step of the way. While he is often in grave peril he never gives in. A person of great vision cannot despair, or he will never succeed. Great drive and persistency are necessary in order to see one's plans through when everything seems bleak. Yosef is just that man, and therefore an important role model for all of us. If we never lose sight of our dreams, we will never give up.

PARSHAT VAYESHEV

Pulling Back from the Brink

Parshat Vayeshev tells the story of Yosef, known in Kabbalah as *Yosef HaTzaddik*, "Yosef the Righteous." Of all of the Biblical characters, why does Yosef merit this title, and how did he achieve such distinction? Equally important is the question of what we can learn from this tzaddik regarding our own *Avodat Hashem.*

Yosef's transformative moment is when he succeeds in escaping the sexual advances of the wife of his employer, Potifar. Potifar's wife was very attracted to the youthful and handsome Yosef. On a daily basis, she tried to seduce this 17-year-old boy, who was alone in a strange land and distant from the morals of his father's home. Yet in spite of all her charms Yosef did not give in. One day, Yosef returned to the house to do his work and found himself alone with Potifar's wife. This time, the temptation was too great for him to bear and he found himself in bed with her, having resigned himself to sin. At the last moment (and according to Rashi, after seeing his father's image), he leaves his cloak in her hands and runs out of the door, escaping sin and reaching the level of a tzaddik, which more than anything else is a reflection of sexual purity.

Our Sages provide us with a much deeper dimension to this story. Rashi quotes *Sotah* 36b, where it states that according to the Talmudic sage Rav, Yosef returned home to do his work and there fell prey to Potifar's wife's enticements. Whereas according to Shmuel, Yosef had already made up his mind to sin and returned home for that very purpose. The Torah's use of the word *melachto* ("his work") is euphemistic. The *Torah Temimah* is bothered by Shmuel's opinion. It would be one thing if the Torah stated that Yosef wanted to sin, but it doesn't. It explicitly states that he came to do his work. Why make Yosef look bad with a forced reading that he desired to sin?! The answer of the *Torah Temimah* is that this approach in fact actually brings **more honor** to Yosef! The very fact that he had descended so much and had

60

already given in to his basest desires, and still managed to extricate himself at the last moment is more meritorious than if he had not been tempted at all. This is reminiscent of the famous Rabbinic dictum that a *baal teshuvah* is greater than a complete tzaddik, for he knows the taste of sin and nonetheless has left it behind.

All of us can and must learn an important spiritual message from the above story. In *Likkutei Halachot*, Rebbe Nachman is quoted as saying that one of the main things holding people back from repenting and actualizing their spiritual potential is the widespread mistaken notion that certain people are born to be tzaddikim, whereas "regular people" cannot possibly ever achieve spiritual greatness. Therefore most people never really try to become righteous and live lives of spiritual mediocrity. The truth is that tzaddikim are not born, they are made! Thus, according to Rebbe Nachman, everyone has the potential to reach spiritual heights, if only they would work as hard as they can.

This theme of setting high spiritual goals and standards for ourselves is also a major component of the educational philosophy of the Piaseczner Rebbe, from *Chovat HaTalmidim* through *Bnai Machshavah Tovah*. We should always strive for greatness, and not sell ourselves short! The *Pachad Yitzchak* is even more explicit. He writes that the Chafetz Chaim was renowned for the purity of his language and for never speaking negatively. Yet who knows of all of the battles, struggles, failures, fallings and retreats that the Chafetz Chaim endured during the war against his evil inclination?! Rav Hutner then switches into English, reminding us of the expression "Lose a battle and win the war." We can glean an additional insight from the *Netivot Shalom*, who tells us that, "In divine service our major task is not the results, but the service of the service (*avodat ha'avodah*) itself." Ultimately, our successes depend to a great extent upon Hashem's providence. This, however, is not our concern. We have to do the best we can and leave the rest up to Heaven.

61

PARSHAT MIKETZ

Waking Up From Our Slumber

In Pharaoh's dream, the seven lean cows devour the seven fat ones and then Pharaoh awakens, *vayikatz* (from a similar root to the name of the parsha, *miketz*, meaning "the end"). The Kozhnitzer Maggid writes that the stories in the Torah guide us to know and serve Hashem. The seven lean cows represent seven forces of the *sitra achra*, the side of evil. They devour the seven ways in which we must serve Hashem, reflections of the seven lower *sefirot*, through love, fear, beauty, victory, thanksgiving, cleaving, and coronation. Parallel to them are seven evil paths that we must avoid. The Maggid continues that when we sin it is as if we are in a state of deep sleep. At a certain point we wake up and do *teshuvah*.

When we are in exile we are also asleep, in a state of darkness and foolishness that leads to sin. The miracle is that we do eventually awaken, realize what is going in, take in the hidden light, and begin to act appropriately. The *Pachad Yitzchak* points out that even in the Holy Land we can be in a state of exile, as in the Greek Exile at the time of the Chanukah story.

Our ability to stand firm in the face of external threats is largely dependent upon internal unity. We need to learn to listen to each other, to really hear each other's voice. As Levinas says, "'we' is not the plural of 'I.'" The majority must be careful not to tyrannically impose its will upon the minority. The Maggid also teaches in the name of the Ari that Yosef's brothers perceived him as being the rejected brother like Yishmael and Esav, so they sold him into slavery. They didn't realize that that stage of Jewish history had ended, and it was no longer necessary for one brother to be excluded. Inclusivity replaces exclusivity as the way of dealing with internal conflict.

Chazal teach us that a dream goes according to its interpretation. We need to begin to remember our dreams, to open ourselves up to dreams and miracles, and become pure vessels for

Hashem's light to shine through. The *Sfat Emet* writes that *Ner, Petila, Shemen* (candle, wick, oil) is an acrostic for *nefesh,* soul. On Chanukah, when this parsha is normally read, all of the Jewish souls, even those who are distant, can be elevated and brought close to Hashem. Now is the time for all of us to wake up from our state of sleep and begin to listen to ourselves, our brothers and sisters, and to Hashem.

PARSHAT MIKETZ

Survival and Resilience

The *Sfat Emet* writes that this parsha teaches us both "to prepare ourselves for the good days in which holiness is revealed, and to enlighten our hearts to prepare for the bad days when holiness is hidden ... before every trial there is enlightenment on how to plan ahead." In this way, Yosef's presence in Egypt helped to pave the way for the Jewish People to survive spiritually, not only there, but also in all of the subsequent exiles, for which the Egyptian exile was the paradigm.

Yosef succeeds in interpreting Pharaoh's dreams where his own great sorcerers had failed. When Yosef is taken by chariot to tour Egypt he is referred to as *Avreich,* implying *Av rach,* meaning "wise in wisdom but young in years." According to Rashi, Yosef also acted as an *Av,* a father, to Pharaoh himself. Later Pharaoh renames Yosef, *Tzefanat Paneach,* "the revealer of mysteries," for as the Rashbam explains, the Egyptian custom was to rename a person when elevating him to a special position.

The Netziv attributes a different meaning to this name, interpreting it as "one whose hidden power to rule is easily revealed." Pharaoh was amazed at Yosef's ability to enter the court after years in prison, correctly interpret the dreams, and give economic advice with almost no transition, despite the dramatic change in his personal circumstances. Most people, even if they are very wise to begin with, undergo mental and emotional decay in prison, and even when they are freed will have tremendous difficulties in adjusting to the new situation.

We cannot even begin to imagine the horrifying conditions of an Egyptian prison thousands of years ago. Therefore, when Pharaoh saw the ease with which Yosef was able to leave prison and begin to function in court, he realized two things. Firstly, Yosef was no ordinary prisoner, but rather a person of extraordinary mental and spiritual powers. Secondly, this resilience of character clearly showed that Yosef was destined for leadership.

While Yosef had not yet been able to maximize his potential, it stayed with him all the time and as soon as he was given the opportunity, his true abilities immediately came to the fore.

When we study this part of the story of Yosef, our thoughts are drawn to another Jewish prisoner - Jonathon Pollard (may Hashem protect him). Mr. Pollard has been languishing in solitary confinement for twenty years for trying to protect Israel from Arab attack. Yet with similar resilience, he continues to comment upon current events and give sage advice, despite his unimaginable suffering. In the same way that Yosef's story is one of survival and resilience, we hope and pray that Mr. Pollard will soon experience a similar, positive reversal of his fortunes.

PARSHAT VAYIGASH

Looking Beyond Our Own Perceptions

At the end of *Parshat Miketz*, the brothers find themselves in a hopeless situation. Binyamin has been framed for stealing the cup and must remain as a slave in Egypt, while the other brothers are to return to Yaakov, knowing full well that the news will devastate, or perhaps even kill him. *Parshat Vayigash* opens with Yehudah's dramatic appeal to Yosef: "And Yehudah approached him, saying, 'Please sir (*adoni*), let your servant speak in the ears of my master (*adoni*), and don't be angry at your servant, for you are like Pharaoh'" (44:18). According to the *Midrash Rabbah* (93:6), Yehudah approaches Yosef with three different tactics: war, appeasement, and prayer. We are of course reminded of the confrontation between Yaakov and Esav in *Parshat Vayishlach* (32:3-21), in relation to which the *Midrash Tanchuma Yashan* (6) states, " He prepared himself for three things; prayer, presents, and war."

It is instructive to note that while Rashi in *Vayishlach* quotes the Midrash regarding Yaakov, he does not quote the parallel *midrash* here in relation to Yehudah. Why not? It would appear that the answer lies in the relationship between the *pshat* (simple meaning) and the *drash* (homiletic meaning) in each case. In relation to Yaakov, the three tactics are clearly seen in verses 8-18, as he divides his camp to prepare for possible attack, sends animals as a present to Esav, and in verses 10-14 prays to God for help, recalling the promise which had been made to him. The Midrash in *Vayigash* is quite different. Here, the proof for this three-way preparation is not found in the *pshat* of the verses. Rather, the Midrash quotes proof-texts from other parts of the *Tanach*, where the word *vayigash* appears in these three contexts. The only connection is linguistic; apparently there is no contextual relevance here.

However, a closer look reveals antecedents of this *midrash* within the text. Rashi comments on verse 18: "'Don't be angry' -

from here you learn that he spoke to him harshly." This word seems to indicate the element of warfare described in the Midrash. In relation to appeasement, one could argue that Yehudah's entire speech in verses 18-34 constitutes words of appeasement, recounting the brothers' journey to Egypt, their previous dealings with Yosef, and of course Yaakov's dire straits. This, combined with Yehudah's self sacrifice on behalf of Binyamin, is of course meant to soften up Yosef and arouse his mercy. In fact, this succeeds beyond Yehudah's expectations, causing Yosef to reveal himself to his brothers, an issue we shall return to shortly.

Here we find war and appeasement, but where is there any hint of prayer on Yehudah's part? Rebbe Elimelech of Lizhensk writes in *Noam Elimelech*, "Since the Torah wrote in a concealed manner, without revealing whom Yehudah approached... we can say that it refers to the Holy One, Blessed be He... 'And he approached Him in prayer,' to pray for himself." Rebbe Elimelech interprets the following verses as referring to God Himself, reading *A-donoi* as God's name rather than "my master," as we had understood it on the *pshat* level.

This idea is further developed by Rav Tzaddok Hakohen in *Pri Tzaddik*:

"All of Yehudah's words can be understood on two levels; on the simple level he was addressing Yosef, but the very same words were intended as a prayer to Hashem... for he understood that the entire event was through Hashem's providence." Rav Tzaddok then goes on to explain the *midrash* with which we began: "What is written in *Bereishit Rabbah*, that Yehudah prepared for war, appeasement and prayer, even though we find no prayer here – rather, the words that he spoke to Yosef were words of prayer to Hashem."

Now let us examine the results of Yehudah's speech/prayer, as seen through the prism of Chassidut. In 45:1-7 we read of Yosef s revelation of himself to his brothers: "And Yosef could no longer restrain himself... 'I am Yosef...' and his brothers could not answer him for they were in shock... and Yosef said, 'Now don't be angry that you sent me here... it was God who sent me here before you.'" In only two words, "*Ani Yosef* -I am Yosef," we have not only the climax of this dramatic scene, but in fact the climax of the entire story that began with the sale of Yosef into slavery. Here, we have the complete reversal of the entire situation that we, through the eyes of the brothers, perceived to be true at the end of *Parshat Miketz*, when all appeared to be lost in the hopeless confrontation between the brothers and the unpredictable dictator of Egypt. The reversal is complete. Not only are they now safe, but in retrospect they were never really in danger! Their entire predicament was, in fact, an illusion, reflecting what Chassidut refers to as *alma d'shikra*, the world of illusions in which we live.

Rav Tzaddok Hakohen's Rebbe, Rav Mordechai Yosef of Ishbitz, discusses this point and its spiritual implications in two passages in his *Mai Hashiloach*. In Part Two, he writes, "with this Hashem teaches us that no one should ever give up hope, even if it seems to him that salvation is very distant." No matter how desperate the situation may seem, Hashem can bring salvation in a mere moment.

In Part One, the Ishbitzer goes a step further: "Yehudah thought that he was standing in front of a Gentile king and arguing with him, but when Hashem sent him salvation, they realized retroactively that they had never been in danger, for in reality they had been arguing with their own brother." Of course, the ramifications of such an outlook are far-reaching, going way beyond the religious imperative delineated in Part Two of never giving up hope. They are, in fact, of a theological nature, relating to the larger question of how we view the reality in which we live, and by implication, our ability to redefine that reality. Continues the Ishbitzer: "and so too in the future, when Hashem will save us and redeem us, then He will show us that we were never in exile and no nation ever ruled over us, only Hashem Himself. The ultimate liberation from slavery, be it personal or national, is rooted in the liberation from *alma d'shikra*, the world of falsehood, by seeing the world through a higher truth, the reality of Hashem's omnipotence.

The message of the story according to the Ishbitzer, is that since the world we live in is highly deceptive, very often we live within the parameters of our own perceptions. Exile may be primarily a psychological category, subject to our ability to redefine it. For example, it could be argued that Natan Sharansky was infinitely freer as a prisoner in the gulag than are many objectively "free" people living in modern technological society. Perhaps this is one interpretation of *Chazal*'s dictum in *Avot* 6:2: "There is no free person except for the one who engages in the study of Torah."

By understanding and acting according to a higher reality we will merit, as individuals and as a people, the ability to truly live freely in this world.

PARSHAT VAYIGASH

The Power of Joy

Yaakov becomes aware of Yosef's existence and status in two stages. First, he sees the wagons that Yosef sent and hears the brothers' description of Yosef ruling Egypt. He then travels to Egypt and meets with his beloved son after decades of longing for him. Rashi teaches that when Yaakov saw the wagons (*agalot*), he remembered that when Yosef had left they were studying the mitzvah of *egla arufa,* the calf whose neck is broken, which is performed when a dead body is found and the killer's identity is unknown. This was a clear sign that it was indeed Yosef who had sent for him. Then Yaakov's spirit came alive. Onkelos translates that the Holy Spirit rested upon Yaakov, and Rashi explains that the Shechinah (divine Presence) that had departed from him now rested upon him again. Only in a state of joy can one receive prophecy. Depression creates static that interferes with the reception of the divine message. When Yosef was lost and as-sumed dead, Yaakov sank into depression, losing his prophetic powers. Now he regained happiness and his status as a prophet. The Netziv therefore shows us that the expression *v'techi*, "came alive,"as alludes to "the root 'alive', always [referring] to happy and joyous living."

When father and son were finally reunited, Yosef fell upon Yaakov's neck and wept. Yaakov, says Rashi, was actually reciting the Shema. The *Maor v'Shemesh* sees this as a Kabbalistic secret. Yaakov represents the *sefirah* of *Tiferet*, beauty, while Yosef is *Yesod*, foundation. For a proper flowing of divine beneficence into the world *Tiferet* must unite with *Yesod,* the conduit to *Malchut*, royalty. The Netziv writes that Yaakov mistook Yosef for Pharaoh and bowed to him. Yosef allowed this to happen in fulfillment of his dream. Yaakov was annoyed, and he read the Shema in order to distract himself and calm down.

The *Sfat Emet* quotes the Maharal that Yaakov reached a state of *deveikut* with Hashem and therefore read the Shema.

Yosef, on the other hand, was accustomed to serving God through everyday activities and didn't need to say the Shema. The Piaseczner in *Derech HaMelech* explains that Yaakov recites the Shema to declare that one can only serve Hashem through joy. Realizing that everything was for the good, he "began anew to fill *Am Yisrael* with holiness and Torah."

It seems that the first stage is bittersweet. Yaakov is reminded of his son's disappearance, and his sons' attempt to wash their hands of responsibility, similar to the *egla arufa* ceremony. The second stage was the pure joy that Yaakov expressed through the Shema, reclaiming both his son and his relationship with Hashem. It is this joy that enhances our relationship with God, as well as with the world around us. We should all aspire to merit serving God only through joy.

PARSHAT VAYECHI

Two Types of Tzaddikim

Before Yaakov's death, he blesses Yosef's two sons, Eph-raim and Menashe. Even though Menashe is the firstborn, Yaakov overrides Yosef's objections and blesses Ephraim first. The *Mai Hashiloach* sees this as reflecting Yaakov's essential quality. His father, Yitzchak, representing the quality of *Gevurah* (strict justice), wanted to bless his firstborn, Esav, despite his being unworthy, for the law takes precedence over any other consideration. Yaakov, on the other hand, representing *Tiferet* (inner truth), insists on blessing each grandson in the manner which is truly appropriate. Rav Y.M. Poupko sees in Yaakov's behavior a redemptive moment in which he corrects his deceitful taking of Esav's blessing. In some Chassidic commentaries (such as the *Shem M'Shmuel*) Ephraim and Menashe represent two approaches to divine service, and Yaakov and Yosef disagree as to which is preferable.

For the *Noam Elimelech*, Ephraim and Menashe are two types of tzaddikim. Menashe represents the mystic who is con-stantly connected to the upper worlds, with no interest in what is happening down below. This is the approach that Yosef prefers. (Given Yosef's personal career, this would appear surprising. Perhaps his own hyper-involvement in worldly affairs caused him to long for the tranquility of quietistic mystical connection with Hashem.) Ephraim, on the other hand, is a different type of tzaddik. While he too reaches a state of *dveikut* with Hashem, his focus is activistic. The goal of his mystical enterprise is not his own experience, but rather the drawing down of a positive influence and blessing to *Am Yisrael*. (In this he is an example of Professor Moshe Idel's "Mystical-Magical Model" of the Chassidic Rebbe.) Yaakov, understanding that the most important compo-nent of leadership is concern for the community, favors Eph-raim's path, and bestows the premier blessing upon him.

We are accustomed to bless our sons to be like Ephraim and Menashe. Some claim that this is because they represent the ability of Judaism to survive even in the diaspora, where they were born. The Netziv writes that Ephraim represents dedication to Torah study, whereas Menashe symbolizes communal leadership. Together they provide the necessary ingredients to lead the Jewish People. Rav Chaim Tabasky once said that the intent of the blessing is to ward off *yeridat hadorot*, the continuous decline of the generations. Since Ephraim and Menashe joined their uncles in becoming the heads of tribes, they indicate the possibility of a generation remaining on the level of the previous one, which is a very appropriate *bracha* to give to our sons.

We can only hope and pray that we merit feeling in our children *aliyat hadorot*, the uplifting of the generations. This exists, writes the *Pri Tzaddik,* as we get closer to the ultimate redemption. As this draws even nearer, we should only have great *nachas* from our children's Torah, *avodah,* and dedication to *Klal Yisrael.*

PARSHAT SHEMOT

Exile and Redemption

The Book of *Shemot*, "names," is in fact amply blessed with names. The Bahag refers to it as the *Chumash Sheni* (Second *Chumash*), despite the fact that he gives the other books more "creative" names. According to the Ramban (at the book's end), it is the *Sefer Hageulah*, (Book of Redemption). Since the Jewish People are still in the desert at the end of *Shemot*, we must, however, determine the Ramban's definition of redemption in this context. In the introduction, the Ramban describes the book as narrating the first exile and the redemption from it. He informs us that, "When they left Egypt, even though they left the House of Slavery, they were still considered exiles, for they remained in a foreign land." Afterwards, we find a fascinating definition of redemption: "When they came to Mount Sinai and built the Tabernacle, Hashem returned and His Shechinah dwelled among them... then they were considered redeemed."

For the Ramban, there are different manifestations of exile and redemption. On the one hand, true redemption can only take place in the Land of Israel, and yet there is also a spiritual, interior redemption which is defined by cleaving to God and the Shechinah. This occurs at the giving of the Torah, and in the Tabernacle, which, according to the Ramban, represents that event.

In the Netziv's introduction he explains the approach of the Bahag. Why is *Shemot* known as *Chumash Sheni* and not by a more exciting name? The Netziv (based upon the Midrash) explains that *Matan Torah* is the completion of the creation. The world was created so that the Jewish People would accept the Torah, and had we not done so, it would have reverted to primordial chaos. Therefore the books of *Bereishit* and *Shemot* are in fact one unit and *Shemot* really is the Second *Chumash*.

Seen through the prism of Kabbalah, the entire saga of human existence is an endless chain of exile and redemption. The very act of creation is the exile of created beings from the endless expanse of Divinity, which was all that had previously existed. Adam and Eve were exiled from the Garden of Eden and the Patriarchs to Egypt. This process then reverses, and we leave Egypt, receive the Torah, and construct the Tabernacle. We thus revive the redemptive state of closeness to God. All of this is a prerequisite for the return to *Eretz Yisrael,* the place of ultimate closeness and permanent redemption.

In our current generation, we aspire to achieve closeness to God through our divine service and by making Aliyah to Israel. We pray that as a result, *Am Yisrael* will soon experience the Final Redemption in our Holy Land.

PARSHAT SHEMOT

Feminine Leadership

Parshat Shemot provides us with several models of human leadership, including that of Pharaoh, who cynically uses his power to exploit and to oppress. On the other hand, we see how the leadership of Moshe and Aharon develops as the parsha progresses. Initially, Moshe takes responsibility, smiting the Egyptian, but after fleeing to Midian he hesitates when God asks him to redeem Israel. Only the addition of Aharon (we don't know how he initially responded to the Divine call) convinces Moshe that he has a chance in the face of both Pharaoh's great power and Israel's despair.

Another model of leadership is revealed in the story of the Jewish midwives Shifrah and Puah. They listen to Pharaoh's evil command to kill Jewish babies at birth, apparently without arguing, and then practice civil disobedience by ignoring this immoral order. For managing to disobey Pharaoh's orders, God rewards them for fearing Him by making them "houses." The Midrash identifies these midwives as Moshe's mother and sister, Yocheved and Miriam respectively, and adds another facet regarding Miriam, who earlier had persuaded her father to remarry her mother, paving the way for the birth of Moshe and the redemption from Egypt. Additionally, according to the Midrash, regarding the mirrors that the women contributed for the building of the laver in the Tabernacle, we see that their dedication to giving birth to children even into the most difficult of realities is "the most beloved" to Hashem.

Regarding the midwives, the *Mai Hashiloach* writes, "When one is afraid of people he has no composure, which is the opposite [of calm]. The fear of Hashem, however, brings calm. Thus God 'made them houses,' for a house represents composure. Since they had composure from their fear of Hashem they had no fear of Pharaoh."

In Kabbalah, women are associated with the trait of *Gevurah* (self-discipline), the source of *yirah*, which is related to the fear of God. The midwives symbolize feminine leadership (as we are told, "in the merit of righteous women we were redeemed from Egypt"), which is based upon the fear of God that leads to calm and composure. The power of this leadership redeems Israel from suffering, replacing the exile with "houses," - the Jewish home and center of divine service.

PARSHAT SHEMOT

The Burning Bush Within Us All

Moshe's mission begins with his encounter with Hashem by the bush that was burning but was not consumed. Why did God appear in a lowly bush and not in a more impressive tree? Rashi explains, "and not in a tree because 'I am with him in his suffering'" (*Tehillim* 91:15). This verse was an important source for the Piaseczner Rebbe when he wrote his celebrated work, *Aish Kodesh*, and he developed his theology of the Holocaust as divine suffering. Moshe's response is, "I will stop and see this great sight." The *Noam Elimelech* applies this verse to our ongoing struggle to improve our character traits: "A person's basis ... is to break his negative traits ... to reach the level of ecstasy and cleaving. The bush was not consumed, for there are still negative traits. 'I will stop and see' means that one must stop these traits entirely, and then he will see great sights." As long as we are filled with negativity, we are prevented from seeing the great sights that Hashem prepares for us, and we are unable to reach an exalted spiritual state. In order to be on fire with passion for God (and perhaps to imagine ourselves in such a state is the greatest sight of all) we need to first perfect those negative personality traits that are holding us back.

Hashem then tells Moshe to "remove the shoes from your feet for the place you are standing on is holy ground." The Seer of Lublin, in *Zicharon Zot*, views this as another hint regarding our service to Hashem. He explains that if we truly sanctify our lives then even our lowly feet, the part of the body furthest from the head and from holiness, can also be elevated and became holy. But how can we do this? Sometimes we feel so low that we don't even feel Godliness in our heads and in our hearts, let alone in our hands and feet! The Chassidic answer is optimistic. As Rebbe Nachman teaches us, "there is no despair at all!" We need to start from where we are now, and work our way upwards. We shouldn't worry so much about the final results; the main thing is to keep growing with intense enthusiasm to serve Hashem. In a similar vein, the Karliner writes in *Beit Aharon* that, "one must always be filled with burning passion, within the bush, even when he is lowly and spiritually dry; nonetheless he should burn with fire!"

As we learned from Rashi, God is in the lowly bush, and he is always with us in our suffering, whether physical or spiritual. What we really need to learn is how to identify the Godliness within us even when we feel so low, in pain, loneliness, or shame. When we do so we are able to transform a lowly bush into a "great sight." All we need to do is be willing to turn aside, open our eyes, and gaze upon it.

PARSHAT VAERA

Rebuking with Love

Parshat Shemot closes with Moshe's dramatic question to God, "Why have You wronged this people, why have You sent me?" *Vaera*, which immediately follows, opens with the divine response, "And God (*Elokim*) spoke (*vayidaber*) to Moshe, saying (*vayomer*), 'I am the Lord (Hashem).'" From this short verse our commentators learned a crucial, ethical lesson. According to Rashi, the words "And God spoke" are words of rebuke in response to Moshe's bold question. The *Ohr Hachaim* reinforces this idea, pointing out that the name "God" represents "the frightening and terrifying Face." Not only does that divine name signify harshness, but also the verb "to speak"(*ledaber*), says the Netziv, symbolizes harsh language.

The commentators also noted the seeming contradictions within the verse, as the verb "to say" replaces the verb "to speak" and the name "Lord" replaces "God." Additionally, they ask, what is the explanation of the enigmatic words "I am the Lord"? Despite these difficulties, Rav Hirsch writes that in the phrase, "I am the Lord," Moshe receives a complete answer to his question. But what is that answer?

According to the Netziv, "saying" represents gentle language. Hashem began by rebuking Moshe with harsh language, but immediately switched to gentle language. With this he hints to Moshe that the world was created with the attribute of judgment, into which Hashem mixed the attribute of compassion, to ensure its continued existence. So too, although the Jews in Egypt are suffering from a situation of excess judgment, nonetheless, compassion, although yet to be revealed, is there as well.

The *Mai Hashiloach* uses both components of this verse, including the verb and the divine name, in order to explain its meaning and teach us an ethical lesson. "After Moshe spoke against Hashem, God rebuked him, as signified by the word 'spoke' ... also the name 'God' ... but He immediately used 'said.'

This is like one who is angry at a beloved friend, but when he sees him shocked and frightened hints to him that his anger was an act … for 'saying' is gentle language … and the 'Lord' is also full of compassion, and my rebuke was only an act, so don't be afraid at all."

From God's words in this verse, we learn that all rebuke must come from a place of love, and that this love must also be expressed. This principle is crucial for educating our children. While we must occasionally rebuke, it must be readily apparent that this is out of love and affection.

It is important for us to learn to find the right balance in our relationships with those whom we love. In the merit of spreading causeless love, we hope to merit the complete and speedy redemption.

PARSHAT VAERA

Exodus and Creation

Parshat Vaera opens with God's address to Moshe, *Vayidaber Elokim el Moshe vayomer elav Ani Hashem*, "God spoke to Moshe and said, 'I am the Lord.'" Numerous commentaries have focused upon the shift in verb from "spoke" (generally harsh language) to "said" (gentler language), and from *Elokim* (God's name of judgment) to *Hashem* (God's name of loving-kindness). Rav Leibele Eiger writes in *Torat Emet* that this is the only place where the Torah says *Vayidaber Elokim* to Moshe instead of *Vayidaber Hashem* or simply, *Vayidaber*. What is the Torah trying to tell us with this unusual form?

Rav Leibele explains that the exodus is, in a sense, a replay of creation. This idea should not surprise us in light of the many sources that see all of creation as leading up to our acceptance of the Torah at Mount Sinai, for which the exodus was a preparation. We could in fact say that if the creation was the universal foundational event, the exodus was our own particular foundational event. To return to Rav Leibele, the creation also begins with the name *Elokim*. Rashi explains that God originally intended to create the world with His attribute of judgment. When he saw that the world could not be maintained in that manner he combined it with loving-kindness, and the name *Hashem* appears. Rav Leibele also reminds us of the law in Rabbinic jurisprudence that the Rabbis are not allowed to ordain a decree that most of the community will not be able to observe. Similarly, God's initial "decree" of judgment needed to be "sweetened" by the mixing in of loving-kindness. Nonetheless, in order that we will appreciate that love, we must first experience judgment. Thus the world was initially created with judgment, a more external manifestation of Godliness, and then its true inner beauty of divine love could also be revealed.

A similar idea is found in the *Imrei Elimelech* of Rebbe Elimelech of Grodzisk, the Piaseczner's father. When the world was initially created, only its physical manifestations were initially apparent. God then revealed Himself in order that humanity would not fall into the tragic error of believing that they were alone in the cosmos, without divine guidance and love. Similarly, the Jews in Egypt were living an existence of harsh judgment, slaving for Pharaoh. Had they not been redeemed when they were, they would have sunken to the irredeemable fiftieth level of impurity. At just the right moment Hashem began the redemption, redeeming not only their bodies, but their faith as well.

As the Ramban points out, the name *Elokim* has the same numerical value as *hateva*, nature. If we look superficially at nature, God may appear to be hidden, and so too, when we look superficially at history. But all of this is an illusion. If God's presence were too explicit, we would be overpowered, robbed of our freewill and unable to function. Hashem wants us to have to search for Him in all of reality, history and nature. That is why He placed us in this world, known in Kabbalah as the *Alma d'Shikra*, the World of Illusion. Only here is our service meaningful. We should aspire to have clear vision to always see Hashem in nature, history, and in everything that happens to us. Then we will merit having our faith, as well as our bodies, redeemed.

PARSHAT VAERA

The Name of God

At the beginning of *Vaera* we learn that the Patriarchs did not know God through His four-letter "proper name," but rather as *E-l Sh-dai*. According to Rashi, they heard God's promises but only now would those promises be fulfilled. For the Ramban, this shows a progression from their perception of God through an unclear lens to Moshe's perception through a clear one. Why does this happen during the Egyptian Exile?

The *Meor Aynaim* relates a common Chassidic motif, that in Egypt *Da'at* (consciousness) was in exile, for the Jews had lost the art of serving God. How does this relate to God's various names? The Ramban writes that *E-l S-hdai* is the name of victory, since God did miracles to save the Patriarchs. In *Chaggigah* 12a, *Chazal* teach us that when God created the world, it continued to expand until He told it, *dai* (enough). This is the origin of the name *S-hdai* (meaning, "it is enough"). Rav Simcha Bunim explains that there had been sufficient creation for the world to recognize God's presence.

The *Pri Tzaddik*, on the other hand, sees this as the key to understanding our forefathers' relationship with God, based upon perceiving Him through miraculous intervention in history. Following an additional comment in *Chazal*, we also pray that God should say *dai* to our sufferings. We need to realize that divine influence is only channeled to us to the extent that we are capable of receiving it. Thus, explains the *Beit Yaakov* based upon the *Zohar,* the name *S-hdai* is based upon the word *shadayim* (breasts), for just as milk flows out through a tiny opening to provide just the right amount for the baby, in the same way God provides us with divine influence in just the right amount, as any more would be beyond our capacity and shatter our vessels.

Later on in the parsha, Rashi quotes the Midrash, placing words in God's mouth as he tells Moshe, "Woe to those who are lost and cannot be found. I mourn the death of the Patriarchs. I often revealed Myself to them as *E-l S-hdai*, and they never asked My Name, whereas you ask My Name." Nonetheless, we are entering into a process in which more consciousness of Hashem is being revealed in the world. For the *Meor Aynaim*, this process begins with the plagues and culminates with the giving of the Torah. Thus the Ramban points out that Moshe does not make use of the name *E-l S-hdai*, for the Torah was given with God's Great Name. And Rav Tzaddok points out that now that the Torah has been given, we are in a position to achieve divine awareness through the study of the Torah, and not only through miracles or historical events. We pray that Hashem will reveal His presence through miracles of salvation. But in the meantime we should connect with Him through the Torah. As the *Nefesh HaChaim* states, "Through our study of the holy Torah, we connect with and cling to God's word and will."

PARSHAT BO

The Liberation of a Tune

In the *Zohar* it is written that in Egypt our speech was in exile. Therefore the redemptive process began when we finally started to groan and to scream. In Rebbe Nachman's essay, *Bo el Paraoh*, he states. "Moshe is the idea of silence which is higher than speech." Moshe is in confrontation with Pharaoh, who symbolizes the ultimate heresy. According to Rebbe Nachman, "Through the tune of the tzaddik ... all heresy is annulled." A tune is a wordless voice, capable of expressing our deepest truths that we are unable to articulate verbally, reminiscent of the shofar on Rosh Hashanah.

The *niggun*, or tune, is a central theme in Chassidism, including the writings of the Piaseczner Rebbe. In one beautiful passage, (*Bnai Machshavah Tovah* 18) the Rebbe bases himself upon the *Beit Aharon* of Karlin when he writes, "The tune is one of the keys to the soul, arousing it and its emotions." While it is true that "there are great cantors and musicians who are far from God", this is because the tune merely opens up the soul, but once opened, "there is no saying what one will do while emotional." Emotion itself is neutral, and it is up to us to use it for divine service.

The Rebbe therefore gives us some practical advice: "Accustom yourself to the song and tune of serving Heaven ... take a tune, face the wall, or simply close your eyes and imagine that you are standing before the Throne of Glory. You pour out your soul to God in song and tune from the depths of your heart. Then you'll feel your soul going out in song ... you'll feel that your soul has begun to sing by itself." In the last analysis, "This is the way of the Chassid. He cries sometimes during a happy song and while dancing, and he dances to the tune of Kol Nidre."

In Egypt we were unable to speak. Our scream began the process of our liberation. One cannot conduct a verbal debate with the heresy of Pharaoh. Victory can only come through the tune, through a silence, not for lack of words, but above words.

Through tune and song to God, I redeem myself from the constricted consciousness of Egypt, from loneliness and depression.

In *Aish Kodesh* on *Parshat Bo*, the Piaseczner Rebbe writes, "Everyone, after learning ... praying, or serving God, should look inward to see if he came close ... to the secret (of the Torah that is meant for him alone)." If we do so and discover that we have in fact come closer to discovering the existential meaning of our own lives, then we have reached a certain level of personal redemption. If not, we should not despair, but continue to search and to sing, to search with a song, until we learn the tune of our own redemption, the tune that we can sing to God and hear Him singing back, just for us.

PARSHAT BO

Sanctifying Time and Space

Rav Tzaddok writes that when the weekly Torah portion discusses the events of a certain holiday, it is as though that holiday is actually taking place. Therefore *Shabbat Bo* is like Pesach, when we celebrate the Exodus from Egypt. *Parshat Bo* includes the famous phrase, *Hachodesh Hazeh Lachem,* "This month is for you," referring to the month of Nisan and *Am Yisrael's* power to sanctify time. According to the *Beit Yaakov* the summer after the winter is like the day after the night. This is related to the *Sfat Emet's* description of exile as a static reality, in which there is no *hitchadshut* (renewal).

To be truly creative, we need to connect with the supernatural source of reality. In *Kohelet,* we read that "there is nothing new under the sun," but apparently above the sun there is! The Jewish People measure time primarily according to the moon. Unlike the sun, which shines forth its own light, the moon merely reflects the light of the sun, as we reflect the light of Hashem. Additionally, the sun is either off or on, day or night, white or black. We know that real life is much more like the moon, with its constant progression of various stages of more and less light, no light, and again a bit of light. With many gray areas and ups and downs, both are very similar.

In *Parshat Bo*, we also learn of the holiness of the *bachor,* the firstborn. Rebbe Yisrael of Rizhin writes that the *bachor* represents the initial stage of the thought process. At this crucial decisive stage one can go either in the direction of *the firstborn of Egypt,* representing impurity, or preferably dedicate our thoughts to holiness, *the firstborn of Israel.* For the *Beit Yaakov,* the *bachor* represents the moment of initial influence, hopefully the moment of instilling holiness. Pesach is the holiday in which we perfect our capacity to give and to influence, as well as our capacity to receive, symbolized by the prohibition of *chametz* and the eating of matza. The success of much of our lives, both in relation to Hashem and to other people, is based upon our understanding of how and when to give and to receive properly.

Our ability to sanctify time represents the Kabbalistic notion of *shana*. The holiness of the *bachor* is *nefesh*, the concept of the individual. Both are stages in our journey from Egypt to reach the holy space of *Eretz Yisrael*, known as *olam*.

We hope that we will all be blessed to sanctify time, space, and ourselves, leaving behind all that limits us from truly serving Hashem.

PARSHAT BO

Finding a Sliver of Light in the Darkness

The *yahrzeit* of the famous author of the *Sfat Emet,* Rebbe Yehuda Aryeh Leib Alter, the second Rebbe of the Gerrer Chassidim, falls on 5 Shvat, which is close to *Shabbat Parshat Bo.* The *Sfat Emet* was so great that Rebbe Elimelech of Grodzisk referred to him as *Melech Yisrael,* the King of Israel. It is therefore only appropriate here to explore some of the thoughts of this giant and incisive thinker on our parsha.

Parshat Bo deals largely with the concept of *kedushat hazman,* "the holiness of time." We find this when Moshe is given the mitzvah of *Hachodesh hazeh lachem,* when we were commanded to sanctify the months and set Rosh Chodesh, "the new month," based upon the appearance of the new moon and to set our calendar accordingly. At the same time, the holidays are also determined by the High Court's proclamation of the new moon. This is well illustrated by the well-known *mishnah* in Rosh Hashanah, in which Rabban Gamliel and Rabbi Yehoshua dispute the proper timing of Yom Kippur due to a disagreement regarding the validity of testimony regarding the new moon. The exception to this rule is Shabbat, whose holiness was sanctified by God Himself at the time of creation. Shabbat continues to occur every seven days and is not dependent upon any human action or declaration.

In this context, the *Sfat Emet* discusses the distinction between Shabbat and Rosh Chodesh. Shabbat, as the Sages tell us, is like The World to Come. Its holiness is set without human intervention, and is readily apparent. Rosh Chodesh, on the other hand, occurs during the week, and is an example of spiritual light appearing in the usually dark, mundane weekdays. (This is obvious also in light of the fact that it begins with the sighting of the tiny sliver of light that is the new moon in the previously dark night). In order for this to happen, says the *Sfat Emet,* human intervention is required. There is, of course, intrinsic holiness in the darkness as well; after all, it is part of God's creation. Yet it is normally hidden and it is our job to find it and activate it. For this reason, we human beings are responsible for the process of sighting the moon and proclaiming Rosh Chodesh. This requires a lot of faith on our part, as darkness also represents a situation in which we feel that God is hidden and we are desperately searching for the light that can help us find our way out of the dark, or that can keep us going until the morning.

Rashi points out that it is very difficult to see the moon during the day. Thus when God first gave this mitzvah to Moshe he showed him the moon at dusk. The *Sfat Emet* reminds us of the verse in Psalms, *v'emunatcha b'lailot*, "your faith is in the nights." During the day it is easy to have faith, but the real test comes at night, when we no longer have the security of "seeing" God's Face. This, according to the *Sfat Emet*, is directly related to the overall context of our parsha, just before the dawn of the Exodus. We all know that "the night is always darkest just before the dawn," and that was certainly true for the overburdened Jewish slaves in Egypt. Yet their ability to find faith even at times of darkness enabled them not only to sanctify time, but also to sanctify themselves, replacing Pharaoh with Hashem, our true Master.

We also live in trying times. Sometimes the darkness seems unbearable. We need to remember that at the end of the month the moon is totally hidden just before it reappears. Difficult tribulations afflict the world before the great light of the Messiah can be revealed. We need to become real *anshei emunah*, people of faith, just like the *Sfat Emet* himself, and we will then merit the rule of the King of Israel.

PARSHAT BESHALLACH

The Song of the Sea

Parshat Beshallach is filled with many particularly significant events. The Jews, just having left Egypt, camp at *Pi Hachirot,* the Egyptians pursue them, and Hashem splits the sea, saving us and drowning the Egyptians. *Chazal* tell us that at this time even the lowliest Jew reached a greater level of prophecy than the prophet Yechezkel. We then sang the famous "Song of the Sea," giving this Shabbat a rare special name, *Shabbat Shirah,* the "Shabbat of Song." Afterwards, Hashem began to feed us with manna. At the end of the parsha the Jewish People had a near fatal encounter with Amalek, destined to become our nemesis throughout the ages. Interestingly enough, this parsha is always read around Tu Bishvat. Here we may ask how all of these seemingly disparate events are related, and what they have to do with Tu Bishvat. Lastly, why does this Shabbat receive the special appellation of *Shabbat Shirah?*

According to the Ari, the Egyptian exile was a rectification of the licentiousness of the generation of the Flood. The throwing of the boys into the water is therefore a kind of replay of the Flood. As we have learned, the Flood itself was kind of like a giant mikvah, purifying the world from all of its terrible sin. Perhaps we can view the passage through the Sea of Reeds, (*Yam Suf,* also known incorrectly as "the Red Sea"), which is the culmination of the exodus process, as also being a kind of ("dry-cleaning") mikvah.

Before arriving at the sea the Jews encamped at *Pi Hachirot,* literally meaning, "the mouth of freedom." Rashi explains that it received this name because it was in that place that *Am Yisrael* really gained their freedom. But is that so, seeing that they were still being pursued by the Egyptians? The *Midrash Mechilta* states that *Pi Hachirot* was a center of idolatry with statues in the form of a man and a woman. The *Mai Hashiloach* elaborates on this point. This was the center of an orgiastic pagan cult. It was named

"Freedom" because the Egyptians mistakenly believed (as do many people even today) that in the place where people can completely let go and fulfill all of their desires, they become truly free. Yet this is a grave error because, as the *Mai Hashiloach* points out, since their desires rule over them, there is no greater slavery.

Here we are reminded of the famous Rabbinic dictum; "There is no free person other than the one who engages in the Torah." Ultimately, liberation from our own desires is the first step towards complete freedom. From there we marched to our freedom at the sea, for the sexual purity represented by *Am Yisrael's* modest behavior, even at *Pi Hachirot,* while incomprehensible to the Egyptians, was in fact the prerequisite to their ultimate freedom. Therefore, as Rav Tzaddok Hakohen states in *Pri Tzaddik,* the ability to sing holy song, as we did after our deliverance at the sea, is a manifestation of *tikkun habrit* and *tikkun hada'at,* the rectification of sexuality and of the consciousness from which it stems.

The next stage in this process, which ultimately leads us to *Matan Torah,* is the eating of manna. As *Chazal* say, the Torah was only given to those who ate the manna. Just as the process of crossing the sea was instrumental in our achievement of sexual holiness, so too the eating of manna was crucial for us to achieve holiness in eating, another prerequisite for receiving the Torah. As Rav Tzaddok explains in *Kuntres Ait Haochel,* sexual desire and the desire to eat are interrelated. This is, of course, clear from the story of humanity's first sin in the Garden of Eden, in which Adam and Chava tasted from forbidden fruit and simultaneously lost their sexual innocence as part of their transition from objective to subjective awareness (as explained by the Rambam in the *Moreh Nevuchim*).

According to the Midrash, Amalek continued to taunt *Am Yisrael* regarding our purity and holiness. His evil must also be overcome before we can receive the Torah. Tu Bishvat, according to Rav Tzaddok, is the day when we begin to correct our eating by rectifying Adam's sin of the fruit. With our Tu Bishvat seders, we overcome this and begin to eat in holiness. This is followed by Purim, in which we overcome Haman (Amalek), and reaches its conclusion on Pesach, when we go out to freedom and begin the march to *Matan Torah* on Shavuot. All of this is encapsulated within the holy song of deliverance and redemption that we sang after crossing the sea. The ability to sing a holy song, in this case a prophetically inspired song, is the true sign of real religious freedom, the freedom to serve Hashem unhindered by evil, external or internal. The combination of Shabbat and *Shirah* is an eternal celebration of all that is good and holy. We join in this celebration when letting our voices ring out in song as we rejoice in our closeness to God.

PARSHAT BESHALLACH

Miriam's Song

After the entire nation sang its song at the Red Sea after they had miraculously crossed it, Miriam the Prophetess led the women in their own special song. What is special about Miriam? Rashi states that the women brought musical instruments with them when they left Egypt, for they were filled with faith that God would do miracles for them. The Kli Yakar notes that the women used musical instruments because the Divine Presence only appears amidst joy. The Piaseczner Rebbe in *Aish Kodesh* explains the Rabbinic dictum that the Jewish People are redeemed in the merit of righteous women to mean that their righteousness is primarily reflected in their mercy.

Miriam is also well known for the well from which we drank in the desert, which appeared in her merit. When Miriam passed away, the water ceased, leading to the incident in which Moshe struck the rock. In that context Rashi tells us that like Moshe and Aharon, Miriam also died by a divine kiss, but this is hidden in the Biblical text because, "It is not proper *(she'aino derech kavod shel maalah)* to say that God kissed a woman." The Piaseczner Rebbe asks why this should make a difference, as we are certainly not dealing here with a physical kiss. His answer is a radical rereading of the Rabbinic text based upon the teachings of his father, Rebbe Elimelech of Grodzisk. Men, who are required to study Torah constantly and to fulfill positive time-bound precepts, receive subliminal heavenly hints. Therefore, even when they think that they have aroused themselves to divine service, the credit is actually God's, and not theirs! Women (such as Miriam), on the other hand, being technically exempt from these commandments, receive no help from above, and when they perform them they deserve all of the credit.

It would therefore be inaccurate to give any credit to Heaven for Miriam's service, which came totally at her own initiative, and was therefore not *al pi Hashem,* by the mouth of

95

God, which is no longer understood to refer to the divine kiss, but rather to divine encouragement to perform the mitzvot! It thus emerges that women's spiritual energy is more praiseworthy than that of men, as they take full credit for their actions and study. This is in line with the thinking of Rav Kook, who writes in *Shabbat Haaretz* that while a mitzvah that has been commanded is on a higher level than one that is not, one who acts voluntarily is emulating the Patriarchs, who observed the Torah before it was given. Such an individual is one who serves Hashem out of love, which is the highest level. Miriam's service flowed from within her like the waters of a natural spring, and the Jewish People therefore received the spring waters in her merit.

This particular *drasha*, composed by the Piasezcner Rebbe, was actually a hidden eulogy for his wife, Rachel Chaya Miriam, the daughter of Rebbe Yerachmiel Moshe of Kozhnitz, who had died five years earlier on *Shabbat Chukat*, the recorded anniversary of Miriam's death. She was a holy woman and a great Torah scholar, who specialized in the study of Kabbalah and Chassidut and helped the Rebbe edit his books. When the Rebbe once left his house in the middle of writing a *drasha*, he returned to find that she had finished it for him! For him this was the fulfillment of the verse, "and they shall be as one flesh."

The *Maor V'shemesh* writes that while Moshe's song was in the future tense, that of Miriam and the women was on a higher level, as it was sung in the present. That which men can only dream of, women are able to connect with in the here and now. We should pray that this feminine spirituality will strengthen itself in our generation, and overflow to the men as well.

PARSHAT YITRO

Receiving the Torah Throughout Our Lives

While we usually think of *Matan Torah* as a one-time event, the *Beit Aharon* teaches that Hashem actually gives the Torah to *Am Yisrael* every Shabbat. In fact, he states, if we prepare ourselves properly on Shabbat the Torah is given to us every day.

The Torah tells us: "In the third month after the Israelites had left the land of Egypt, on that very day they entered the wilderness of Sinai. They journeyed from Refidim and encamped in the wilderness ... in front of the mountain."

Rebbe Elimelech of Grodzisk explains in *Imrei Elimelech* how these verses guide us in our personal preparations to receive the Torah. In order to understand this we must first grasp some basic definitions. "Good" is whatever brings us closer to Hashem. "Bad" is whatever takes us away from Him. "Humility" brings us closer to Hashem, while "arrogance" takes us away. Based upon this, Rebbe Elimelech delineates several stages in the process. Firstly, we must become like the desert, which is a place of utter desolation. This is the ultimate humility, which is necessary to nullify the ego that prevents us from opening ourselves up to Hashem.

Once we have achieved this level of *bittul*, ego nullification, we need to make ourselves into a vessel that will be capable of receiving the light of divinity. We can achieve this by becoming like an *ani*, a poor person, who is always ready to receive sustenance. In fact, the word *ani* has the same numerical equivalent as the word *Sinai*. So too, the true servant of God, while always feeling inadequate, nonetheless is always ready to receive the divine influx. But how is this accomplished? The *Imrei Elimelech* tells us that we need to contemplate just how much Hashem loves every single Jew. He informs us that the numerical equivalent of the acrostic of the ten *sefirot* is equal to the word *Yisrael*, which reminds us of the grandiose origins of the Jewish soul. This realization leads us to a state of *deveikut,* cleaving to Hashem, making us ready to receive the Torah.

The *Imrei Elimelech* also gives us another important tip. When we are traveling from Refidim to get the Torah, we need to think quickly about *teshuvah* and then run away from the evil inclination in order to receive it! This is not the time to get bogged down in fixing all of our sins; there will be time for that later. If we worry too much about the past at this point, the *yetzer hara* will have time to catch us and we will have a hard time moving on.

The Grodzisker's son, the Piaseczner Rebbe, writes in *Derech Hamelech* that our acceptance of the Torah must become perpetual, for we always need to find newness within it. By integrating his father's advice into our lives we will be able to accomplish this holy task. Instead of celebrating *kabbalat haTorah* once a year on Shavuot, we will experience this on a weekly or even a daily basis.

In fact, according to the *Beit Yaakov,* God proclaims the Ten Commandments continually. Normally we can't hear them, due to the background noise in our lives, which was turned down during *Matan Torah.* If we can succeed in turning down this noise ourselves, we will have accomplished the ultimate good, bringing ourselves ever closer to Hashem.

PARSHAT YITRO

The Dual Aspect of Shabbat

The giving of the Torah is, in many ways, the climax of *Sefer Shemot*. Although all of the mitzvot were given on Mount Sinai, the Torah emphasizes the Ten Commandments, which were inscribed upon the tablets of the law. These Ten Commandments are repeated in the book of *Devarim* in the context of Moshe's farewell speech to *Am Yisrael*.

Subtle differences appear between the two versions. According to the Netziv in *HaEmek Davar Shemot* 34:1, the second version was written upon the second set of tablets, the first having been shattered in response to the sin of the Golden Calf. We will explore the differences regarding the mitzvah of Shabbat in order to reach a deeper understanding of this central mitzvah:

Shemot 20:8-11: <u>Remember </u>the Sabbath day, to keep it holy. Six days shall you labor, and do all your work: but the seventh day is a Sabbath to the Lord your God... <u>for in six days the Lord made heaven and earth,</u> the sea, and all that is in them, <u>and rested on the seventh day:</u> therefore the Lord blessed the Sabbath day, and hallowed it.	*Devarim* 5:12-15: <u>Keep</u> the Sabbath day to sanctify it, <u>as the Lord your God has commanded you</u>. Six days you shall labor, and do all your work: but the seventh day is the Sabbath of the Lord your God ... <u>And remember that you were a servant in the land of Egypt, and that the Lord your God brought you out </u>from there with a mighty hand and a stretched out arm: therefore the Lord your God commanded you to keep the Sabbath day.

We will focus on three differences:

1. In *Shemot* the word *Zachor* (meaning "remember") is used, as opposed to *Shamor* (to "keep"), which appears in *Devarim*.

2. The reason given for Shabbat in *Shemot* is to remember creation, while in *Devarim* it is to remember the exodus from Egypt.

3. In *Devarim* we find the phrase *Ka'asher Tzivcha*, ("as the Lord your God has commanded you"), which has no parallel in *Shemot*.

In order to shed light on the first two points, we will begin by examining the third. According to the simple explanation, *Devarim* reminds us to observe Shabbat, about which we were already commanded at Mount Sinai, as was recorded earlier in *Shemot*. Yet this explanation is clearly incorrect. Rashi on *Devarim* 5:12 dismisses this idea, reminding us of a phrase that we all sing in *Lecha Dodi*: *Zachor Vishamor Bedibur Echad Ne'emru* – "*remembering* and *keeping* were stated simultaneously."

Devarim is not only a second reading of the Ten Commandments; it is a restructuring of what was also expressed at Mount Sinai. Conversely, everything that was stated in *Shemot* is also alluded to in *Devarim*. To what, then, does the phase *Ka'asher Tzivcha* refer? Rashi, based upon the *Gemara* in *Sanhedrin* 56b, tells us that the mitzvah of Shabbat was given to *Am Yisrael* at Mara, after the crossing of the Reed Sea, before reaching Sinai. The Shabbat experience is therefore so crucial that it is actually a prerequisite to receiving the Torah. (A personal parallel to this concept is that a brit milah takes place on the eighth day of life, after the baby has experienced one Shabbat.)

Rav Hutner, in *Pachad Yitzchak, Shavuot* 12, explains the differences between the two versions. Basing himself on the Maharal's *Tiferet Yisrael*, he reminds us that *Devarim* is also called *Mishnah Torah*, which is usually translated as the "Repetition of the Torah", since this book, as Moshe's farewell speech, reviews many of the mitzvot previously stated in the earlier books. While the book of *Devarim* is also the verbatim word of Hashem, it is stylistically different than the first four books. Here, Moshe speaks in the first person, and the divine words are spoken as though they were his own. According to the Maharal, the Torah's pristine divine teachings are being restated here in more human, earthly terms. So in *Shemot* the reason given for Shabbat is the "divine" reason of creation, whereas in *Devarim* it is the more "human" reason of the Exodus from Egypt. Only after leaving Egyptian servitude was *Am Yisrael* capable of sanctifying time and observing Shabbat.

Regarding the change in verbs from *Zachor* (remember) to *Shamor* (keep), the Maharal's explanation is as follows: From *Zachor* the Rabbis learned the positive mitzvot of Kiddush and Havdalah, expressing the requirement to verbally proclaim the holiness of Shabbat. From *Shamor* they learned the prohibition of 39 categories of *Melachah* - creative labor. As stated previously, *Zachor* and *Shamor*, the mitzvah of *Kiddush* and the prohibition of labor, were stated simultaneously, and are in fact, two aspects of the same commandment. The Maharal explains that the function of the negative commandments is to keep us from falling to a lower spiritual level, whereas the active performance of the positive commandments is meant to elevate us to a higher spiritual level, to bring us closer to Hashem. This is similar to the famous comment of the Ramban, that negative commandments are an expression of *Yirat Hashem*, the fear of God, and positive commandments are an expression of *Ahavat Hashem*, the love of God. Therefore, in *Shemot* we are given the positive mitzvah of *Zachor*, elevating us closer to the Divine, and in *Devarim*, written in more human terms, the emphasis is on *Shamor*, the negative, to help us maintain our basic human level.

The phrase *Ka'asher Tzivcha* ("as the Lord your God has commanded you") does not appear in *Shemot*, according to Rav Hutner, even though Shabbat had already been commanded at Mara, for a similar reason. Since the mitzvah was given before the Torah was revealed, it is in a sense similar to the Oral Law. Therefore it is referred to only in *Devarim*, which is written in a human style and is somewhat reminiscent of and a transition to the Oral Law.

Let us now focus on the relationship between *Zachor* and *Shamor*, between the positive commandment of Kiddush and the prohibition of *Melachah*, creative labor. People often wonder as to the need for the countless and highly detailed restrictions on our Shabbat behavior, and they ask what spiritual purpose they are meant to serve. Rav Hutner deals at length with this question in *Pachad Yitzchak Shabbat* 1. The prohibition of labor functions as an external vessel that contains the deeper meaning of Shabbat, which is that Hashem created the entire world and is still present in it, albeit in a hidden manner. While engaging in our daily labors six days of the week, our sensitivity to Hashem's presence in the world may be dulled. Shabbat serves as the weekly reminder of this ultimate truth, serving to help us reconnect with Hashem. How is this achieved?

The highest expression is that of *Zachor*, the recitation of Kiddush, the announcing of Hashem's presence, but the framework that enables this is *Shamor*. By refraining from labor, by totally changing our lifestyle, we are able to de-emphasize the physical, and elevate our spiritual consciousness, reconnecting with our divine source.

A similar idea is found in the writings of the Chassidic master, Rebbe Yaakov of Ishbitz, in *Beit Yaakov, Terumah*, 1, where he states:

Now the body does not feel the holiness of Shabbat to clearly realize that there is a Creator who rules over every single thing. Only the Jewish soul feels the holiness of Shabbat through observing its mitzvot. For when the body rests from worldly matters, the soul is empowered to look to its source. This is the "extra soul," which is more powerful than the body and shines upon the body. But in the future, in the "day that is totally Shabbat," then it will be clear that also physical matters are for Hashem.

If we were on a higher spiritual level, we would fulfill the mitzvah of *Zachor* – Kiddush – "God-consciousness" in the following way. On Friday night we would take a cup of wine to make Kiddush, and proclaim that God created the world and is still present within it. Kiddush would last for a full 24 hours until it ultimately blended into Havdalah, announcing the end of Shabbat. Were we able to maintain such a heightened state of consciousness the entire day, there would be no need for *Shamor*, the prohibition of labor. We would have neither the time nor the inclination to work, being in a complete state of *deveikut* (literally, "cleaving"), a very close bond with Hashem. However, since we are human, and are incapable of 24 hours of intense concentration and *deveikut*, we need a framework to remind us. This framework is *Shamor*, the prohibition of labor, which is the vessel that contains the inner meaning of Shabbat. By refraining from our daily labors, we remind ourselves of the true purpose of creation and of our lives - to serve Hashem. By feeling the closeness of Hashem's presence on Shabbat, this infuses meaning into all aspects of our lives.

PARSHAT YITRO

The Ultimate Unity with God

The highlight of our parsha is the giving of the Torah on Mount Sinai. This was not only the transmission of information and the initiation of a covenant, but also a peak mystical-prophetic experience for each and every Jew. We can glean some insights as to the experiential aspects of that unique event from the *Maor V'shemesh*, written by Rebbe Kalonymos Kalman [K.K.] of Cracow, the great-grandfather of the Piaseczner Rebbe, who also bore his name. Prior to receiving the Torah, *Am Yisrael* is referred to as *Am Segula*, the "Treasured People." Many interpretations have been given for this name, but for Rav K.K. this means that we constitute the inner dimension of all of the worlds. Knowing this will help us to understand how he describes the intense mystical experience of *Matan Torah*.

Before we actually received the Torah, we made the famous pronouncement of *naaseh v'nishma*, "we will do and we will listen." Here, Rav K.K. describes a religious phenomenon with which we are all familiar. When we are davening together in shul, we have a tendency to fall into the trap of thinking that our *tefillah* and *avodah* is the highest in the room, that only we have real *kavanah*. This is highly destructive. We should always make the opposite assumption, that we are the lowest in the congregation, and need to learn from everyone else around us. If all of us were to think like this, we would constantly inspire each other to greater and greater levels of divine service. This idea is related to Rav K.K.'s theory of community (that had a great impact upon the Piaseczner Rebbe as well). At Mount Sinai, every Jew screamed *naaseh v'nishma* with their own personal *kavanah*, thus revealing their own special aspect of the Torah, and so should we.

Just before the revelation, we are told that Moshe brought the people out towards God. Rashi comments that, "the Shechinah went out towards them like a groom goes towards his bride." The *Maor V'shemesh* explains, using Kabbalistic terminology, that "by saying "*naaseh v'nishma*," they raised feminine waters, revealing parallel masculine waters... for the bride raises feminine waters and receives influx from the groom. Thus *Am Yisrael* raised feminine waters and the Shechinah went towards them, and they received the Torah." Here the rapturous nature of mystical union is described in overtly sensuous terms and in a rare usage of masculine gender imagery to describe the Shechinah.

The actual experience of divine speech is described as *roim et hakolot v'et halipidim*, "hearing the voices and torches," a synesthetic experience in which they reached a place so high that the distinction into sensory differentiation had not yet occurred. For the Netziv, this means that they saw sparks of fire in the forms of the letters. For Rav K.K. the verse doesn't describe their vision of the divine voice, but rather of their own! "They witnessed their own voices as they said *naaseh v'nishma*, and they visualized the letter combinations created by their speech, and the angels created by those letter combinations. And the torches, this was their own enthusiasm."

While we tend to view *Matan Torah* as a one time historical event, this is an error. The *Kli Yakar* states that the reason why the Torah does not reveal the date when it was given is that we need to realize that it is constantly being given to us anew. According to Rav Soloveitchik, every time we read the Torah in shul we are reenacting *Matan Torah*. Of course, for this to be a powerful and meaningful experience we need to make it happen as well. The *Beit Aharon* writes that Hashem gives us the Torah every single day, when we accept God's light upon ourselves. When we do so then we ourselves play the role of *Am Yisrael* at Mount Sinai, to whom the Shechinah went out like a groom to meet the bride. In this way, we are able to experience that great moment of unity with God in our own lives.

PARSHAT MISHPATIM

True Piety: Concern for Our Fellow Man

The literary structure of *Sefer Shemot* is primarily narrative. Beginning with the slavery of the Jews in Egypt, it continues with the Exodus and the splitting of the sea. Afterwards the Jewish People receive the Torah at Mount Sinai, commit the sin of the Golden Calf, and finally build the *Mishkan* (Tabernacle), the place of the indwelling of God's presence. Most of the mitzvot given in *Shemot* (with the exception of *Parshat Mishpatim*) are directly related to the narrative. Examples of these are the laws of the Pesach sacrifice before the Exodus, the Ten Commandments at Sinai, and the many mitzvot pertaining to the service in the Tabernacle.

Regarding the Tabernacle, the Ramban writes: "The secret of the *Mishkan* is that the (divine) glory which dwelled upon Mount Sinai will dwell upon the *Mishkan* in a hidden fashion." The purpose of the *Mishkan* is to be a permanent symbol of the Divine revelation at Sinai. Just as Hashem revealed Himself to *Am Yisrael* at Sinai, He continuously reveals Himself in the *Mishkan* as well.

In light of the above, *Parshat Mishpatim* seems entirely out of place, disrupting the narrative flow. *Mishpatim* contains almost no narrative at all. Instead it deals with a wide-ranging list of interpersonal mitzvot, such as damages and financial obligations. We find details about damages caused by fire, animals, and pits, and the fines levied upon the negligent party. Why are such details included here? *Sefer Shemot* is a beautiful narrative of the spiritual growth of *Am Yisrael*. From the degradation of the Egyptian exile, we emerge to cross the Reed Sea, witnessing a tremendous revelation of God's presence. We receive the Torah at Mount Sinai, hearing the voice of God. Ultimately we build the *Mishkan*, so that the Shechinah, God's presence, can dwell permanently within the camp. Why break up this beautiful and moving narrative with an entire parsha of financial laws about slaves and animals? Why not flow from the Divine revelation at Sinai directly to the *Mishkan* that represents it without this detailed legalistic disruption? At first glance, this parsha would appear to fit better in *Sefer Vayikra* or in one of the legal sections of *Bamidbar* or *Devarim*.

In *Baba Kama* 30a we read: "Rav Yehudah says, 'Whoever wants to be a Chassid (pious one) should fulfill the words of *Nezikin* (damages).' Rava says, 'The words of *Avot* (ethics).' And some say 'the words of *Berachot* (prayer and blessings).'" Both the Maharsha and the Maharal explain that this threesome indicates the need to perfect one's relationship with others, with oneself, and with Hashem.

The first on the list is *Nezikin*, damages, the types of interpersonal mitzvot that we learn in *Parshat Mishpatim*. What the Gemara is teaching us is that true piety is not dependent only upon a spiritual relationship with Hashem, but first and foremost upon building a just society, a society in which people's financial and property rights are respected, in which all are acutely aware of their moral obligations to each other. Indeed the *Mai Hashiloach* teaches that *Parshat Mishpatim* calls upon us to achieve such a state of holiness, that even our property is sanctified, so that it will not harm others.

This is the message of the placement of *Parshat Mishpatim*. The Jewish People have had some very intense and sublime spiritual experiences, peaking at Mount Sinai. And the goal of these experiences is to create the *Mishkan*, a permanent home for the divine presence, and the physical and spiritual center of the Jewish nation. However, before this can happen Hashem tells us to pause for a moment. There is an in-between stage that cannot be skipped. Spirituality is beautiful, but only when predicated upon a true concern for the other. An unjust society cannot hope for the Divine presence in its midst. Only by rigorously enforcing the type of worldly ethic described in *Parshat Mishpatim* can we aspire to the ultimate spiritual experience of God's permanent presence in our midst.

PARSHAT MISHPATIM

The Jewish Slave

After the giving of the Torah in *Parshat Yitro*, we jump right into the civil and criminal laws of *Mishpatim*, beginning with legislation regarding the *eved Ivri*, the Jewish indentured servant. Rav Leibele Eiger explains the concept of *eved Ivri* as it applies to our service of Hashem, *al derech ha'avodah*. He explains, "One must remove from himself all other types of slavery … other than his slavery to Hashem." As the Torah explains, the *eved Ivri* goes free in the seventh year, and Rav Leibele relates this to our experience of Shabbat, the seventh day: "And on the seventh he goes out to freedom – on the holy Shabbat every Jew goes out from all the things that enslave him."

For the Grodzisker Rebbe in *Imrei Elimelech* the essential lesson is the need for *tikkun ha'avdut*, rectifying slavery. We are told that the *eved Ivri* must work for six years. This teaches us to rectify each of the six lower *sefirot* from top to bottom, beginning with *Malchut*, royalty, up through *Gevurah*, self-discipline. (*Shana*, year, is numerically equivalent to *sefirah*). When we have accomplished this we then go up to the seventh, *chessed*, loving-kindness, achieving love of God and going out to freedom from the oppression of the *yetzer hara.*

His son, the Piaseczner Rebbe, asks in *Derech HaMelech* why the famous verse of *naaseh v'nishmah*, "we will do and we will hear," is written in *Parshat Mishpatim*, after the giving of the Torah, and not beforehand in *Parshat Yitro*. He quotes the Baal Shem Tov that "it is a great miracle that a person remains alive after prayer, that his soul has not left him from the great cleaving." This reminds us of a story that Rav Neria tells about Rav Kook. Rav Kook was once staying at a hotel in Europe. Although his custom was to always daven in the morning immediately upon arising, on this particular morning Rav Kook first came down to the lobby and spoke to the manager for a few minutes. When asked for an explanation, he replied that he woke up in such an intense state of *deveikut* that he was afraid that were he to daven right away, he might, God forbid, not survive the experience. He needed to deal with earthly matters until it was safe for him to pray!

The Piaseczner Rebbe continues with a story from his father-in-law, Rebbe Yerachmiel Moshe of Kozhnitz, regarding his grandfather, the holy Kozhnitzer Maggid. When the Maggid was a young man, he had a friend. The two began at the same spiritual point and yet while the Maggid grew in stature his friend remained at the same level. The Maggid later explained that this was because his friend would pray, and after prayer he would return to the same level he was at before prayer, thus remaining at this same point his whole life. The Maggid, on the other hand, would try to remain on the same level he had achieved during prayer. The result was that each prayer brought him to higher and higher levels of *kedushah* until he reached true spiritual greatness.

This, according to the Piaseczner Rebbe, explains why *naaseh v'nishmah* is reported now, after *Matan Torah*. Even after receiving the Torah, we have to be careful not to go back down to where we were before, but to always keep growing. Our prayers and our learning always carry us to new heights and continuous growth, as we correct ourselves and get closer and closer to Hashem. While the laws in *Mishpatim* therefore represent the details of the Torah that has already been given, at the same time they represent a new gate of higher service for us to enter.

PARSHAT MISHPATIM

Serving God with Joy

The end of *Parshat Mishpatim* records a bizarre event that occurred at the time of *Matan Torah*: "Moshe and Aaron, Nadav and Avihu and the seventy elders went up and they saw the God of Israel ... and upon the nobles of the children of Israel He laid not His hand, and they beheld God, and ate and drank." According to Rashi these "nobles" are Nadav, Avihu, and the elders, and they deserved punishment for gazing upon God disrespectfully, while eating and drinking. While according to Onkelos, they didn't actually eat and drink, but rather luxuriated spiritually in an overly sensual way, the intent is the same. They did not keep the proper distance from Hashem and should have been punished. This position can be supported by *Midrash Tanchuma*, which states that the later death of Nadav and Avihu was actually the punishment for their behavior here, but was delayed so as not to mar the giving of the Torah.

Other commentators are more positive. The Ramban writes that, "They saw what was appropriate for them ... they rejoiced and made a holiday as is fitting for *Matan Torah*." From here we learn that all of our *Avodat Hashem* needs to be joyful. Similarly, Rav Hirsch (for whom the verses describe all of *Am Yisrael*) states that they felt the closeness of Hashem by eating from the sacrifices. This symbolizes the fact that the Torah wants us to sanctify our physical lives as well, and to serve God with every facet of our existence.

This concept is known in Chassidut as *avodah b'gashmiut*, "service through corporeality." This idea expands the realm of serving Hashem from the purely "spiritual" to everyday activities as well, such as eating, drinking, work, and sexuality. Of course all of this is predicated upon the assumption that these activities are done in strict adherence to Halachah. Furthermore, there is a thin line between *avodah b'gashmiut* and hedonism. It is less risky to serve God through prayer and other mitzvot than through physicality. Yet this holistic approach, if done truly *l'shem Shamayim*, for the sake of Heaven, is ultimately the highest level.

We should aspire to merit fulfilling all of these concepts in our own service of the Divine. We should always perform the mitzvot in the way God wants, with great joy. Moreover, our joy should be truly *simcha shel mitzvah*, spiritual joy for the sake of heaven. The pleasure that we feel when we serve Hashem should also permeate every facet of our lives.

PARSHAT TERUMAH

Half a Shekel

In *Parshat Terumah*, we are commanded to give a contribution to help build the *Mishkan*, as God says, "Build me a Holy Place (*Mikdash*) and I will dwell (*Shochen*-as in *Mishkan*) in your midst." Here we may ask how human beings can build a Sanctuary that is more than just a splendid building. According to the *Sfat Emet*, we must first correct the concept of building, or doing, which is central to our physical world. By so doing, we will merit that God will dwell in our midst. God's presence will dwell among us in response to our perfection of the world.

Here, Rav Shimshon Raphael Hirsch points out a crucial grammatical distinction. We aren't really commanded to make a *Mishkan*, but rather a *Mikdash*, meaning a "holy place," (from the same root as *kedushah*, holiness). The *Mishkan* is God's response - that He will dwell in our midst. According to Rav Hirsch, our job is to create the reality of a *Mikdash*, a holy society, for both the individual and the collective. When we succeed in sanctifying society, the Divine response is that of indwelling, representing the two sides of the covenant of the Torah.

The Ramban's statement that the *Mishkan* is the ongoing representation of the revelation at Sinai is very well known. But what is the connection between the *Mishkan* and the Torah? Of all the vessels in the Tabernacle the most important would seem to be the Holy Ark, in which the Tablets of the Law are contained. Interestingly, all of the measurements of the Ark are halves (one-and-a-half by two-and-a-half, and so forth). The *Mai Hashiloach* explains, "All of the measurements of the Ark are halves, since in order to receive the Torah one must know that he is lacking ... and that without the Torah he is incomplete. For God only transmits the Torah to one who knows that he is lacking and that he requires the Torah to complete that lack." Someone who feels that he is already complete is not prepared to receive the Torah.

Real internalization of the Torah can only occur when one makes himself into an empty vessel ready to be filled.

His son, the *Beit Yaakov,* has a different approach. The Ark is built with halves since "God left space for every single Jew to build. The Jew, through his service, completes and perfects this lacking." The half measurements represent man's challenge. The Torah is in a sense incomplete in the world unless we fulfill and apply it. This is similar to the words of the *Beit Yaakov's* son, the *Sod Yesharim,* on *Parshat Shekalim,* that we give a half-shekel to symbolize our service. The "other half" is God's will. These complete each other to form a complete shekel.

We only hope that we will be blessed to fulfill both of these explanations. Although we must know that we are lacking and in need of Torah, the Torah also "needs" our learning and doing in order to reach its completion in the world. By striving to make it complete, we fulfill the objective of the creation of the world.

PARSHAT TERUMAH

The *Aron* and the Nature of Humankind

The *Aron* (Ark) is central to the vessels of the Tabernacle, and is constructed from three boxes. The innermost and outermost are gold, while the middle is wood. For the Maharal, this symbolizes the human being, who has a pure soul (like gold) on the inside of his physical body (like wood). The external gold box may stand for the transcendental holiness that surrounds us. Rav Hirsch, on the other hand, writes that the *Aron* represents the Torah that it contains. The wooden tree of Torah can only grow straight when it is supported by strength and stability, like gold. In addition, the gold symbolizes the prohibitions, and the wood, the positive commandments.

The *Mai Hashiloach* sees in the *Aron* various leadership models of the Jewish People. The King is on the inside, and the High Priest on the outside. Each suffers from a different type of spiritual danger. The King is in danger of becoming obsessed with the physical pleasures of this world, and may forget that his task is to represent the Kingdom of God on Earth. The High Priest, on the other hand, is in danger of neglecting the dictates of the physical world as he reaches higher and higher levels of connection with the spiritual realm. This is also a serious problem, for he needs to continue to serve Hashem and help the Jewish People in this world as well. In the middle is the tzaddik, the righteous one, who knows how to balance the physical and the spiritual. His job is to influence both the King and the High Priest, in order that both of them stay on track and avoid the pitfalls of their jobs.

The *Mai Hashiloach*'s student, Rav Tzaddok Hakohen, explains that the wood of the *Aron* is acacia, *shittim* in Hebrew. While wood itself refers to the Torah, acacia, *shittim*, is related to *shtut*, foolishness, in other words, to the evil inclination that opposes it. The gold that surrounds it inside and out is the Torah scholar, described as one whose inside is identical with his outside, a model of sincerity and consistency. It is this quality which enables one's Torah to overcome one's evil inclination, to elevate it to participate in divine service.

We should all strive to attain the qualities of both the tzaddik and the Torah scholar, striking the proper balance in every aspect of our lives.

PARSHAT TERUMAH

To Embrace the Divine

Parshat Terumah contains a detailed description of the Tabernacle and its holy vessels. Inside the Holy of Holies is the *Aron*, which houses the Torah. On top of it sits the *Kaporet* (the gold covering on top of the *Aron*), upon which are the *Kruvim*, the Cherubim. The Torah tells us, "You should make two Cherubim of solid gold at each end of the *Kaporet*.... And the *Kruvim* will spread their wings over the *Kaporet* facing one to the other." Rashi here states that the *Kruvim* had faces like children, while the Ramban describes their bodies as being like birds. The Gemara in *Baba Batra* 99a teaches that when the Jewish People would do the will of Hashem the *Kruvim* would face each other, and if not (God forbid) they would face away from each other. In *Yoma* 54a they are described as actually embracing each other, and there Rashi explains that they were clinging together, holding and embracing like a man hugging a woman. Here the implication is that the *Kruvim* were formed like a man and a woman, with the masculine figure (so to speak) representing God and the feminine form symbolizing *Am Yisrael* (and/or the Shechinah, the "feminine" presence of God).

A medieval Kabbalistic source can help us to understand this idea. Rav Shem Tov ibn Gaon (14th century) writes in his *Badei HaAron* that, "Adam and Eve were created together, *du-partzufim* [like hermaphroditic Siamese twins], embracing. This is hinted at in the form of the *Kruvim*." Rav Shem Tov brings two insights here. Firstly, he views the *du-partzufim* creation of Adam and Eve as the two of them embracing. This is quite different than the usual description (such as in the Ramban in *Bereishit*) that describes them as being back-to-back. Secondly he provides us with the highly creative idea that the *Kruvim* are meant to represent Adam and Eve in this state. Even after we have provided them with gender identity, the usual understanding is that they somehow represent Hashem and *Am Yisrael*, and for them to also symbolize the human genders in an embrace is a most startling image. Some two hundred years before, the Raavad had already described the *du-partzufim* as representing the Divine traits of *chessed,* loving-kindness (masculine) and *gevurah,* self-discipline (feminine).[2] Thus in the Kabbalistic view of a dual-gendered Divinity, the way is paved for a detailed symbolic labyrinth in which God, Adam, and Eve, the Jewish People, individual men and women, as well as the *Kruvim,* all participate in the same arena. *Midrash Tadsheh* further sees the two *Kruvim* as representing two different names of God that correspond with the aforementioned divine attributes. A bit after the Raavad, Rav Eliezer of Worms wrote in his commentary to *Sefer Yetzirah* that the purpose of the *Kruvim* was to increase fertility amongst the Jews.

In light of the above we can understand a beautiful *drasha* of the Seer of Lublin in *Zichron Zot.* As we saw above, the *Kruvim* spread their wings over the *Kapporet.* The Seer teaches that wings symbolize mitzvot that fly upward when performed with love and fear. The wings of the two *Kruvim* that are spread upwards there-fore represent the divine names and attributes that are associated with love and fear, in the same way that they were described earlier. However we sometimes get bogged down thinking about our sins and then we can't serve Hashem with proper joy. The antidote is to spread our wings, doing mitzvot with love and fear. This will help us to forget the past and move forward, achieving enthusiasm and joy in our service.

The Seer then moves onto the description of the *Kruvim* facing each other and the gender imagery we saw above. They are both man and woman, the microcosm of Hashem and *Am Yisrael,* and thus they simultaneously represent the relationship of Hashem and the Jewish People, as do every husband and wife when they are united. This fits with Rav Shem Tov ibn Gaon's

---

[2] See Moshe Idel, *Kabbalah: New Perspectives,* New Haven, Yale University Press, 1988, pp. 128-131.

vision of the *du-partzufim*, not as back-to-back, but as in the *panim-el-panim* embrace in which each gazes into the other's face, the part of the body that most intensely manifests God's image within the human being. The result, states the Seer, is the process of interaction between the male influencer and the female receiver, who in turn gives to the male and stimulates an even greater influence to descend. *Am Yisrael* performs mitzvot, which gives pleasure to Hashem, who in turn sends down influx and blessing into the world, providing for all of our needs. We respond and the process goes on and on. All of this is symbolized by the *Kruvim* in the Tabernacle and afterwards in the Temple.

Unfortunately there are no *Kruvim* today. All of us must therefore redouble our efforts, religiously and politically, to rebuild the Temple. In the meantime we still have a role to play, as we are the *Kruvim,* in our marriages and in our relationships with Hashem. Let us spread our wings in a loving embrace with the Divine and fly up to Hashem.

PARSHAT TETZAVEH

The Pure Fragrance of Our Divine Service

The three main topics of *Parshat Tetzaveh* are the *Ner Tamid* (Eternal Light), the priestly garments, and the incense altar. What does this order teach us? Since the holy vessels were already described in *Terumah*, we may also ask why the incense altar is mentioned only now. The Chezkuni writes that the eternal light comes to illuminate the *Mishkan* just as Hashem lit up the world at the time of creation. Here we see that the *Mishkan* is a microcosm of the entire world. Since light symbolizes holiness and wisdom, it was necessary at the very onset of creation. In the same way, it is necessary to have light before we can begin the service in the *Mishkan*. The priestly garments are so crucial that *Chazal* declare that a Kohen (priest) is only really considered to really be a Kohen when he is wearing them. In fact, working in the *Mishkan* without them carries a penalty of death. As we know, the Kohen symbolizes the *oved Hashem*, "the true servant of God," and we are all striving to emulate him and learn from him how to properly worship Hashem.

The Gemara in *Arachin* 16a states that, "Just as the sacrifices atone, so do the priestly garments atone. Therefore, the Ephod (a shirt with two shoulder straps, to which the golden breast plate was attached) atones for idolatry, the tunic for bloodshed, the breeches for sexual immorality, the breastplate for financial wrongdoing, the turban for haughtiness, the robe for negative speech, the headband for brazenness, and the sash for immoral thoughts." This list highlights the crucial areas of our behavior that must be perfected if we are to be, like the Kohen, true *ovdei Hashem*.

The incense altar comes as the climax of both *Terumah* and *Tetzaveh* together. Rav Hirsch explains that the *rayach nichoach*, the pleasing fragrance, can only arise at the end, after all else has been completed. The incense altar stands, facing the *Aron*, between the *Menorah* and the Table of the showbread. Thus we see that that the

Torah in the *Aron* influences both our spiritual (*Menorah*) and our physical (Table) lives. This is what enables us to serve Hashem with a pleasing fragrance. The *Mai Hashiloach* explains that only after the priestly garments have filled the Jewish People with the awe of Hashem, "they are now able to receive the joy and love that come from the power of the incense." The Hebrew word for incense, *ketoret,* actually means "connection," as the incense helps to create a deeper connection between man and God, in itself the greatest source of joy and love.

When we look at the totality of the Tabernacle, its vessels and the priestly garments, we find the image of the sensory feast that went on there to be overwhelming. The vessels and garments provided visual beauty, and the bells on the priest's robe, in addition to the Levitical music, created auditory stimuli. The incense provided the sweet scent, and the sacrifices themselves, touch and taste. It is clear that the *Mishkan,* and later the Temple, were created in such a way to create a maximal meditative experience upon entering, one that was most conducive to achieving *deveikut,* cleaving to Hashem. We should only hope that we will be blessed to reenter this meditative space in the near future.

PARSHAT TETZAVEH

The Priestly Garments and Ourselves

After learning about the *Mishkan* and its vessels in the previous parsha, we travel further inward to study the uniform of the Kohanim. The Rabbis teach us that only when uniformed are the priests really priests, and without proper garments they are liable to the death penalty. Rav Y.M. Poupko taught us that the function of a uniform is to de-emphasize the individual in favor of his role, and that in the *Mishkan* everything must be done exactly as the Torah dictates, for if not, it may be idolatry.

One of these garments is the *avnet*, a sash worn around the waist. The Chassidic *gartel*, a cloth sash worn around the waist, is a close modern-day equivalent to this. The Gemara states that the *avnet* atones for sinful thoughts, and it is often said that that the *gartel* separates one's higher spiritual half from the lower physical one. The *Beit Yaakov* takes this idea a little further. There are three centers in the human body. The brain is the spiritual center, while the heart is the seat of the emotions, and the genitals express the most powerful of the physical urges. The ultimate question is; where does my heart go? Is it primarily elevated due to the influence of the brain, or is it drawn towards hedonistic pursuit by the intense influences of the body? The *avnet* (or *gartel*) is worn around the waist as a statement that the wearer wants to direct his heart upwards towards the spiritual brain, and not downwards to the physical body. One of the reasons some Chassidim don't wear neckties is to prevent the brain from being divided from the heart, and one of the reasons for *peot* is to connect between these two. The *avnet* is, however, worn only at times of prayer or Temple service. One's physical side must also find proper outlets that are themselves another aspect of holistic *Avodat Hashem*.

The *Mai Hashiloach* points out that the High Priest wears both the *tzitz*, a headband with the Name of God inscribed upon it, and *michnasayim*, breeches, in order to cover the genitals. This teaches us that even one who has reached the spiritual level of having God's Holy Name inscribed upon him must nonetheless always be on guard to protect his basic moral behavior. In a society in which we are endlessly bombarded by immoral messages, we always need to be on guard not to sully our Torah with anything that is not strictly sanctioned by Halachah. Woe to those who blur Halachah to permit what is forbidden, weakening us as "a kingdom of priests and a holy nation." By fulfilling this lofty ideal in addition to the actual service of the Kohanim in the *Beit Hamikdash*, we maintain our purity and spiritual existence as a nation.

PARSHAT KI TISSA

When the Tablets Were Smashed

Parshat Ki Tissa contains one of the most dramatic moments in the Bible - Moshe's smashing of the two divinely given Tablets of the Law, in response to the sin of the Golden Calf. After all of Aharon's stalling tactics had failed, he was forced to announce that "tomorrow will be a holiday for God," hoping to gain one more day so that Moshe could return from Mount Sinai and prevent this horrible debacle. The Ari understands Aharon's words as a cryptic prophecy that in the future all of the fast days, including 17th Tammuz, when this occurred, will become days of celebration.

When Moshe came down from the mountain and saw the wild dancing around the calf, he instinctively threw down the tablets, shattering them. Much has been written in the commentaries regarding this fateful moment. For example, Rashi gives the simple explanation that if an estranged Jew is forbidden to eat from the *korban pesach,* then certainly the Jews, so estranged from God at that moment, could not possibly receive the tablets, which represent the entire Torah and mitzvot! The *Meshech Chochmah* writes that the Tablets had to be destroyed, because they would have otherwise become the object of idolatrous worship. This idea later became an important source for Professor Yeshayahu Leibowitz's radical approach in which he denied the possibility of there being holiness in any object, even in the Land of Israel itself (God forbid).

What were the repercussions of Moshe's act on the future of the Torah? On the one hand, our Sages teach us in *Eiruvin* 54a that any forgetfulness of Torah learning is the result of Moshe's act. When the Tablets were broken, the letters were loosened from their physical anchor and in later generations from the minds of Torah scholars. On the other hand, in *Menachot* 99a-b, Reish Lakish tells us that Hashem endorsed Moshe for breaking the Tablets, and sees this as an example of the paradoxical rule that occasionally the nullification of the Torah is its very foundation. This rule, used only rarely in history and only by the greatest of all halachic authorities, is also cited in relation to Rabbi Yehudah Hanasi's decision to transcribe the Oral Law into written form so that it would not be forgotten in the wake of the Hadrianic persecutions.

Rav Tzaddok Hakohen, in *Resisei Lilah* 56, sees a connection between these seemingly contradictory sources. Not only are they not really a contradiction, but they actually complement and explain each other. Moshe and Rabbi Yehudah Hanasi are actually two sides of the same coin. When Moshe destroyed the Tablets upon which were engraved the Ten Commandments by God Himself, he took the ultimate Written Law, and removed it from its written quality. This caused the forgetting of the Torah, as a result of which, many generations later, Rabbi Yehudah Hanasi was forced to commit the Oral Law, now in danger of being forgotten, into writing. This was an inverse parallel to Moshe's original act and brought the process around full circle.

While forgetting the Torah would seem to be a grave problem, it has its advantages as well. Rav Tzaddok, here and in his *Pri Tzaddik,* as well as Rav Hutner in *Pachad Yitzchak* on Chanukah, discuss the fact that forgetfulness of the Torah actually leads to a situation in which much more learning occurs and many new *chiddushei Torah*, novella, are produced. For example, when Moshe died, hundreds of laws were forgotten until Otniel reconstructed them with Torah analysis. The results were not only the laws themselves, but also a tremendous amount of original Torah scholarship that enriched the world, just as the Oral Law continues to do so today.

Similarly, when there is a legal dispute, sometimes resulting from forgetfulness, the result is that each side works hard to support their position and more and more Torah learning is created. Therefore, while the incident of the Golden Calf and the shattering of the Tablets initially appear to us as a grave tragedy, the greatness of our Sages is the ability to see that good that comes out of everything, in this case for the Oral Law and Torah study in general. We also need to learn to maintain this balance, on the one hand fighting evil whenever we encounter it, but on the other, always maintaining an optimistic posture regarding everything that happens to us as a nation and as individuals.

PARSHAT KI TISSA

Looking Behind the Mask

Thirty days before a holiday begins, we start studying its laws. This is not only a technical matter, but also indicates that the spiritual reality of the *chag* begins to descend upon the world as well. Therefore, when we read *Ki Tissa,* usually around Purim, the *kedushah,* holiness, of this festival has already begun to permeate our existence. When we examine the parsha, we uncover various hints of Purim within it.

The most famous custom of Purim is the wearing of masks, which dates back to medieval times. In *Ki Tissa* we encounter two instances of face-hiding or mask-wearing. The first is with regard to Hashem Himself, when Moshe requests, "Please reveal Your glory to me." According to Rashi, Moshe requested that Hashem should reveal a visual manifestation of His Glory. However, Hashem responds, "You cannot see My face, for no person can see Me and live … You will see My Back, but My Face you shall not see." The Rambam explains that Moshe desired to reach such a clear perception of Hashem's reality that he would understand His very essence. Hashem's response was that no human being, even the most perfect, could achieve this level. Instead of revealing His Face, Hashem would only reveal His Back, enabling Moshe to perceive how He differs from other beings, but not His essential quality. In this way, Hashem hides His Face from Moshe, an example of *hester panim*, the hiding of the Divine Face, an expression in which *Chazal* see an antecedent of Esther (*hester*) in the Torah.

At the end of the parsha we read, "And when Moshe had finished speaking with them, he put a veil on his face. But when Moshe went in before the Lord to speak with Him, he took the veil off until he came out. And he came out, and spoke to the children of Israel that which he was commanded. And the children of Israel saw the face of Moshe, that the skin of Moshe's face shone: and Moshe put the veil upon his face again, until he went in to speak with Him."

Moshe achieved the ultimate spirituality so that the light of his soul shone through his face (*panim* - face, reflects a person's *pnimiut*, or inner quality) transforming his skin (*ohr* written with *ayin*) into light (*ohr* written with *aleph*) as is discussed by the *Pachad Yitzchak*. This overpowering light was too much for the people to bear, and Moshe covered his face with a mask, in a different sort of *hester panim*.

The challenge faced by the generation of the Jews in Persia was to seek out Hashem's hidden "face" in a generation of *hester panim*. On Purim we are reminded, perhaps by our masks, to always search deeply for Hashem's hidden message for our generation. Additionally, we can perhaps learn to stop taking each other for granted, and to realize that a great light is hidden inside every Jew. By seeing each other in masks, we are reminded not to accept a superficial relationship with each other, but to strive for this essential inner quality. This will lead us, as Rav Kook writes in *Orot Ahavat Yisrael*, to a greater love for the Jewish People, and thus to the unity necessary to defeat our enemy of Amalek-Haman (*Sfat Emet*).

PARSHAT VAYAKHEL

Shabbat and Harmony with Hashem

From the juxtaposition of the prohibition of labor on Shabbat and the commandment to build the *Mishkan*, the Rabbis derived the 39 categories of *Avot Melachot*, the prohibited creative labors on Shabbat. Although there is some difference between the Babylonian and Palestinian Talmuds on this point, the accepted position is that those acts done in order to build the *Mishkan* may not be done on Shabbat. Here we see the categories of space and time intersecting in holiness with *Am Yisrael*, the representatives of personal holiness.

In Chassidut, we learn that the 39 *Avot Malachot* represent the perfection of the creation of this world. During the week, the *Beit Aharon* states, we engage in *birurim*, clarifications of worldly reality, but on Shabbat there are no *birurim*. The essential *birur*, according to the *Mai Hashiloach*, is to clarify that everything we do stands in unity with the will of God. This world is referred to as the *Alma d'peruda*, world of separation, in which we lack harmonious connection with Hashem, other people, nature, and even with ourselves. Our goal is to bring everything back to its essential state of *achdut*, cosmic unity, thereby achieving *deveikut* with Hashem and living cohesive lives. This position is diametrically opposed to the post-modern ideal of the fragmented self.

In this way, explains the *Sfat Emet*, the *Mishkan* itself also represents this process, as it is composed of numerous details that comprise one whole. This explains why this parsha was given *behakel*, in front of the entire Jewish People, to emphasize the importance of unity. Ultimately the *Mishkan* unites not only *Am Yisrael*, but also man and God, symbolized by the *Kruvim* [Cherubim] on the Ark. The destruction of the Temple, according to the Gemara in *Sanhedrin*, had negative manifestations, not only on the cosmic, or even the national level, but directly impacted on interpersonal relationships as well; limiting even the enjoyment a married couple shares with each other.

It is crucial that we redouble our efforts to sanctify all aspects of the reality in which we live; time, space, and ourselves. We also need to work on our relationships from the inside out. First, we must connect deeply with ourselves, then with other human beings (beginning with those with whom we share close relationships), and finally with Hashem.

PARSHAT VAYAKHEL-PEKUDEY

The Merit of the Mirrors

The laver of the Tabernacle is discussed in both *Vayakhel* and *Pekudey*, which are often read together. In *Vayakhel*, it is made from mirrors donated by the Israelite women, and in *Pekudey* the Priests sanctify their hands and feet from its waters before beginning their divine service. The simple reason for the use of mirrors, according to the Ramban, is that the shiny brass looks very beautiful in a vessel filled with water.

Rashi quotes the *Midrash Tanchuma*, which states that the Jewish women in Egypt originally used these mirrors for the lofty purpose of helping them to bring more Jewish children into the world. The women would beautify themselves in front of these mirrors to become more attractive to their weary husbands, who were suffering under the burden of slavery. While Moshe initially rejected these mirrors as associated with the "evil inclination," God instructed him to accept them, as they "are the most beloved objects of all." Eventually the water from the laver would be used to restore harmony between man and wife in the situation of the *sotah*, a "suspected adulteress." According to the *Kli Yakar*, this closes an unseemly situation in which certain gentiles suspected Jewish women of committing adultery with the Egyptians. Rav Hirsch continues Rashi's reasoning, seeing the laver as the means through which the body and the senses are elevated to divine service.

Ibn Ezra has an entirely different approach. The women contributed their mirrors because once they had reached a high level of spirituality they were no longer interested in worldly vanities.

The *Kli Yakar*, (also following Rashi as do most of the commentators) gives us another fascinating insight. Mirrors are used for the laver since water, like a mirror, reflects one's image. Here, in fact, the waters reflect one's spiritual image. (Incidentally, the British author, Oscar Wilde, had a similar idea in his book, *The*

Picture of Dorian Gray.) This is also related to the concept of *sotah*, for "just as a mirror reveals to a woman if she is beautiful or not, the waters of the laver reveal if she has been faithful or not, and if her deeds are pure." The test of the *sotah* is a miraculous process (Ramban), and, similarly, gazing into the waters of the laver miraculously reveals one's "true face."

The *Talmud Yerushalmi* tells us that we read *Parshat Parah* before *Parshat Hachodesh* because *Parah* represents the purity of *Am Yisrael*, whereas *Hachodesh* marks the beginning of the holiness of Jewish time. The *Sod Yesharim* explains that purity is simply the lack of impurity, a neutral concept. It is an empty vessel that we fill with holiness, which is pure light. This is achieved when we, in the words of Rav Hirsch, sanctify our bodies and our senses, making them all a part of our service of Hashem.

PARSHAT PEKUDEI

The Cloud of Glory

Parshat Pekudei closes the book of *Shemot*, and with it the narrative that is largely interrupted by the laws in *Vayikra* and which resumes in *Bamidbar*. *Pekudei* is largely a review of the priestly garments, commanded in *Tetzaveh* and executed now. It is also, according to the *Mai Hashiloach*, the completion of *Vayakhel*, as those vessels constructed in *Vayakhel* are first used here in *Pekudei*. Afterwards, we are told of the erection of the *Mishkan* on *Rosh Chodesh Nisan* in the second year after the Exodus. After all of the vessels are placed in the *Mishkan*, this parsha (and the book of *Shemot*) close with a description of the *Anan Hakavod*, the Cloud of Glory, the Tent of Meeting, and the presence of the Shechinah in the *Mishkan*. The final verses read:

"The cloud covered the Tent of Meeting, and the Presence of the Lord filled the Tabernacle. Moses could not enter the Tent of Meeting, because the cloud had settled upon it and the presence of the Lord filled the Tabernacle. When the cloud lifted from the Tabernacle, the Israelites would set out on their various journeys, but if the cloud did not lift they would not set out until such a time as it did lift. For over the Tabernacle a cloud of the Lord rested by day, and fire would appear by night, in the view of all the house of Israel throughout their journeys."

The Netziv explains that the Tent of Meeting and the Tabernacle are essentially one. From the human perspective, it is the Tent of Meeting, but it is also referred to as the Tabernacle, the *Mishkan*, to indicate the indwelling of the Shechinah, God's presence. In the words of the Ramban, "the glory rests inside the cloud that is inside the Tabernacle." Thus the Ramban continues his famous approach that the *Mishkan* is a continuation of the revelation at Sinai. There, as well, a great cloud rested upon the mountaintop and Moshe needed a special divine invitation in order to enter. Here, as well, a cloud covers the *Mishkan*, the symbol of Mount Sinai, and Moshe is enjoined from entering without special permission.

In addition to indicating to Moshe whether or not he could enter the Tabernacle, the cloud also guides *Am Yisrael* in their journeys. Of course all of our journeys are primarily spiritual and only geographical in a secondary sense. The *Beit Yaakov* uses this idea to explain our verses. "In the building of the *Mishkan* one must understand the great holiness, for it was apparent where God was dwelling ... and everyone understood exactly what Hashem wanted from him, how to behave in every aspect. This is normally shown only to great tzaddikim after much endeavor, but then every Jew knew exactly what God expected from him at every step."

This idea is an application of a central theme in Ishbitzer Chassidut of the *Beit Yaakov* and his father, the *Mai Hashiloach*. Our goal in this world is always to follow the exact will of God in every single thing that we do, large or small. Regarding matters of Halachah, that is relatively easy once we determine the correct law. The difficulty becomes acute in general matters. Normative Halachah leaves those largely up to individual preference, but as the *Beit Yaakov* states in *Ki Tetzei*, "In truth, in depth there is really nothing that is optional. Rather every thing that it is good for a person to do is really a mitzvah. And everything that it is bad for him to do is really a transgression. There is really nothing that is an inconsequential option having no significance." Thus it should come as no surprise that the *Beit Yaakov* celebrates the situation at the end of our parsha, in which every Jew knew explicitly just what Hashem demanded of him at each moment. "We can understand the great joy that Israel had ... that they saw explicitly what Hashem wanted, and this joy is just a hint of what will be in the future."

This description must not be viewed as only a past experience, for it is the experience that we strive for today. We all desire that God's presence be palpable, and that it be centered upon the Temple, the permanent replacement of the Tabernacle. When we merit this again then God's word will go out to all of humanity, and we all know what is expected of us and how to serve Him in peace and tranquility. May that day come very soon.

PARSHAT VAYIKRA

The Value of a Sacrifice

In the book of *Vayikra,* we enter the world of sacrifices, the reason for which was hotly debated by the medieval authorities. According to the Rambam, the sacrifices are an educational compromise, designed by God to wean the Jewish People away from idolatry. If we follow this approach it would appear as if the sacrifices had no intrinsic value apart from being an educational tool for teaching us a powerful lesson.

The Ramban strongly disagrees with this opinion, and he refutes the Rambam's approach by showing that sacrifices have always been a central part of religious ritual. Long before humanity had ever dreamed of idolatry, Adam and Noach both brought sacrifices to Hashem. Even Bilaam brought sacrifices in his attempt to turn God away from the Jewish People. Furthermore, the Torah describes the sacrifice as "a sweet smell to Hashem," and the Ramban insists, "God forbid that they have no benefit other than to refute the idolatry of foolish people." Instead, their secret meaning is that in Hashem's great mercy He is willing to accept an animal instead of the sinner himself, who deserves death for daring to violate the divine will. In addition, they positively impact upon the cosmos with their spiritual energy.

The *Meshech Chochmah* ingeniously tries to harmonize these two positions. He differentiates between sacrifices offered in the Temple, and those offered upon private altars: "Sacrifices offered upon private altars are to refute idolatry ... this is not so regarding sacrifice in the Temple, which comes to unify the worlds and bring the lovers (Hashem and *Am Yisrael*) together." While this distinction is fascinating, it is not a convincing resolution of the Rambam's philosophical position with the Kabbalistic one of the Ramban.

Rav Tzaddok Hakohen provides some justification for the Rambam's view, connecting it to the idea of prayer. "The essence of prayer is the desire and yearning to pray ... the idolater wished

to benefit his god by feeding him. Similarly, *Am Yisrael* desired to
... benefit Hashem ... and Hashem permitted them ... although
He lacks nothing ... sacrifice reflects their desire and longing ...
and thus prayer is in place of sacrifice ... and this desire to pray is
Hashem's desire."

The essence of both sacrifice and prayer is the desire to give
something to Hashem, who, while needing nothing, accepts our
desire as His own. This desire is born out of our awareness that
we, although infinitesimally small and utterly dependent upon His
mercy, nonetheless are driven to "do something for Him in
return." But what can we do for a Being that is perfect and
therefore needs nothing? The truth is that there really is nothing,
and yet we are not willing to accept that. Thus we give sacrifices
and pray, not only for our own needs, and not only for the
experience of closeness that they bring, but also, in our most
humble way, to offer up something of our own in thanks for
Hashem's beneficence.

PARSHAT VAYIKRA

The Nature of Sacrifice

Much has been written about the verse, "When a person from among you offers a sacrifice to Hashem" that opens the laws of the various sacrifices in the book of *Vayikra*. The main discussion centers on the words *adam,* person, and *mikem,* from among you. Rashi quotes the Midrash regarding the word *adam* as hinting to the first man: "Just as Adam didn't sacrifice from stolen property, for everything was his, nor should you sacrifice from stolen property."

The *Sfat Emet* elaborates on this seemingly banal point. The Torah is actually addressing a deep and fundamental problem here. How can we achieve atonement of our wrongdoings by offering an animal in our stead? What is our relationship with the animal kingdom? This goes back to Adam Harishon. He was responsible to lift up all of the levels of creation. These are collectively known as *dzch"m,* an acrostic signifying inanimate, plant, animal and speaker (man). We see Adam's deep connection with the animals, as it was he who named them, declaring their essence. His interdependence with them, while not being allowed to eat them (this was only permitted after the flood), did enable him to bring sacrifices from them.

But what about us today, asks the *Sfat Emet*. As imperfect beings, what gives us the right to offer an animal upon the altar? Is this not by definition theft, stolen from nature herself? This is where the phrase *from among you* comes in. As individuals we really do have limited merits and rights. However, if we nullify ourselves to *Klal Yisrael,* and approach the sacrificial act as part of the nation, we are able to do so justifiably. Similarly, the *Mai Hashiloach* writes that this teaches us that one who comes to sacrifice should not desire haughtiness to be greater than his fellow, but should rather make himself equal with all of Yisrael.

Elsewhere, the *Mai Hashiloach* reminds us that the word *korban,* sacrifice, comes from *karov,* to be close. As he explains, the

Torah is teaching us how a person brings himself close to Hashem. Basing himself upon *Chazal*, he teaches us that we can learn from the various sacrifices that in order to approach Hashem we need to be free of sexual immorality, haughtiness, improper friends, depression, and anger. It is certainly not sufficient to merely offer up an animal and to walk away. A true sacrifice comes with the profound awareness that Hashem, in his great mercy, allows us to offer an animal instead of ourselves. Similarly, all of our *avodah* must include some aspect of self-sacrifice in order to be real and meaningful. Lip service and rote fulfillment of the mitzvot is insufficient. With this point in mind, we can only hope that we will all become truly worthy to fulfill the mitzvot in the way that will bring us close to Hashem.

PARSHAT TZAV

Study and Service

Parshat Tzav completes the description of the various sacrifices that began earlier in *Vayikra*. Afterwards, there is a description of *shivat yemai hamiluim*, the seven days of the dedication of the Tabernacle. This was also the period of initiation for Aharon and his sons, the priests, into the Tabernacle service. Moshe also participated and, according to Rashi, dressed in a white robe the entire week, reminiscent of the High Priest on Yom Kippur, who also wears white garments. Rashi's source is in the *Gemara, Avodah Zarah* 34a, and there he states that Moshe did not wear the priestly garments, which were only to be used by Aharon. *Tosafot* disagree, arguing that Moshe in a sense had the status of High Priest at that time, and in any event, the priestly garments had not yet been sanctified to be worn only by Aharon.

The Kohanim are also commanded to guard the *Mishkan*, and not to leave it for the full seven days. The Ramban sees this as a mitzvah for all generations that a priest is enjoined not to leave the Temple during the time of his service. According to the Netziv, the purpose of their remaining in the *Mishkan* the entire week is to study Torah, specifically the laws of the sacrifices that they are to offer, so as not to err in the future. He points out that the in-depth study of Torah is also called *mishmeret,* a guarding.

Rav Hirsch also sees a lesson about Torah study in these verses. Moshe teaches and instructs Aharon and his sons in all of their duties. This is a precedent for the future relationship between Torah scholars and priests: "Moshe was to appear to them in the role of 'transmitter of the Law,' as in the future the priests in Jewry as such were subordinate to the teachings of the Torah and the teachers of the Torah. The essential office of the Jewish priest is the carrying out of the Law rather than the study of it. The office of the student of Torah is attached to no particular ancestry or tribe." We therefore know that even a *talmid chacham* of the lowest lineage is to take precedence over an ignorant High Priest.

At the beginning of the service in the newly erected Tabernacle, we are reminded of the interplay between study and service, and of the multi-faceted role of the Jew. Taking both Moshe and Aharon as our models, we are reminded of the absolute necessity of in-depth Torah study, of the centrality of *avodah*, service, and of the importance of accepting higher Torah authority. That authority is not inherited; it is earned by hard work and dedication. Essentially we are all invited to enter the Tabernacle of Torah study, *ohalei haTorah,* and to actively participate in the great service of God that we engage in when we study His holy word.

PARSHAT SHEMINI

From Pesach to Iyar

Parshat Shemini is usually read immediately after Pesach, on the Shabbat when we bless the month of Iyar that follows Nisan. One of its main topics is the laws that determine which animals are kosher or not. As the timing of the reading of the *parshiyot* is never a coincidence, we may ask why *Shemini* is the appropriate transition from the holiday of Pesach to the month of Iyar.

The *Maor v'Shemesh* writes that the holiness of Pesach radiates onward in time and influences *Isru Chag* [the day after the holiday], the following Shabbat, Rosh Chodesh, and the entire month of Iyar. Rav Eliyahu Ki Tov discusses the custom of placing a key in that week's challah, or of making challot in the shape of a key on the Shabbat when we bless Iyar. This symbolizes the key to *parnasa*, earning a living, since the manna began to fall in Iyar. Since the manna replaced the matza that was eaten when we left Egypt, this is a clear continuation from Pesach into the new month. We are also reminded that according to the Maharal, the leader of the Seder is to drink a fifth cup of wine, representing the *parnasa* that is needed even after the Redemption.

The *Mai Hashiloach* writes regarding Pesach that the rectification of eating that we experience helps us to guard our eating throughout the entire year. His student, Rav Leibele Eiger, continues that the holiness we achieved by eating matzot on Pesach is actually revealed on this Shabbat. The *Maor V'shemesh* explains that the laws of Kashrut therefore appear in *Shemini*, for now that we have rectified our eating, we are ready to receive and uphold them properly.

Rav Tzaddok Hakohen teaches that each Shabbat contains the holiness of the following week. This idea also includes Rosh Chodesh, which contains the holiness of the whole month. In the case of Iyar, this includes *Yom Ha'atzmaut*, the holiday of our national independence. This is in keeping with the words of the *Sfat Emet*, who wrote that all of the Torah holidays have Rabbinic equivalents. Sukkot has Chanukah and Shavuot has Purim, but Pesach, the holiday in which Hashem gathers the Jews in from the exile and returns them to the Land of Israel, is still lacking its modern version. Less than sixty years later, his prayers were answered and *Am Yisrael* was not only home, but even had their own state after 2,000 years of wandering.

On *Shabbat Shemini*, we therefore leave Pesach behind and travel into Iyar. By so doing, we utilize our rectified eating to observe Kashrut properly. We also, with Hashem's blessings, hope to have an abundant and steady source of income for our families for the rest of the year. And most importantly, the process of the redemption continues to move forward to its inevitable climax, the Messianic era, the Temple, and the perfection of humanity and the cosmos.

PARSHAT SHEMINI

Serving God with *Bittul*

Parshat Shemini is sometimes read on *Shabbat Parah*, when the portion of the Red Heifer used for purification from contact with the dead is also recited. Is there a connection between both of these *parshiyot*? *Shemini* has two main topics. The first of these is the bizarre deaths of Aharon's sons, Nadav and Avihu, for offering *strange fire*, an improper incense offering. The second is the list of kosher and non-kosher animals. The connection between these two subjects is that both the story of Nadav and Avihu and kashrut teach us a lot about self-discipline in our divine service.

The dietary laws are classified as *chukim*, laws for which there are no explanations in the Torah, and they are observed as an expression of Hashem's will. While some (notably the Rambam in *Moreh Hanevuchim*) have offered rational explanations, they are often not very convincing, and we are on safer ground simply accepting them as God's commandments, meant in some mysterious way to bring us closer to Him and make us better Jews.

Nadav and Avihu's deaths teach us that even when we come to serve Hashem with enthusiasm and creativity, we must limit ourselves to that which is sanctioned by Halachah. If not, we are in danger of an ego trip that borders on idolatrous self-worship. Paramount in our *Avodat Hashem* must be the awareness that it is Hashem's word (as interpreted by *Chazal* and the Halachah) that guides us, and not our own desires, however holy we may feel them to be. This reflects the central Chassidic concept of *bittul*, the nullification of the ego.

The *Parah Adumah*, the red heifer, is the ultimate *chok*, so strange that even the wise King Shlomo was unable understand it. The *Sfat Emet* points out that *Parshat Parah* also teaches us the lesson of *bittul*. Rav Nechemia Polen has written that whereas "rational" philosophers, such as the Rambam, want to turn the *chukim* into *mishpatim* by giving them logical explanations, many

143

Chassidic authors take the opposite path, emphasizing our obedience to divine law as a matter of faith, even where the Torah does give explanations. Notable in this hermeneutic posture is the Piaseczner Rebbe in *Aish Kodesh*, where he relates it to the radical annulment of human understanding in the face of the most inexplicable event of all- the Holocaust.

We should always endeavor to aspire to the level of *bittul*, serving Hashem in truth, for pure reasons and without ulterior motives.

PARSHAT TAZRIA

The Power of Renewal

Parshat Tazria often coincides with *Parshat Hachodesh*, which follows *Parshat Parah*, which speaks about ritual purification. As pure vessels, we are ready to receive holiness, which is higher than purity. We therefore now read *Hachodesh*, regarding the holiness of time that begins with Rosh Chodesh Nisan.

The first mitzvah given to us as a people is *Hachodesh hazeh lachem* - "This month (Nisan) is the first month for you." For Rashi, this teaches that the new moon signals the beginning of a new month, and that Nisan, the month of spring, is the first month. We Jews mark time primarily by the moon. The *Pri Tzaddik* writes that we are like the moon. Just as the moon has no independent light, but rather reflects the light of the sun, we too reflect the light of Hashem. We can add that the moon, with its constant waxing and waning, is the most appropriate symbol for our spiritual lives, a constant cycle of light and darkness, ups and downs. In this endless pattern of *razo v'shov*, running and returning, we experience both closeness and the distance that brings us to greater yearning. We then achieve even greater closeness until …we begin again. The Ramban therefore stresses the importance of living our lives in time with our own holy calendar, and not with that of the nations.

The *Mai Hashiloach* writes that *Hachodesh* teaches that we have the power of *chiddush*, renewal and creativity. How are we to activate this in our daily lives? For the *Beit Yaakov*, when summer comes after the winter, it is like waking up in the morning. The Maharal explains in *Gevurot Hashem* that in the spring we witness renewal and rebirth on many levels, in nature, in Torah and for *Am Yisrael*. Therefore, every Pesach, every exodus, is our rebirth.

Parshat Hachodesh is our alarm clock. After spiritually hibernating all winter the time has come to wake up, open our eyes and stretch! Now is the time of rebirth, not only in the realm of nature, but also in the realm of the supernatural, in all that pertains to Torah and to our service of Hashem.

Parshat Tazria appropriately opens with a discussion of childbirth. *Rosh Chodesh Nisan* is a time of rebirth, a time when the words of our sages will be fulfilled: "In Nisan we were redeemed, and in the future we will be again redeemed in Nisan!"

PARSHAT TAZRIA-METZORA

The Cycle of Light and Darkness

In *Metzora* we learn about the ritual impurity and purification of the *niddah* (menstruant woman), detailing the cycle of the family purity laws. According to Rebbe Nachman, in the drama played out in the laws of family purity the woman represents faith and the man intellect. The cycle of family purity teaches us that when faith is weak we must refrain from the use of intellect and focus on strengthening our faith. Once strengthened, our faith becomes a strong vessel capable of containing our intellect.

The Jewish People count time according to the moon with its constant cycle of darkness and light, concealment and revelation. The *Darchei Moshe* teaches that the blessing of the new moon is like a wedding and therefore we dance, for the cycle of family purity parallels the cycle of the moon.

In our private and national lives we also experience constant ups and downs, periods of light and darkness. This is one manifestation of the Baal Shem Tov's saying, "continuous pleasure ceases to be pleasure." Therefore we could not have left the Egyptian exile without first experiencing it, and apparently Israel could not have arisen until the end of the European exile. Needless to say, it is similarly impossible to divide between Yom Hazikaron and Yom Ha'atzmaut, both of which fall around the time that this parsha is read. The idea that we could achieve or maintain our state without sacrifice is a dangerous illusion.

It is important to emphasize the vast difference between the sadness of Yom Hashoah and that of Yom Hazikkaron. Rav Gustman, *zt"l*, once called on a family sitting *shiva* for their son killed in Lebanon. He pointed out that while his own son had been passively murdered in the Holocaust, their son had died as a heroic soldier in the IDF defending the people of Israel and the Land of Israel. This same point was made on Yom Hashoah in more recent times, when the mother of soldier Shmuel Weiss, killed in Jenin, eulogized him at his funeral. This distinction does in fact comfort us.

The *Sfat Emet* writes that every Torah holiday has a parallel Rabbinic one. Sukkot, centered in the Temple, has Chanukah. Shavuot, the reception of the Torah, has Purim. "And from Pesach we are still hoping for a holiday as it says, 'like the days when I took you out of Egypt I will show you wonders.'" Fortunately, our generation has merited seeing the fulfillment of his holy prayer.

PARSHAT METZORA

Parshat Penuyah

Rav Leibele Eiger, a grandson of Rav Akiva Eiger and a fore-most disciple of the Ishbitzer, was much attuned to the unique nuance of each Shabbat. In *Torat Emet* he writes that the Shabbat between the *Arba Parshiyot* and *Shabbat Hagadol* is called *Shabbat Penuyah*, which could be translated as "the Free Shabbat," i.e. that which *does not* have a special designation. Alternatively, it could be a reference to a single woman, known as a *penuyah*. Lastly, it could be translated as the "Shabbat of Turning," from the root *l'fnot*. For Rav Leibele the first option is irrelevant, as the whole point is to articulate what *is* special about this Shabbat.

The *Arba Parshiyot* constitute a purification process to help us prepare for Pesach. For Rav Leibele Pesach symbolizes *eirusin*, the betrothal of *Am Yisrael*, the bride, with Hashem, the groom. This Shabbat is *Penuyah*, read as *Penu Y-ah*, "turn to God," as we turn to Hashem, yearning for Him to bring us to close, to bring us into the holiness of Pesach. In this, we play the role of the bride, who must be free of any binds in order to enter the realm of her husband. (This idea is reminiscent of the famous explanation of the Ran for how the act of betrothal takes effect, an idea that we will not elaborate upon here.) This was our posture before leaving Egypt. The divine response was *E-hiyeh*, "I Will Be." In other words, "I do." With this, Hashem declares His intent to take us as His bride. We then move to *Shabbat Hagadol*, which is like the *Aufruf* before the wedding.

Parshat Metzora discusses a woman's monthly spiritual impurity that is followed by immersion in the mikvah. One of the reasons for this separation is so that the night of immersion should be as romantic as the night of the wedding, which also follows ritual immersion. When we hear the Torah reading, we should try to experience the feeling of separation and the anticipation of unification implicit in our preparations for Pesach. We should make ourselves free of all other bonds and ready for Hashem to (as stated in *Shir HaShirim*) take us to His chambers on Seder night

149

PARSHAT METZORA

Metzora and Mezuzah

In *Parshat Metzora,* we read about the affliction called *metzora,* commonly translated as "leprosy," that affects people, clothing, and houses. *Chazal* teach us that *metzora* is a punishment for speaking *lashon hara,* derogatory speech, as we saw when Miriam was punished for speaking against Moshe. According to the Midrash, Moshe himself is smitten when he speaks against the Jewish People at the burning bush. The *Sfat Emet* points out that we are dealing here with concentric circles, with the human body on the inside, protected firstly by clothing, and even more externally, by the home. Of course, even the body is an externality, guarding the innermost soul. Thus, states the *Sfat Emet,* when a person was malfunctioning spiritually his house would be stricken first, and if he didn't repent, his clothing would then be affected, followed by his body. All of this was in order to encourage repentance before the soul was negatively affected.

Regarding house leprosy, the Torah begins with the words, "when you come into the land of Canaan," from which *Chazal* learned that house leprosy only occurs in the Land of Israel. There is a view that it had a side benefit, that when the walls would be taken apart as part of the purification process, hidden treasure left by the Canaanites would be discovered, enriching the homeowner. Yet if leprosy, including that of a house, is a punishment for *lashon hara,* prohibited everywhere, not just in the Land, it too should be applicable everywhere.

Perhaps another halachah can help us to elucidate this law. We know that in Israel we are required to put up mezuzot immediately upon entering a new house, whereas in the Diaspora, this requirement is only incumbent after thirty days. Similarly, in Israel it is customary to celebrate the *Chanukat Habayit,* dedication of a house, as soon as possible upon moving in, sometimes even on the same day. But why is there a distinction? If all houses are required to have mezuzot, why is there a thirty-day dispensation outside Israel?

The answer is clear. For a Jew the only real homeland is Israel, and therefore his only real home can be in Israel. Outside Israel we are merely transient guests. Our houses are not really our own, and we may be forced to pick up and move at any time. As it says in *Sefer Eretz Yisrael* in the name of Rebbe Nachman, "The holiness of the Land of Israel is sufficient for everyone ... there is our life, our holiness, our homes, our country, our land, and our fate. But in *chutz l'aretz* (outside the Land), we live like guests searching for a place to sleep, loitering in the courtyards, marketplaces, and streets, since it is not our land and portion. Therefore [the Diaspora] is called 'outside the Land,' for we literally stand outside, with no one to bring us inside to the house, until we return to our holy Land."

If this is the case, we should not be surprised that we can take our time putting up a mezuzah in the Diaspora, or that the laws of house leprosy do not apply. For all laws of ritual impurity ultimately are a reflection of innate purity and holiness that has been damaged. A home in the Diaspora, lacking the intrinsic holiness of a home in *Eretz Yisrael,* is paradoxically not worthy of leprosy! We need to daven and work for the day when we will fulfill the verses of "when you come into the Land," when all of the Jewish People will come home to *Eretz Yisrael* and build houses of holiness throughout the Land.

PARSHAT ACHAREI MOT

How to Stay in the Land

Parshat Acharei Mot continues the narrative that left off in *Parshat Shemini* with the death of Aharon's sons, Nadav and Avihu. It opens with laws pertaining to the Kohanim and their Tabernacle service. The Kohanim are given strict guidelines regarding exactly how, when and with what dress they may approach the holy locale, all in order that *they will not die*. As Rashi explains, a doctor wishing to make an impression on his patient will warn him exactly how to behave, because if he does not do so, the patient may die, like so-and-so who didn't follow the rules. In the same way, the sudden and tragic deaths of Nadav and Avihu, who didn't follow the rules, serve as a clear warning to future generations of Kohanim to be exacting in the Temple, for the consequences of sloppy religious behavior are indeed grave.

The bulk of the parsha is devoted to a detailed description of the Priestly service in the Temple on Yom Kippur, carried out almost entirely by the High Priest himself. Today, lacking the Temple, we mistakenly believe that Yom Kippur is simply about fasting and its related laws. A quick look at the Mishna in *Yoma* is enough to correct this misimpression, as seven of its eight chapters are dedicated to the Temple service, with only the last one pertaining to fasting! One aspect of the Kohen's service that has been retained today is confessional prayer, so central to the liturgy of Yom Kippur. Regarding these prayers, Rav Kook writes in *Orot Hateshuvah* that one of the fundamental principles of *teshuvah* is the willingness to take responsibility for our actions, which are born of free will. This is the meaning behind the articulation of our sins in the *vidui*. The result, writes Rav Kook, is that "thus he clears the way before himself to return to Hashem, renewing his life along the correct lines ... connecting with the holiness of the light of the Torah, that revive the soul."

One of the highlights of the High Priest's service on Yom Kippur is the selection, by lots, of the two goats, one to be offered in the Temple, the other sent as a scapegoat (known as the *Azazel*) to die in the wilderness. These two goats must begin as exactly identical animals, yet their career ends in diametrically opposed circumstances. Regarding this, Rav Hirsch writes insightfully that, "All of us are placed at the entry to God's Sanctuary to decide between Hashem and *Azazel* [the opposite of God's Will], between God and the power of our senses... We can decide for God, gathering together all the powers... to be near God, to belong to God, to be like God... keeping pure and doing good of our own free will... Or the decision can be made *l'Azazel*... against these demands of His will ... And the decision is not made for anyone beforehand." Thus these two goats represent none other than us ourselves, and the life-choices that we are constantly called upon to make. Everything rests upon our choosing properly; our entire lives and more hang in the balance.

Acharei Mot concludes with the list of *arayot,* prohibited sexual relations, which we read at Minchah on Yom Kippur. If we do not follow these laws we are told that the Land will vomit us out, just as it did the immoral Canaanite nations that preceded us here. As Rashi explains, "like an allegory of a prince that was fed disgusting food. Since he cannot digest it he vomits it out. Similarly, *Eretz Yisrael* cannot maintain sinners."

Unfortunately our moral behavior in *Eretz Yisrael* today is in dire need of vast improvement. Certain leaders of secular Zionism articulated the goal of transforming *Am Yisrael,* destined to be a Kingdom of Priests and a Holy Nation, into a nation like all others. Unfortunately this misguided dream has been far too successful. Those who are committed to Torah values share a great responsibility to do everything in their power to bring all of the Jewish People to the realization that our continued existence in *Eretz Yisrael* is dependent upon our following the Torah and observance of the mitzvot. We have already learned the hard way that "religious coercion" tends to backfire, and we need to find the proper balance between love and strength in dealing with the broader community, much of which is starved for spiritual meaning and guidance. With God's help, we will be successful.

Thanks to Rabbanit Chana Henkin for pointing out some of the sources in this drasha to me.

PARSHAT KEDOSHIM

Sanctifying our Lives

Rashi teaches us that we become holy by refraining from forbidden relationships and prohibited activities, in other words, by following Halachah (Jewish Law). The Ramban disagrees, arguing that one who follows the letter of the law but not the spirit of the law can be a *naval b'reshut haTorah*, "a disgusting person within the Torah." Holiness for the Ramban is therefore dependent upon *kadesh atzmicha b'mutar lach*, "being holy in that which is permissible." To be holy, we need to sanctify our everyday lives. In Ishbitz, they say that we should always ask ourselves whether any act will please Hashem or not, and if it does not, we should not do it. As the *Beit Yaakov* says, there aren't really any optional acts; everything is on the level of either being a mitzvah or a prohibition! Rashi's and Ramban's positions seem to follow their interpretations of why a Nazirite brings a sin offering when completing his period as a *Nazir*, for Rashi to atone for his sin of asceticism, whereas according to the Ramban for returning to normal life.

The Netziv points out that *kedushah* is a highly personal matter. Unlike normative Halachah, holiness cannot be legislated, and the Torah left it to the individual as a personal decision. For the *Mai Hashiloach*, being holy is not only a commandment; it is also a promise from Hashem, that we will be holy. His student, Rav Leibele Eiger, quotes from the *Zohar* that when the Rashbi [Rabbi Shimon Bar Yochai] and his students would reach *Parshat Kedoshim* they would be filled with special joy, realizing that this seemingly elusive holiness was ultimately achievable, for one can attain unity with the Divine.

One of the most relevant teachings about holiness is that of the *Maor V'shemesh*. For him, holiness is dependent upon the community. A Jew only achieves holiness as part of a community that serves Hashem together, through prayer, study, mitzvot, and loving-kindness. The idea that one can separate himself from the community and achieve holiness is a dangerous illusion. We all need to constantly inspire each other to greater heights of *avodat Hashem*, which is ultimately meaningful only in the context of the covenantal community. This teaching greatly inspired his descendant, the Piaseczner Rebbe, for whom the building of a holy community for group service of the Divine is a central component of Chassidut.

Through our connection with other Jews, our family and friends, who also aspire as we do to serve Hashem in truth, we should merit to find true holiness in our personal lives and to build holy communities based upon *ahavat Yisrael* and mutual support.

PARSHAT KEDOSHIM

Loving Our Neighbor As Ourselves

Regarding the verse, "You shall love your neighbor as yourself; I am the Lord," Rebbe Yisrael of Rizhin would tell the following story (*Irin Kadishin*):

"There were once two friends who loved each other so deeply that their souls were bound up together. They were physically distant from each other and one was falsely accused of a crime and sentenced to death. It was decreed that all of the citizens should come to witness the execution, and his friend also came. When he saw that it was his friend he cried out loudly, 'Let him go! I committed this crime, not my friend!' Their case came before the king, who ordered the two to be brought before him. Only one could be guilty, so why would the other want to die for naught?

"The friend explained, 'I know that my friend could not have committed this crime because his temperament is incapable of such a deed. It is certainly a false accusation, and if so it is better that I should die and not witness his death since our souls are bound together. I, in fact, must be deserving of death if I have been fated to see my friend die.' The other also made the same declaration to the king. The king set them both free, adding his own request: 'I also want to join your circle of loving friendship. Please bring me into your fellowship and I will also share this great love with you.' So too, when we reach the level of loving your neighbor as yourself the Lord requests to dwell among us so that we should share our love with Him as well, and He will also be our faithful Friend."

Parshat Kedoshim is usually read during the month of Iyar, which the Lubavitcher Rebbe pointed out as the only month that is fully within *Sefirat Haomer*, the period in which we mourn for 12,000 pairs of Rabbi Akiva's students who died for not showing each other proper respect. We must strengthen our *ahavat Yisrael* and fulfill the words of Hillel to the convert, "Do not do unto others what is hateful to yourself." The Chassidim added that Hillel's words also teach us not to do anything that is hateful to Hashem, so as not to distance ourselves from Him.

We hope that we will merit transforming the days of *Sefirat Haomer* into days of pure preparation for the receiving of the Torah - in the Ramban's words, an extended *Chol Hamoed* between Pesach and Shavuot - with no hatred, sadness, or mourning at all.

PARSHAT EMOR

Learning from Contact with Death

Parshat Emor opens with the laws of the Kohanim, including their prohibition of contact with the dead. What can all of us, especially in these difficult times, learn from this Halachah?

Both the *Meor Aynaim* and the *Mai Hashiloach* view the Kohen as the paradigmatic servant of Hashem. Therefore, we who wish to dedicate ourselves to the service of the Lord need to learn from these priestly guidelines as well.

The *Mai Hashiloach* teaches us that the prohibition of the Kohen's contact with the dead comes to distance him (and by philosophical extension, us as well) from three common emotional/spiritual reactions to death, suffering and tragedy in the world. The first issue is that of theological doubts and the weakening of faith. Paradoxically, the atheist or the one who does not believe that Hashem directs the world views tragedy as unfortunate coincidence or mere "bad luck," but not as a theological challenge. In contrast, one who believes that all events in the world are the result of divine guidance may reach a state of dissonance in attempting to bridge the chasm between his expectations of goodness and the evil he encounters. The second problematic response is that of the sadness and depression that often results from the reality of death and suffering. Thirdly, contact with death can lead to dangerous passivity. The dead person is utterly passive and those around him may also be driven to passivity, a common symptom of depression. Therefore, the Torah legislates that the Kohen, (hinting to us as well), should avoid these destructive states of mind: weakened faith, depression, and passivity. Instead, we are urged to reaffirm life and vigorously embrace divine service based upon their opposites - strong faith, happiness and an active stance towards life's issues.

The *Aish Kodesh* writes that although we intellectually understand that everything that comes from Hashem is in fact *chessed*, we are not always strong enough to withstand such "hidden *chessed.*" We therefore pray to our merciful Heavenly Father to send us an influx of "revealed *chessed*" so that we can serve Him with perfect faith, great joy and a powerful activism.

PARSHAT EMOR

The Service of the Incomplete

One of the laws of the Temple service is that a Kohen who is a *baal mum*, physically deformed, may not actually participate. The Torah gives a long list of physical deformities to which this law applies, and Rashi adds that even those not listed disqualify the Kohen. Rashi also states that as soon as his deformity is cured the Kohen is fit to resume his participation. Explaining this prohibition, the Sforno quotes the verse from *Esther* that states that a person "may not approach the king's gate dressed in sackcloth." This means that only an individual who appears fully dignified can approach, rather than one who is deformed.

Rav Hirsch discusses this prohibition in relation to a parallel law that disqualifies deformed animals from being sacrificed. According to his interpretation, neither the sacrifice nor the person who brings it can be anything less than physically perfect. If this were not the case, people would receive the mistaken impression that the purpose of the altar is to cure the sick and deformed, when in fact, as Rav Hirsch states, "life and strength, not death and weakness, live at the altars of God." The *Meshech Chochma* points out that the sacrificial laws are *chukim*, seemingly illogical laws. It is therefore possible that a Kohen might not really believe in them, in which case his service would be invalid. God therefore gives physical deformities to those priests whose service might otherwise be secretly invalid, preventing this problem. The *Mai Hashiloach's* son, Rav Shmuel of Biskovitz, writes in *Neot Desheh* that if such priests were allowed to serve, people would arrive at the dangerous assumption that one can achieve spiritual perfection through sadness. Therefore only one who appears to be complete (and presumably happy) is allowed to serve in the Temple.

Even after all of these explanations, however, we may still retain an uneasy feeling that an injustice has been done. As the *Mai Hashiloach* writes in Part Two of his work, "There is a complaint in the hearts of the disfigured priest; why has he been distanced from the service?" As he goes on to explain, we are not discussing a priest who disqualified himself through sin, in which his responsibility is clear. As this priest may have been born with a deformity, which is no fault of his own (despite the difficult words of the *Meshech Chochma* above), why should he be sent away from serving God like his brethren? The answer comes at the end of these verses, when we are told that this priest, although prohibited from offering sacrifices, is allowed to eat from the sacrifices and all of the consecrated foods. The *Mai Hashiloach* continues his explanation: "Internally you lack nothing ... if it is God's will that he not serve he should not be angry, for thus is God's will fulfilled, but inside he is not distant and eats the hallowed foods." He further explains in Part One that we all need to realize that if we serve Hashem truly for the sake of Heaven, then even if we perceive that we are being sent away by God, we actually are serving Him by refraining from service because that is His will at this time. In other words, we need to internalize the truth that the service of God has to be on God's terms (as expressed through Halachah) and not on our terms. Putting our own spiritual desires first may in fact be an ego trip bordering upon idolatry!

The *Mai Hashiloach's* grandson, in *Sod Yesharim*, continues this line of reasoning and explains that even though externally this priest appears to be incomplete, the fact that he eats the hallowed food shows that internally he is entirely holy (unlike the interpretation of the *Meshech Chochma*). From here we learn two crucial spiritual lessons. Firstly, we should not pass judgment based upon externalities. It is what is going on inside that really counts. Secondly, in a world focused upon self-gratification, we need to constantly remind ourselves that we are here to serve Hashem, and not ourselves. Sometimes we perceive that that the Halachah somehow excludes us. If so, we should understand that on a deeper level we are being asked to serve Hashem in a different, but not inferior way. When we truly internalize this deep message, we will not only be better servants of God, but will feel much happier with our lives.

PARSHAT BEHAR

Creating a Just Society

The mitzvot of *Shemittah* and *Yovel* (Sabbatical and Jubilee Years) have many explanations. It is certainly true that they come to deepen our *emunah* and *bitachon* in Hashem, and to strengthen our connection with *Eretz Yisrael*. Additionally, they guide us in creating a more just society in which all members are treated with compassion and in which equality is not merely an empty slogan. This is a major theme of Rav Shagar's *shiurim* on *shmittat kesafim*, the annulment of debts at the end of the *Shemittah* year.

During the *Shemittah* period all produce is *hefker*, ownerless, and anyone can enter my property and avail themselves of the fruits on my trees. This not only reminds me of my duty to care for the poor, but it actually enforces it. This is also the case with the law that during *Yovel* all fields are returned to their original owners and all slaves must be set free, which is a great equalizer in society. No one, no matter how wealthy, can amass great amounts of property or control other Jews as slaves. Every few years everything must "go home," as the land reverts to its original owners and the slaves go to their homes.

Nowhere is this idea as clear as in *shemittat kesafim*. All debts are cancelled, in effect freeing the poor from financial "slavery" to the rich, and perhaps preventing the possibility that they will one day need to sell themselves into slavery to pay off those debts. The Torah also warns the creditor not to refrain from giving loans for fear of not being repaid. So powerful is this concept that when Hillel the Elder saw that people stopped giving loans, he enacted the *Prozbol*, saving the wealthy from sin and ensuring that the poor could still receive loans.

In Israel, poverty is rampant and constant government proclamations of "economic growth" are of little comfort to the poor, elderly, single parents, and new immigrants who cannot feed their families. The exploitation of foreign workers also continues. If Israel is to be a "Light unto the Nations," it is imperative that we create a just society that cares passionately for the needs of its weakest members, treating them with true compassion. In the "Prague Spring" of 1968, Alexander Dubcek introduced *Socialism with a Human Face*. Israel today is desperately in need of *Capitalism with a Human Face*. As Levinas writes in the name of Rav Yisrael Salanter, "The physical needs of the other are my spiritual needs."

PARSHAT BEHAR-BECHUKOTAI

Trusting God through His Laws

The main issues in *Parshat Behar* are *Shemittah* (the Sabbatical Year), *Yovel* (the Jubilee Year), and *ribit*, the prohibition of taking interest on loans. The *Mai Hashiloach* explains that through these mitzvot we learn to place our trust in Hashem in all aspects of reality. In the realm of space, we do not work our fields during the year of *Shemittah*, and the fruit that grows there is ownerless. This teaches us that even the land we buy is ultimately not ours, and we must rely on Hashem for sustenance. On the personal level, we let all of our Israelite slaves go free during *Yovel*, internalizing the message that control over other Jews is not a legitimate way to get ahead. In terms of time we cannot take interest, and we come to realize that we cannot make money by trying to manipulate time because interest is essentially "money for time." It is important to emphasize that the mitzvah of *Shemittah* is a major statement of our faith and trust in Hashem. Without these qualities, it is impossible for us to exist in *Eretz Yisrael*, where everything happens through direct divine providence.

Later on, in *Bechukotai*, we read of the punishment of exile that results (also) from violating *Shemittah*. One way or another, the Land will get to keep its Shabbat. After reading of the rebuke and exile we may feel like worthless beings, so the parsha ends with the mitzvah of *Erechin*, explaining how much people are "worth" if they dedicate their worth to the Temple, reiterating that all of us are indeed beings of intrinsic value.

"If you walk in My statutes ..." The *Mai Hashiloach* gives three interpretations to this verse. Firstly, "My statutes should be engraved (*nechkak*, a play on words) upon your hearts," i.e. that we reach the level of serving God naturally. On the other hand, "if" implies a doubt, for who can really hope to fathom the Divine will and fulfill it in every situation? Nonetheless "if" is also the language of prayer, for "God, so to speak, prays, 'if only they would walk in My ways and understand My deepest intentions.'"

By strengthening our belief and faith, we will reinforce our hold on the Holy Land. This is only achieved by walking in God's statutes, serving Him in truth and joy.

PARSHAT BECHUKOTAI

Rebuke and Exile

Most of *Parshat Bechukotai* is devoted to the horrifying re-buke, the *tochachah*, which *Am Yisrael* must endure as a result of sinning, and of not repenting in the face of punishment. The Rambam writes that at a time of suffering, the community must understand that it is being punished for sin, and must repent. Failure to do so, and the assumption that suffering is mere happenstance, is no less than "cruelty, causing people to cling to their evil ways and bring even more suffering upon themselves." Rav Yehuda Henkin, in his *Chiba Yetara,* uses this idea to explain the word *keri*, which appears repeatedly throughout the *tochachah*. *Keri* is related to *mikreh*, coincidence, and denotes our refusal to believe that Hashem is punishing us and that we must repent. Instead we insist upon viewing our suffering as mere happen-stance. Ultimately this brings Hashem to treat us with *chamat keri,* the anger of coincidence, removing His providential protection and leaving us vulnerable to the cruelties of the fate we claim to be experiencing.

The Ramban writes that this parsha is a prediction of the Babylonian Exile after the destruction of the First Temple, whereas the *tochachah* in *Parshat Ki Tavo* describes the Roman Exile after the Second Temple was destroyed. In chapter 26: 42-46, we are told that despite the horrific sufferings of the Exile, God will remember His covenant with us and never allow us to be wiped out. He will eventually return us to the Land when it is ready (having rested to make up for the Sabbatical Years in which it was abused) and the Jewish People are sufficiently cleansed in order to return to its holiness. This process can also be excruciatingly painful. In a famous prophetic passage written in the early 20th century, the *Meshech Chochma* predicted the assimilation and destruction of European Jewry: "When the Jews forget their heritage, cease to study their religion, study foreign languages, and think that Berlin is Jerusalem … a great storm will come to uproot them."

In verse 42, we read "And I will remember My covenant with Yaakov, and even My covenant with Yitzchak, and even My covenant with Avraham, and I will remember the Land." The martyred Rav Yissachar Teichtel, in his *Aim Habanim Semachah*, written in Budapest during the Holocaust, used this verse to explain the letter that Rebbe Schneur Zalman, the first Lubavitcher Rebbe, wrote to Rebbe Levi Yitzchak of Berditchev when the former was released from Czarist prison. In it, Rebbe Schneur Zalman stated that it was the merit of *Eretz Yisrael* and its inhabitants that had saved him, and that in general saved the Jews from misfortune. Rav Teichtel writes that our verse is the source of this idea, since it progresses from Yaakov to Avraham, ending with the Land, "For the merit of the Land of Israel stands above all of our merits, and is even greater than *Zechut Avot*, the merit of the Patriarchs." Similarly, Rav Charlop writes in *Mai Marom*, even when we are unfortunately lacking the attributes of the Patriarchs mentioned in the verse, "if they have only this one merit, that they return to the Land to rebuild it, for this alone God will have mercy and redeem them, returning them to Himself and to His holy Torah." May the merit of *Eretz Yisrael* continue to protect all of the Jewish People, and may all of us return speedily to Hashem, His Torah, and His land.

PARSHAT BAMIDBAR

The Desert Experience

Parshat Bamidbar is always read before Shavuot, just as the Torah was given in the desert. We may ask what is significant about the desert experience. The *Mai Hashiloach* writes that the desert is a place of snakes, scorpions, and thirst, and yet *Am Yisrael* entered the desert to show that even in such a wild and seemingly ownerless place Hashem is present and there is potential for holiness that must be actualized. Therefore, continues Rav Leibele Eiger, the desert teaches us that there is nothing in the world that exists outside the Divine realm. The *Mai Hashiloach* further points out that the book of *Bamidbar* is filled with stories of great people who fall, for no one can rest upon their laurels and be too sure of themselves. Again, the desert seems to break down all of our assumptions about reality and truth.

On the other hand, according to the Kozhnitzer Maggid, the desert is the place where physicality is broken down and one can achieve *deveikut,* connection, with Hashem. In the desert we are *hefker,* ownerless and ready for the Holy One to bring us into His realm, much as the groom brings the bride into his realm under the *chuppah,* as the Ran explains.

The *Aish Kodesh* addresses the famous question of why the Torah was given in the desert and not in *Eretz Yisrael.* Had it been, we would have thought that we are only obligated to fulfill the mitzvot under optimal conditions. Instead we learn that our obligation to the Torah and mitzvot is a constant, irrespective of the difficulties of specific times or places.

Midbar, desert, is also related to the word *midaber*, speaker, which typifies the human being. Through our words of prayer and study we are also able to enter the divine realm and achieve *deveikut,* as our ancestors did at *Matan Torah.* When you read the Torah this Shabbat, try to picture yourself in the desert. Visualize a time when you were there, only this time you are not traveling in a bus with food and water. In spite of your apparent vulnerability

Hashem is always there to take care of you, and there is no one else you can rely upon. This type of relationship opens you up to really being ready to receive the Torah deeply, internalizing every word.

PARSHAT NASO

Learning from Our Mistakes

Parshat Naso discusses two major topics: the *Sotah*, the "suspected adulteress," and the *Nazir*, the person who takes on vows of abstinence from haircuts, contact with the dead, and the consumption of wine. In the Torah, *Sotah* appears before *Nazir*. However, in the Mishna the Rabbis placed *Nazir* before *Sotah*.

The Gemara in *Sotah* 2a discusses the relationship between the two topics. "Why is *Nazir* [in the Torah] discussed after *Sotah*? To tell you that whoever witnesses a *Sotah* in her disgrace should take the [Nazirite] vow to abstain from wine." The Gemara then asks why the Torah's order has been reversed and gives a technical answer.

The Chassidic Masters, Rav Mordechai Yosef of Ishbitz and his student Rav Tzaddok Hakohen, discussed this question in several places. Two issues concerned them. Firstly, is there a deeper reason for the reversal of the order from *Sotah-Nazir* in the Torah, to *Nazir-Sotah* in the Mishna? Secondly, the Gemara's statement that one who witnesses the disgrace of the *Sotah* should take on Nazirite vows is very puzzling. We could all understand that a person involved in immoral behavior due to the influence of alcohol should be on guard against the slightest possibility of drunkenness, but why should an "innocent bystander" need to become a *Nazir*?

The Ishbitzer (*Mai Hashiloach* part 1, *Naso*) explains: "*Sotah* teaches that one should analyze his faults and then take vows and set limits for himself. Therefore, in the Torah we find *Sotah* and then *Nazir*, as it says in *Gittin* 43a, 'no one is stable in Torah until he first makes a mistake.' However, *Chazal* ... who love people and desire to help them, arranged *Nazir* before *Sotah*, teaching that one must limit himself before he makes a mistake in Torah." The role of the Torah is to describe the human reality that all too often we are negligent about taking steps to protect our spiritual welfare until the problem has already manifested itself. *Chazal*, on the other hand, interpret the Torah in a way that makes it applicable to human needs and warn us in advance of how to avoid serious pitfalls.

In *Likkutei Mai Hashiloach* on *Gittin* 43a, the Ishbitzer relates to the second question: "Regarding those words of Torah that one becomes stable only after a failure, it is not necessary that he himself be the one who fails. Even by witnessing others fail he can arrive at these Torah matters and stabilize himself." The Jew must go through life with open eyes, constantly asking himself what he can learn from everything he encounters. If he sees others stumbling he should ask himself how to prevent himself from arriving at the same situation, thus avoiding the problem to begin with. Rav Tzaddok Hakohen takes this idea a step further. In *Pri Tzaddik, Naso* 13, he tells of Reb Zusha, who was once out walking when he witnessed a Gentile trying to pick up a wagon that had tipped over. When the Gentile asked him for help, Reb Zusha replied that he was unable to assist him. The Gentile retorted, "You could help, but you really don't want to." Reb Zusha said to himself, "This is a hint regarding the lower (letter) *hey* (of Hashem's name). It has fallen and I am able to restore it, but I don't really want to."

What is the message of this bizarre tale? Why did Reb Zusha reinterpret the simple words of a non-Jewish peasant as a deep and personal Kabbalistic message? Explains Rav Tzaddok: "Everything that a person witnesses is a hint from above... Therefore in *Torah shebichtav, Sotah* comes before *Nazir*, for since the person 'happened' to see the *Sotah*, surely he must take a vow not to drink wine. But in *Torah shebaal peh, Nazir* is arranged before *Sotah*, as it explains in *Avot* that the good path is *Haroeh et hanolad* (to be able to realize the implications of events, and take proper action in due time)." The wisdom of *Chazal* teaches us to prepare ahead in order to guard ourselves properly.

Rav Tzaddok's interpretation is startling. Everything we see or hear contains a hidden message for us. If not, we would not have been present to witness the event or have heard about it. We have all experienced that after witnessing a car accident (God forbid), we tend to drive more carefully, at least for a while. According to Rav Tzaddok, we should learn to do this instinctively in all matters.

With Hashem's help, we should become sensitized to the constant messages He sends us all the time. When He gives us the wisdom to learn from the experience of others, we learn the proper lessons from our own failures so that we can use them as a vehicle for growth.

PARSHAT NASO

The Lessons of the *Sotah*

Parshat Sotah, "the suspected adulteress," which appears in *Parshat Naso*, continues to generate controversy, both for the seeming disproportionate treatment of the wife and for its apparent "trial by ordeal" method. Yet this law is often misunderstood.

The Biblical focus on the wife's adultery stems from the fact that in Biblical law a man may marry more than one woman at a time. The reverse is not true in order to avoid patrimonial doubts. The woman in our story, while not necessarily guilty of adultery, is not one of high moral caliber either. Her flirtatious behavior has already led her husband to formally warn her not to seclude herself with a certain man (in any event forbidden as *yichud*). Disregarding his warning, they again seclude themselves and there is now a halachic presumption that relations have taken place. If this is the case, her husband must divorce her. The *Sotah* procedures come in order to **permit** husband and wife to remain together. According to Levinas, the importance of this procedure is that the case is taken out of the hands of the husband (who in the ancient world could simply murder his wife), and placed under the responsibility of an outside judicial body.

In the Temple, the *Sotah's* hair is uncovered as a reflection of her immodest behavior. From here, the Rabbis learned that a married woman must cover her hair when in public (completely, according to the Chatam Sofer, based upon the *Zohar*, or all but a handbreadth according to Rav Moshe Feinstein). The priest encourages her to admit her culpability if she is guilty. If she does so she will need to divorce, but no other penalty will be applied, as there is no independent testimony that she actually committed adultery. If she insists upon her innocence she drinks water from the laver (for which the women donated their mirrors, happily accepting the law of *Sotah* upon themselves) mixed with a drop of earth and into which a scroll containing God's Name has been inserted. This is the source of the statement that God's Name is erased to make peace between husband and wife.

While it is true that if she is guilty she dies a supernatural death, this is hardly trial by ordeal, in which a suspected witch was bound and thrown into the water. The assumption in such a case was that if she were innocent, God would perform a miracle to save her. But naturally she would die. Our situation is entirely different. Firstly, it is the woman who opts to drink the water despite encouragement not to do so. Secondly, the water is not poisonous, so it requires a miracle on God's part for her to be punished. Naturally, nothing would happen to her. If she drinks and is found innocent, not only will she not die, but also she and her husband will be blessed with a child. So powerful was this idea, that the childless Chana "threatened" God that if she did not naturally conceive she would become a *Sotah* and "force His hand"!

The Rabbis added several insights to the above. Firstly, if she was guilty, not only would she die, but her illicit lover would perish as well, in the same supernatural way. Secondly, if her own husband was also guilty of sexual misconduct the waters would have no effect upon her. Regardless of his own morality, the Chizkuni faults him for letting the relationship deteriorate to this extent. According to the Ramban the whole procedure of *Sotah* is a unique case in which the Torah relies on a miracle for halachic purposes. This is done not only to preserve a threatened marriage, but also to help maintain a holy and modest society in which the Shechinah can dwell. It only worked at a time when *Am Yisrael* was characterized by sexual purity. To our great consternation, that is no longer the case and *Sotah* no longer exists. Nonetheless, the moral lessons of modesty, the sanctity of marriage, the caution needed in dealings between men and women, and the extent to which we must go to preserve *shalom bayit*, domestic tranquility, are every bit as relevant today as they were in Biblical times.

PARSHAT BEHAALOT'CHA

Striving Toward Heaven Like a Flame

According to the *Mai Hashiloach*, "One could spend his entire life on this parsha [*Behaalot'cha*], for all the essentials of the Torah are dependent upon it." One of these "essentials" is found in the section dealing with the menorah. Aharon is commanded to light the menorah in the Tabernacle, and Rashi informs us that the candles must be lit so that the flame will go up by itself. This is a lesson to us on how we must burn with the upward motion of *itoruta d'litata*, an arousal from below, in our divine service. The mitzvah of *Pesach Sheni* in the parsha is therefore given in response to those who were legitimately exempt from bringing the Passover sacrifice but nonetheless insisted upon doing so.

When the Levites began their Temple service, all of their hair was shaved off. The *Mai Hashiloach* points out that this is the opposite of the Nazirite in the previous parsha, *Naso*, who was not allowed to cut his hair. Since both the Levite and the Nazirite are dedicated to serving Hashem, why are they commanded to behave differently from each other? Like many issues in Judaism, this is one of finding the proper balance. In the Kabbalah, hair represents anger (the complete opposite of popular philosophy in the sixties, a time of many misunderstandings). The Nazirite, tending toward sensual temptation, grows long hair so that his excess *chessed*, loving-kindness, will be balanced by more *gevurah*, self-dicipline. For the Levite, in contrast, who insists on perfect truth and tends toward anger, his hair is removed to generate more *chessed*. This is similar to the situation in a marriage, where the masculine *chessed* and feminine *gevurah* balance each other in a harmonious whole.

Later on in the parsha, we learn that despite receiving a generous portion of manna (the perfect food) each morning, not everyone was satisfied. Some demanded meat, bringing down a deluge of quail that became an overwhelming plague. This shows

175

us that food must be a way of serving God, not only a vehicle for sensual pleasure.

Still further, the parsha describes how Aaron and Miriam slandered Moshe, and Miriam was punished with leprosy. (Why Aaron was not punished would require a separate discussion.) Moshe prayed to Hashem and Miriam was healed. Rav Leibele Eiger teaches us that all healing flows from this parsha.

The overriding lesson that we learn from *Parshat Behaalot'cha* is that we should strive toward serving Hashem with properly balanced sexuality, eating, and speech, rising heavenward like a flame. Through our endeavors, we should ultimately be healed from all of our physical and spiritual ills.

PARSHAT BEHAALOT'CHA

Aspiring to Prophecy

After Moshe emanates part of his spirit to the seventy elders, Eldad and Medad remain in the camp and prophesy. What were they doing there? Regarding this question, there is a dispute in *Sanhedrin* 17a. According to the first, anonymous opinion, they remained at the ballot box after not having been chosen among the seventy elders. According to Rabbi Shimon (quoted in Rashi), they remained behind due to their extreme humility, feeling unworthy to join the elders even though they had been chosen. For this, they were rewarded with the experience of prophecy. The Torah then describes how "the youth" (according to Rashi, Moshe's son Gershom, and according to others, Yehoshua) ran to inform Moshe that the two were prophesying. Yehoshua then advises Moshe to imprison them. In his eighth *drasha*, the Ran points out that according to the position of Rabbi Shimon, Yehoshua completely misjudged the situation. He perceived them as rebelling against Moshe when, in fact, their prophecy came as a result of their humility and feeling of unworthiness. Moshe understands the situation, responds calmly, and states, "Are you jealous for me? If only all of God's people would be prophets, that God would give them his spirit."

It is clear, even according to the anonymous position in *Sanhedrin*, that Eldad and Medad were not chosen, that Yehoshua's reaction was extreme, and Moshe's was correct. Moshe is not concerned about the possibility of an alternative spiritual leadership as long as all is truly for the sake of Heaven. He also realizes that if Hashem chose to grant them prophecy, they were obviously deserving of it (even if they did not deserve to be chosen among the seventy elders). Certainly, no evil would come from such prophecy. In fact, the opposite is the case. Moshe understands that the goal of being a "nation of priests and a holy people" also includes the aspiration to be a prophetic people. In addition to the obvious aspect of prophecy, i.e. receiving open divine messages, there is another aspect, as explained in detail by the Piaseczner Rebbe in *Mevo Hashaarim*. Prophecy also includes the prophetic lifestyle, a life in which one is acutely conscious of the presence of the Divine and lives with the constant desire to achieve *deveikut*, a connection with Hashem. The Rebbe goes on to explain that Chassidism is actually a continuation of prophecy, of the intense spiritual lifestyle to which every Jew should aspire.

I would like to offer an additional insight in the spirit of Levinas. Eldad and Medad may represent radical difference and otherness. Yehoshua views them as strange and perhaps frightening, and he responds accordingly. Moshe, in contrast, as an older and more seasoned leader, does not feel threatened by their strangeness. He not only tolerates them, but he loves them as well. And so should we when we are confronted by Jews who seem strange in their behavior or attitudes. We should greet all Jews with tolerance and love. In so doing we will merit being a holy people, living according to the Torah, divine connection, and prophecy.

PARSHAT SHLACH

Seeing the True Picture

One of the most perplexing stories in the Torah is that of the *Meraglim*, the spies. With their evil report about *Eretz Yisrael*, they caused forty years of wandering in the desert. According to *Chazal*, this event took place on Tisha B'Av, paving the way for the subsequent destruction of the Temples and the exiles. Our commentators have offered numerous theories to answer such questions as: How could such great men have failed so miserably? What exactly did they do wrong, since they were sent to spy? Why was the punishment so harsh? Also perplexing is the story of the *Maapilim*, those "illegal immigrants" who chose to disregard Moshe's warning and attacked *Eretz Yisrael*, only to be defeated. Why was their *teshuvah* not accepted? In our answer we will attempt to delineate a certain trend within the Chassidic commentaries.

The *Mai Hashiloach* points to a similarity between the Land of Israel and the Torah itself. The Torah's laws sometimes appear to be exceedingly harsh. Yet when studied more deeply, they reveal their inner quality of love and connection with Hashem. So too, the Land of Israel, which superficially appears to be *Eretz Ochelet Yoshveha*, a land that consumes its inhabitants, reveals itself through penetrating vision as a place filled with love, holiness, and Torah. The spies were not sent to give a military report, but rather a description of the inner quality of the land, which is all goodness. Because of their superficiality they reacted angrily, condemning the land and bringing catastrophe upon *Am Yisrael*.

The *Sfat Emet* tries to "get into the head" of the spies. After all, they faced a real dilemma. On the one hand, they had heard that *Eretz Yisrael* is a "very, very good land," but what they saw appeared to be very different. They saw an *eretz ochelet yoshveha*, an exceedingly harsh land. As "seeing" is very often "believing," how were they to reconcile such a contradiction? The *Sfat Emet* gives an amazing answer to this question. The spies should have made a "leap of faith." They should have understood that the *middat hadin* (attribute of justice) that they witnessed was for the Canaanites, and that when *Am Yisrael* would enter the land, it would be transformed into a place of mercy for its rightful owners. And why were the *Maapilim* unsuccessful? Their *teshuvah*, says the *Sfat Emet*, was on a very low level. Their attitude was one of, "What have we got to lose? Hashem is going to kill us all in the desert anyway." There was no remorse, understanding, or appreciation for the greatness of *Eretz Yisrael*, and this type of *teshuvah* was not acceptable to Hashem.

Rebbe Nachman explains the Gemara's statement that, "*Eretz Yisrael* is acquired through hardship." He asks what the main hardships are that one must endure in order to inherit the land. The answer he gives is to overcome those who slander *Eretz Yisrael*. Interestingly enough, so little seems to have changed. Just as in the time of the *Meraglim*, many people still focus on the externality of *Eretz Yisrael* and its seeming harshness, neglecting to draw inspiration from the love, miracles, and Torah that are present here in every rock and every blade of grass. This negativity is one factor that holds us back from a deeper connection with the land and discourages aliyah. (In a somewhat similar vein, the French-Jewish philosopher Emmanuel Levinas, in an article entitled "Promised Land or Permitted Land," describes the *Meraglim* as the first "post-Zionists." Amazingly, his article was written in 1965). It is imperative for all of us, especially now, to focus on the good and to maintain a positive attitude.

We will close with a *drasha* from the Piasenczner Rebbe given in the Warsaw Ghetto in June 1940: The following is the text from *Aish Kodesh*.

" 'We must go forth and occupy the land,' [Caleb] said. 'We can do it!' (Numbers 13:30)

Let us attempt an understanding of this episode. If the spies spoke with reason, saying, 'the people living in the land are aggressive, and the cities are large and well fortified,' (*Bamidbar* 13:28) why did Caleb not enter into a debate with them, trying to demolish their argument and their reasoning? Why did he limit himself to the simple statement, 'We must go forth'?

This is how the faith of a Jew must always be. Not only when he sees reasonable openings and paths for his salvation to take within the laws of nature must he have faith that God will save him, and take heart – but also, God forbid, when he sees no way for salvation to come through natural means, must he still believe that God will save him, and strengthen himself in his faith and his belief. In fact, at just such times it is better not to look for natural paths for salvation to take, for if such a way is not apparent and, God forbid, a person's faith should become damaged, a blemish in the person's faith and in his belief in God may actually prevent the salvation from happening, God forbid.

A person needs to say: 'Yes, all the logic and facts may indeed be true. The people and the land may be very strong, and their cities well fortified, and so forth, but still I believe in God, who is beyond any boundaries and above all nature. I believe that He will save us. We must go forth and occupy the land. We can do it!' He must say this without rationalizing or theorizing, for it is this kind of faith and belief in God that brings our salvation close."

More than half a century later, despite the radical differences between life in the Warsaw Ghetto and our current life in Israel, the Rebbe's words still ring true with their simplicity, clarity and power. May we merit proper *emunah*, faith. May we merit inheriting *Eretz Yisrael*, to live in true peace and to build a just Torah society that will be worthy of *Mashiach*.

PARSHAT SHLACH

The Spies' Moral Dilemma

In 1965, long before the term *post-Zionism* had been coined, the French-Jewish philosopher Emmanuel Levinas diagnosed the *Meraglim* as suffering from that very syndrome in his article, "Promised Land or Permitted Land." Based upon the Talmud, *Sotah* 34b-35a, Levinas sees three motivations for the spies' plot: atheism, fear, and moral relativism. Regarding the first, he writes, "The revolt of these men: a crisis of atheism, a crisis much more serious than the crisis of the Golden Calf. The Golden Calf, that was still religious: one switched gods. Here, nothing is left; one contests the very attributes of Divinity." The spies express this through the demystification of sacred history, denying the past accomplishments of Hashem.

Fear, the most obvious aspect, is a direct result of the Diaspora experience: "The strength of the inhabitants of Canaan frightened these puny Jews, just out of the Egyptian ghettos. How could they oppose them in the name of a God who, Heaven knows, never shows Himself ... Of what worth are all the abstractions and subtleties of revelation before the splendid appearance of the children of the Earth who wear the sun as a medallion?" The spies, suffering from an inferiority complex, saw themselves as grasshoppers, and assumed that all who saw them shared their self-deprecation.

The most interesting idea is that of moral relativism. "Perhaps the explorers had moral qualms. They may have asked themselves whether they had the right to conquer what others had so magnificently built." Even the evident fact of Israel's moral superiority is irrelevant in such an approach. "One can also doubt that moral superiority ... permits an expropriation ... the invocation of rights due to moral superiority of Israel is improper." Or perhaps there is no such moral superiority. Who has the right to decide that one moral system is any better than another? "By what right are we going into this land? What moral advantage do we have over the inhabitants settled in this country?"

How are these three aspects related? "An overly pure conscience ...begins to doubt God because God's command asks us either what is above our strength or what is beneath our conscience. The Promised Land is not permitted land."

For Levinas, the Israeli project is inherently moral. "We are going into this land to ascend to heaven. We will not possess the land as it is usually possessed; we will found a just community ... to sacralize the earth ... to accept the Torah is to accept the norms of universal justice ... the very contestation of moral relativism. What we call the Torah provides norms for human justice. And it is in the name of this universal justice and not in the name of some national justice or other that the Israelites lay claim to the Land of Israel."

Levinas interprets the Talmudic statement that the spies claimed that the Canaanites were too strong for God to remove them not only as a military claim, but primarily a moral one. "The right of the native population to live is stronger than the moral right of the universal God ... one cannot take away from them the land on which they live, even if they are immoral, violent, and unworthy, and even if this land were meant for a better destiny." We are reminded of today's moral relativism, which, among other faults, weakens the West's resolve to fight the terrorism that threatens to destroy it. "Must freedom be granted to those who want to kill freedom? The explorers, in the purity of their egalitarian conscience, denounced as anti-democratic the wisdom that excluded from freedom the murderers of freedom."

In the final analysis, "Did the crime of the explorers consist of being too pure and of having thoughts that they did not even have rights to this land? Or did these people back off from a project which seemed to them utopian, unrealizable ... in both cases, the explorers were wrong."

Levinas's prophetic words can help to guide us in today's quandary. We need to face our great challenges courageously with deep faith in Hashem and in the justice of our cause. Our conquest of *Eretz Yisrael* certainly infers upon us great moral responsibility for all who live here. Nonetheless, we cannot abdicate our rights or our responsibilities. In order to be a Light unto the Nations we first have to be capable of seeing our own light. That light can shine only when *Am Yisrael* lives in *Eretz Yisrael* according to *Torat Yisrael*.

PARSHAT KORACH

A Diverse Band of Rebels

Who are the rebels described in *Parshat Korach*? What are their motivations, and when does this story take place? For R. Chananel, the 250 men were Levites who desired to be priests. On the other hand, Rashi writes that Datan, Aviram, Ohn (later saved when his wife exposed her hair and frightened away the rebels), and most of the 250 men involved were from the tribe of Reuven. Camped near Korach, they succumbed to his influence, as we are told, "Woe to the evil one, woe to his neighbor!" Ibn Ezra dispenses with chronological order in the Bible and dates this rebellion as taking place after the transgression of the Golden Calf. Moshe's tribe of Levi didn't worship the Golden Calf, and they replaced the firstborn sons as spiritual leaders. Korach and the 250 men were firstborn sons. Datan, Aviram, and Ohn were from Reuven, Yaakov's firstborn son. In fact, Korach's statement that "all of the people are holy" refers to the firstborn.

Ramban disagrees with R. Chananel since it is wrong to impute evil motivations to the Levites, who were themselves holy. In his view, Ibn Ezra also errs since we must maintain the chronological integrity of the Bible except when absolutely necessary. The revolt took place after the debacle of the spies and the decree of wandering in the desert. This is not a rebellion of the firstborn tribe of Reuven, for Yosef had replaced Reuven in that function generations before. Korach's jealousy was directed primarily against Eltzafon and was only secondarily against Aharon. Datan and Aviram joined out of refusal to accept the Divine decree of desert wandering.

The Netziv sees Korach as the greatest of his generation, yet his jealousy and hunger for power destroyed him. Datan and Aviram, by contrast, were opportunists who had always hated Moshe. The 250 men, on the other hand, were truly righteous. They sincerely desired the priesthood in order to come closer to

Hashem. Burning with the flames of spiritual desire, they were consumed by heavenly fire like Nadav and Avihu before them.

In *Pirkei Avot* we learn that the dispute between Hillel and Shammai was for the sake of Heaven, whereas that of Korach and his fellows was not. The *Maor V'shemesh* quotes Rebbe Elimelech that Hillel and Shammai loved each other. Korach and his fellows hated each other, and banded together in an uneasy coalition of rebels; as we say, "politics makes strange bedfellows." From the unfortunate story of Korach, we can learn how all of our disagreements should only be for the sake of Heaven.

PARSHAT KORACH

The Blue and the White

At first, Korach's complaints to Moshe, as described in *Parshat Korach*, appear to be justifiable demands for democratic reform and equality. However, this is not really the case, for, as the *Mai Hashiloach* points out, Korach did not protest when his own tribe of Levi was elevated to a special status. According to the *midrash* quoted by Rashi, Korach asked Moshe if an entirely blue tallit would require a thread of blue, and according to other *midrashim* he also asked if a room full of Torah scrolls would require a mezuzah. The Maharal explains in *Tiferet Yisrael* that Korach hoped to trick Moshe into giving answers that would serve him in his campaign to remove Moshe from power. He writes that the blue thread symbolizes Aharon (divine service) and the mezuzah represents Moshe (Torah study). Korach assumed that Moshe would answer that a blue thread and a mezuzah are not needed and he would have responded that a holy people therefore has no need of religious leadership. However, Moshe's response was the opposite. The thread is found on the corner of the garment and the mezuzah at the entrance, to show that even a holy people requires separate leadership.

The *Pri Tzaddik* has a similar, but not identical explanation. He argues that any words written in the Torah, even if spoken by an evil person like Korach, must be true on some level. It's true that the people are all holy, for they have the fear of heaven, and they are like a tallit. It is also true that the Lord is inside them, for they are filled with Torah just like a room that is filled with scrolls. Nonetheless they still require a separate thread so as not to forget, and a mezuzah to guard the doorway.

Rav Hirsch takes the opposite approach. Korach's words are all a lie. The people are commanded to be holy, but they are not yet holy! "They must not confuse the goal with the reality ... their holy mission must remain before their eyes as a distant goal and aspiration."

According to Rav Soloveitchik, the white strings represent clear situations and the blue doubtful ones. Korach argued that no one needs Rabbinical authority, for every Jew has the right to make halachic decisions for himself. Moshe rejected this position, arguing forcefully that everyone needs a Rav to whom he must turn to with his questions.

Our goal should be to succeed in reaching the proper balance between democracy and leadership, and between the feeling of holiness and the aspiration for holiness. We should also pray that all of our conflicts are only for the sake of Heaven.

PARSHAT CHUKKAT

The Problem with Leadership

What exactly was the sin for which Moshe and Aharon were punished and not allowed to enter the Promised Land? Our commentators bring numerous explanations. According to Rashi, Moshe hit the rock instead of speaking to it, whereas the Ibn Ezra writes that he struck the rock twice. The Rambam sees Moshe and Aharon's sin in the inappropriate anger that was expressed in response to the legitimate request for water. The Maharal follows the Rambam, adding that anger is a sign of lack of faith. It is well known that "anger is like idolatry," for anger shows that one insists upon his own desires being fulfilled instead of accepting the will of Hashem. According to the Ramban the sin consisted of saying, "*we* will bring forth water" instead of "*He* will bring forth water," thus taking credit for the miracle.

The Abarbanel has an entirely different approach. The punishment of not entering Israel was only announced now, but it was actually for other sins. In Moshe's case, this was the sin of the spies and in Aharon's, the sin of the Golden Calf. In both cases the severity of the punishment is related to their leadership role and they, to some extent, are being punished for the sins of the whole generation. In light of all of the above (and more), the Italian Rabbi Shadal wrote that the Torah says that Moshe and Aharon sinned once, but the commentaries have already found thirteen sins. He did not want to add another to their load. ...

Rav Menachem Liebtag has written convincingly that this story is representative of the leadership crisis which plagues Moshe and Aharon throughout the book of *Bamidbar*. Apparently, the generation was not worthy of great leaders of their stature and they did not always succeed in bridging the gap. The story of the desert is therefore that of one crisis after another until in the end only a new generation under new leadership was able to enter the land.

Today we often seem to have the opposite feeling. We perceive our leaders as being small-minded, lacking in faith and vision. We feel that we deserve better. Nonetheless, "Yiftach in his generation is like Shmuel in his," so we will continue to daven for great leaders while working together with those that we have.

PARSHAT BALAK

Active and Passive

A quick glance at *Parshat Balak* reveals that it contains no mitzvot, only narrative. It opens with the story of Balaam and ends with that of Pinchas, an entirely different type of character.

The *Mai Hashiloach* writes that although Balaam always wanted to curse the Jews, he passively waited for someone to hire him to do so. In fact, Balaam is a completely passive and greedy individual. The bizarre story of the donkey is described by Robert Alter in *The Art of Biblical Narrative* as an example of "high comedy." According to Alter and also to Rav Elchanan Samet, the story of the donkey serves as a foreshadowing of the story of the attempted cursing through a type of simulation game in which the donkey "plays" Balaam, and Balaam "plays" Balak. Yet Balaam, the great prophet, cannot even see what is visible to his own donkey. This great sorcerer, who aspires to destroy an entire nation with his words, laments the lack of a sword in order to kill a donkey. And while it is true that Balaam is a great orator, his donkey is also quite eloquent! In fact, many of the commentators argue that the entire story was recorded for one purpose only - to make fun of Balaam. From the above, Balaam emerges as an evil but pathetic figure, weak, passive, and controlled by others.

The zealous Pinchas, on the other hand, represents the opposite, not only in his righteousness, but also in his activism. When he sees a problem, and that "there is no man" to fix it, he takes immediate action. While it is certainly true that zealotry is a dangerous quality, in this case there was a plague and many people were dying. A great *chillul Hashem* had been created, and the Torah was being disgraced. Everyone stood around crying, not knowing what to do. Pinchas (who according to *Chazal*, consulted with Moshe, the top halachic authority) took the initiative, risked his life, and saved the Jewish People. God then rewarded him with the Covenant of Peace and the High Priesthood.

The activism and self-sacrifice of Pinchas is a strong example to us all, while the self-serving passivity of Balaam should be avoided. It is often easier for us to remain passive in the face of adversity. This, however, runs counter to the Torah's entire aim of *Tikkun Olam*, perfecting the world. Only by actively confronting the world around us, with the willingness to take risks in order to fight for what is right, can we really achieve a *kiddush Hashem* and bring the world closer to its ultimate perfection.

PARSHAT BALAK

How Goodly Are Your Tents ...

Balaam's most famous words appear in his unintentional blessing, "How goodly are your tents, Yaakov, and your dwelling-places, Yisrael." These verses are so beautiful that we recite them upon entering the synagogue for morning prayers. This seems to imply that his words allude to houses of prayer. What, in fact, are these tents and dwelling-places? Are they physical houses or spiritual dwellings, and why are they associated with Yaakov?

The Chizkuni points out that Yaakov is known as the "tent-dweller," and is therefore associated with these tents as well. Rashi sees both the physical and spiritual in Balaam's words. Quoting from *Chazal*, he states that the tent openings faced away from each other in order to ensure maximum modesty and privacy for each family. (One modern example of this is Moshav Keshet in the Golan Heights, where the houses are designed with this principle in mind.) Rashi further informs us that this verse refers to the Tabernacle and the Temple, which retain spiritual potency even when they are destroyed. According to Sforno, Balaam is referring to spiritual "houses," – the study halls and synagogues that are "goodly" for *Am Yisrael*. Rabbeinu Bachaye follows his usual approach and brings numerous levels of interpretation. On the simple level, the verse refers to *Eretz Yisrael,* and homiletically to the tent openings that face away from each other. On the Kabbalistic level, we are referring to the configurations of the Sefirot, the upper and lower realms.

The Netziv also brings two interpretations, and sees the reference to separate tents for men and for women, or to centers of spiritual and political leadership. Rav Hirsch focuses upon the morality and modesty the tents represent. The camp is divided according to the Tribes, for in *Am Yisrael* there are no patrilineal doubts, and everyone therefore knows their place. All of this stands in direct contrast to Balaam's own vulgar immorality, as we see at the end of the parsha and as depicted by *Chazal.*

Balaam is unable to defeat us at this point, due to our unique combination of morality, spiritual and political leadership, and consciousness of the Temple's holiness. In addition, the Tribes dwell together in peaceful unity, our most powerful weapon against adversity.

Let us aspire to this sorely needed harmony today, both in the spiritual and political sense.

PARSHAT PINCHAS

Striking at the Root of the Problem

At the close of *Parshat Balak,* we found the Jews engaged in two severe sins: immorality with the daughters of Moav, and the idolatrous worship of the deity of Baal Peor. *Midrash Tanchuma* graphically describes how Balaam used Moabite women used their charms to entice the Israelite men to worship idols. This is reminiscent of *Chazal's* words that the Jewish People only engaged in idolatry in order to participate in public licentiousness as well. Pinchas steps in, killing Zimri and Kozbi, who were engaged in immorality, thus stopping the plague. As a result, Hashem rewards Pinchas in the following parsha, *Parshat Pinchas*, with the Covenant of Peace and the High Priesthood.

In *Netivot Shalom*, the Slonimer Rebbe points out that Pinchas chose to act against the sexual infraction and not against those who were worshipping idols, despite the fact that technically the worship of idols (for which one must give his life rather than transgress) is a more severe halachic infraction than relations with a Gentile woman. Why did Pinchas choose this tactic, and why did it stop the plague? The Slonimer Rebbe answers that faith in Hashem (the opposite of idolatry) and holiness in sexual matters are two of the major foundations of Judaism, and that the proper observance (or lack thereof) of one directly impacts upon the other. Pinchas correctly decided to attack the sexual immorality that was the root cause of the idolatrous behavior, instead of attacking the idolatry, which while more severe, was the result of the earlier misconduct. The Slonimer Rebbe also states that in our era of *Ikvita deMeshicha*, (the footsteps of the Messiah), these two areas are the major tests that we are faced with constantly, and we must all work to perfect ourselves in these areas of faith and holiness.

Parshat Pinchas is always read during the Three Weeks. As we know, the First Temple was destroyed due to idolatry, immorality, and violence. The first two of these transgressions appear in our story. The violence displayed by Pinchas in this story is an exception to the general use of violence, which is severely prohibited and can destroy the fabric of society. Needless to say, none of us are on the level of Pinchas, and cannot therefore mete out justice in the same manner. Our aspiration should be to grow in our holiness and faith, and uproot violence, hatred, and immorality from our midst.

PARSHAT PINCHAS

Turning Sadness into Joy

Parshat Pinchas is usually read during the three-week period between 17th Tammuz and Tisha B'Av. The *Maor V'shemesh* teaches us that the Shabbatot of these three weeks are the loftiest of the year, elevating all of the sadness of the weekdays and revealing the hidden potential of this period. It contains 21 days, parallel to the 21 days from Rosh Hashanah to Hoshanah Rabbah. In *Beit Aharon* we learn that the Three Weeks are connected with the three higher *sefirot: Chochmah, Binah,* and *Da'at.* This explains why their intrinsic holiness is so hidden; yet we read Pinchas, which tells of the holidays, symbolizing the future redemption when these days will reveal their true holy nature. Sometimes, Pinchas is read on the eve of 17th Tammuz, when Aharon told those preparing to worship the Golden Calf, *Chag l'Hashem machar,* "Tomorrow will be a holiday for God." The Ari explains that this was a prophecy of the future, when all the fast days will become holidays.

Another incident described in *Parshat Pinchas* is when Tzelafchad's five daughters approach Moshe, asking for their father's inheritance in the land. From here, *Chazal* learn of the great love of Jewish women for the Holy Land. The Apter Rav in *Ohav Yisrael* looks at the significance of the names of Tzelafchad's daughters. *Machla* comes from the root that means "forgiveness" and is also related to the word for "dance." *Noa* implies "motion", and signifies that all illness should be removed from the Jewish People. *Chagla* can be divided into *Chag l'Hashem,* the happiness that comes from "celebrating" the Divine. *Milka* is related to the "Kingdom" of Holiness. Lastly, *Tirtza* is interpreted to mean that the deeds of *Am Yisrael* will be "desirous" to Hashem.

Forgiveness, dance, healing, happiness, proper Torah government, and deeds that find favor in Hashem's Eyes are the ingredients for elevating the *Bein Hametzarim* [the three weeks between 17th Tammuz and Tisha B'Av] to the level of the High

Holidays and bringing the redemption which will transform the fast days into holidays. The redemption of the Holy Land is dependent, not only upon political struggle, but also upon these special ingredients. We will need all of them in the future in our loving struggle for *Eretz Yisrael.* May we merit Hashem's blessings.

PARSHAT MATTOT

The Power of Speech

The uniqueness of the human being is in the power of abstract speech, as expressed by Onkeles and Rashi regarding the creation of humanity. *Parshat Mattot* contains the laws pertaining to vows, whose non-fulfillment, says Rashi, is tantamount to "profaning one's speech." The *Mai Hashiloach* explains that in general the laws of the Torah apply to all Jews, but through vows the individual is capable of creating additional personal Torah law to help him deal with particularly difficult temptations.

As beings characterized by speech, we must recognize its incredible power for good or for bad. We speak during prayer, while studying Torah, and in our interpersonal relationships, but we are also capable of misusing speech through slander, profanity, scoffing, and verbal violence. The world was created through speech and we too have the power to create (or destroy), depending upon how we use this most precious gift.

The First Temple was destroyed in part due to violence, and the Second Temple through hatred. Both include an element of slander that, according to the Rambam, "is a grievous sin which causes the deaths of multitudes of Jews." Ultimately this misuse of speech and its destructive results can be traced back to the spies who slandered the Land of Israel on Tisha B'Av, beginning the process that culminated in the destruction of both Temples.

The *Divrei Elimelech* (the father of the Piaseczner Rebbe) points out that Aharon Hakohen died on *Rosh Chodesh Av*. Aharon was characterized by his intense love for the Jewish People and was known for his ability to make peace between enemies. His death on this day serves as a reminder of the dangers of slander and violent speech. More importantly, however, it serves as an inspiration that specifically now, during the Three Weeks before Tisha B'Av, we must redouble our efforts to rectify our speech and strengthen our *Ahavat Yisrael*, thus correcting the slander and hatred which have caused us so much harm during our history. If we all succeed in doing so, we will perhaps merit the fulfillment of the words of Zechariah, and will, *be'ezrat Hashem*, be able to celebrate on Tisha B'Av instead of fasting.

PARSHAT MATTOT

The Spirit of Folly

In *Parshat Mattot, Am Yisrael* wages war against Midian who, under Balaam's leadership, led us astray with harlotry and idolatry. The *Mai Hashiloach* teaches us that Midian represents *dimyon,* imagination or illusion. What does this mean? Imagination seems crucial. For the Rambam, a highly developed imaginative faculty is a prerequisite for receiving prophecy. It is our ability to imagine that enables us to transcend reality, as we usually perceive it, and to open up new possibilities for creative growth. The visualization-meditation of the Piaseczner Rebbe is based largely upon our ability to develop a powerful imagination, *machshava tova,* and use it to influence the rest of our religious persona and help us get close to Hashem. What, then, is the problematic *dimyon* referred to above?

Chazal teach us that, "No one ever sins unless a foolish spirit *(ruach shtut)* enters him." What is this foolish spirit? God created the world in order to have a *dirah b'tachtonim,* a dwelling in the lower realm. To accomplish this, human beings need free will so that they can serve Hashem out of choice. To have free will, we need God's presence to be hidden. The Hebrew word for "world" is *olam,* which is from the same root as *helem,* meaning "hidden." In the Kabbalah our world is called *alma d'shikra,* the world of illusions. The illusion is that God is not really present in our lives. This is the spirit of foolishness that enables us to sin.

Of course our *yetzer hara,* evil inclination, is quite clever and uses more subtle tactics. Rav Tzaddok Hakohen writes that we are sometimes convinced that a sin is actually a mitzva. The Rebbe Rashab teaches in *Kuntress U'Maayan* that we often delude ourselves into thinking that even if we transgress a little it won't really impact upon our relationship with Hashem. This is a dangerous illusion against which we need to be on our guard. Rav Soloveitchik writes in *Al Hateshuvah* that the word for sin, *chet,* is related to the expression *lihachti et hamatara,* to miss the target. We feel that through sin we can gain physical pleasure, honor, or ego satisfaction. In reality, after the momentary pleasure of sin has worn off, we realize that we have missed the mark, and are left feeling more empty and alienated. Rebbe Nachman even called the *yetzer hara* the *koach hamidameh*, the power of illusion.

An additional profound insight is added by Emanuel Levinas, who refers to "the temptation of temptation." Often, it is not even the forbidden act or object that so seductively beckons to us, but more the thought of it, and the maddening curiosity to personally experience what it would be like to sin. This seems to be the mechanism through which Adam and Chava were driven over the edge to eat from the Tree of Knowledge, and it continues to plague us even to this day.

The antidote is *shiviti Hashem lenegdi tamid*, to place God in the forefront of our consciousness. When we really internalize God's constant presence in our lives we will succeed in liberating ourselves from the *dimyon* of Midian and from the alluring illusion of sin.

PARSHAT MATTOT

Mutual Dependence

At the end of *Parshat Mattot*, the Tribes of Gad and Reuven approach Moshe with a special request. Due to their extensive cattle, they wish to remain on the eastern side of the Jordan. Moshe is very surprised by this request. After forty years of wandering in the desert, is the sin of the spies about to be repeated? In the end, a compromise is reached. The two tribes will enter the land and participate in its conquest with the rest of *Am Yisrael*, only afterwards returning to settle on the eastern bank.

Besides the "Zionist" issue here, there is another significant point. We often find tension between the needs of the community and those of the individual (or in this case, the sub-group). On the one hand, the two tribes do have legitimate special needs, and on the other hand, *Am Yisrael* needs their help as well. The model that is offered by the compromise reflects both of these needs. The two tribes agree to contribute their share to *Am Yisrael*, and in return, their special needs are also guaranteed. Perhaps they also realized that their individual success on the eastern bank was ultimately dependent upon the successful conquest of the rest of *Eretz Yisrael*.

In today's community, there is often tension between communal and individual needs. The Piaseczner Rebbe writes in *Tzav V'Ziruz* that ultimately the community exists to serve the needs of the individual, and is not an end in its own right. Nonetheless, any attempt to completely sacrifice either one for the sake of the other is doomed to failure. Our joint success is dependent upon the realization of each individual that they also depend upon the community, as well as the community's realization that it exists primarily to serve the needs of its members. In this way each one of us not only contributes to everyone else but benefits as well, and we all grow maximally, both as individuals, and as a community.

PARSHAT MASAI

Rebuilding the Land of Israel

Parshat Masai is usually read at the beginning of the month of Av, at the start of the nine days of heightened mourning that culminate with Tisha B'Av, the anniversary of the destruction of both of the Temples. In *Bamidbar*, 33:53, we read, "And you shall dispossess the inhabitants of the Land, and dwell in it; for I have given you the Land to possess it." Ramban, both here and in his additions to his *Sefer Hamitzvot*, sees this verse as the source of the Biblical commandment to conquer and to settle *Eretz Yisrael*. In his view this obligates every Jew today to make aliyah.

Chazal teach us that the sin of the Spies peaked on Tisha B'Av when, as a result of their slandering the Land, the Jews cried out to return to Egypt. This day was then cursed as a day of crying throughout the generations. Rav Uzi Kalheim, *zt"l* explains in *Be'er Megged Yarechim*, that, according to the Maharal, we have continued to fulfill the mitzvot that we accepted joyfully in happiness. For this reason, *Am Yisrael* always celebrated leaving Egypt and receiving the Torah. Coming to Israel, on the other hand, having been disrupted by the spies, causing the subsequent decree of wandering, has always been illusive and difficult for many Jews.

Amongst the desert camps we read of in *Parshat Masai* are *Charada* and *Makhelot* (33:24-25). The *Mai Hashiloach* explains the symbolism of these names. *Charada* [trembling] indicates the historical stage when the Jews are in exile and unsure of what Hashem expects from them. They therefore remain passive and do not move to Israel. *Makhelot* [choirs] is the next stage, when the Jews are filled with the clarity that the time has come to actively leave exile and make aliyah. The *Mai Hashiloach,* written in the mid 19th century, ends with a prayer, *Halavei sh'tihiyeh b'karov b'yameinu,* "let it be soon in our days." One generation later, his student Rav Tzaddok Hakohen noted in his *Tziddkat Hatzaddik* that this process was already taking place as masses of Jews had begun to return to Israel after two thousand years of passivity in Exile. In his view this mass aliyah was a sign of the imminence of the Messianic Redemption.

In 1914, Rav Kook wrote a poem for *Rosh Chodesh Av* in *Megged Yarechim*. Although it loses much in translation, the following lines are still particularly meaningful: "The people's rejoicing at slivers of light of salvation will uplift that which was destroyed by senseless crying." Rav Uzi explains that the rectification for the slander against *Eretz Yisrael* and the subsequent crying comes through the love of *Eretz Yisrael* and the joy at seeing it being rebuilt. We can only pray that we will be blessed with the joy of seeing *Eretz Yisrael* being built in love and be spared experiencing any further anguish from the uprooting of people from their homes and the destruction of their communities. During the month of Av, it is our hope that Zechariah's prophecy be fulfilled so that Tisha B'Av will be the greatest celebration.

PARSHAT DEVARIM

A Book of Ethics

The Ramban begins his introduction to the book of *Devarim* by pointing out that this *sefer* is also known as *Mishneh Torah*, the Second Torah. While it is not an exact repetition of the mitzvot that were previously taught, it comes to warn the Jewish People to keep those commandments that were already given, to clarify various details, and add several new mitzvot. Everything is recorded in *Devarim*, which is essentially Moshe's farewell speech to the Jews before they were to enter the Promised Land under Yehoshua's leadership.

The Netziv explains that the expression *Mishneh Torah* comes from the phrase *shinun shel Torah*, the repetition of the Torah, and its main message is to encourage us to engage deeply and profoundly in intensive Torah study. In addition, we learn many ethical messages from this book for, "from this book in particular one can extrapolate all types of *mussar*, ethics." This point is also noted in the Chassidic tradition. Rav Tzaddok writes in his *Pri Tzaddik* that, "the Holy Jew (of Pshischah) would learn several verses of *Devarim* daily, and said that this was his *sefer mussar* [book of ethics]." When we consider that this *mussar* and rebuke was spoken by no less than Moshe Rabbeinu himself, in the Name of Hashem, it makes perfect logical sense that *Sefer Devarim* should be the ultimate book of ethical guidance throughout the generations.

The *Mai Hashiloach* focuses on the difference between the Jewish People at the time the Torah was given on Mount Sinai, and their status now, many years later, when they are about to enter *Eretz Yisrael*. At *Matan Torah*, the people mistakenly believed that their acceptance of the Torah was total on both the intellectual and the emotional levels. Yet this was incorrect, "for at the reception of the Torah the hearts of the Jews had not yet been purified to completely follow Hashem's will; they merely understood intellectually that it was in their interest to fulfill Hashem's will. However, when they entered the land, then their hearts were purified." This is achieved, he states, since "*Eretz Yisrael* hints at the internalization of the words of the Torah within the body." This explains how the Jews were capable of making the Golden Calf only forty days after receiving the Torah, and the other tribulations of the desert era. Ultimately this entire process is necessary, according to the *Mai Hashiloach,* in order to purify us completely, emotionally as well as intellectually, so that "the words of the Torah would be totally internalized on a permanent basis, even without effort, such as when one is asleep."

From these words we can already take one crucial element of *mussar* from *Devarim.* Intellectual understanding of the Torah, while crucial, cannot replace the deep emotional connection necessary to sustain one's faith and commitment in times of stress or doubt. Especially in education, this point needs to be emphasized. We must raise our children and students to love Hashem and His Torah with a powerful personal, emotional quality. This is much more important than the dry, intellectual scholarship that is sometimes the nearly exclusive interest of the yeshiva world. Once, when the Rogatchover Gaon was a young man, he came before Rav Tzaddok Hakohen, and proceeded to recite from memory every place in Rabbinical literature where a certain phrase appeared. Rav Tzaddok gently rebuked him, stating, "When I was a young man I also pulled stunts like that. It doesn't impress anyone. *Rachmana liba bayeh,* Hashem wants your heart!"

When we read the portion of *Devarim* and the rest of this *sefer,* we should close our eyes and try to imagine that we are sitting in the desert, preparing to finally enter *Eretz Yisrael* after a lifetime of wandering. Moshe Rabbeinu is speaking, exhorting us to love God and to fulfill His commandments in the Holy Land. His powerful words will fill our entire being, not only entering the brain, but the heart as well.

PARSHAT VE'ETCHANAN

Two Sets of Tablets

Parshat Ve'etchanan is blessed with two wonderful gems, the Shema and the Ten Commandments. The Kozhnitzer Maggid writes that since we are forbidden from learning Torah on Tisha B'Av, which always falls right before *Parshat Ve'etchanan*, we read the Ten Commandments in order to reaccept the Torah, and the Shema to reaccept the "yoke of Heaven."

According to the Midrash, the Ten Commandments recorded here are the version that was inscribed on the second set of Tablets. The version of the First Tablets, which were shattered, was recorded in *Parshat Yitro*. The first were given as *itoruta dele'ala*, an arousal from above. Due to their pristine holiness, this set was inapplicable to this world and was broken. The second set was given after the sin of the Golden Calf and following Israel's subsequent punishment and *teshuvah*. As such, this second set represents *itoruta deletata*, an arousal from below. As the Netziv points out, although they were less holy than the first, they represent the partnership of *Am Yisrael* with Hashem. The second set of Tablets contains the basis of the Oral Law as well as that of the Written Law, and Moshe himself chiseled it. This more "earthly" Torah is that which sustains us throughout history, developing with us as we move through exiles and redemptions, slowly making our way toward the ultimate rectification of reality. It is therefore fitting that the period of the Three Weeks begins with the shattering of the First Tablets on 17th Tammuz, and ends with the reading of the version of the second Tablets on Shabbat Nachamu, immediately after Tisha B'Av.

Ultimately, full closure for this difficult period is achieved on Tu B'Av, right after Shabbat Nachamu. The Mishna compares Tu B'Av with Yom Kippur, which is the day that the second Tablets were given in response to our repentance. The earthly weddings that we celebrate on Tu B'Av are a microcosm of the cosmic wedding that takes place between Hashem and His bride, the people of Israel, on Yom Kippur. Actually, according to Rav Tzaddok, Yom Kippur is not the *chuppah*, but represents a deeper and more intimate stage, the *yichud*, when the bride and groom are alone together for the first time after the ceremony.

The *Maor V'shemesh* writes that the Shabbatot of the Three Weeks are the highest of the year, for the yearning that results from the separation of exile is so powerful that it can take us to places we never thought possible. Afterwards on Tisha B'Av we achieve such closeness to Hashem that the *Mashiach* is born, as stated in *Bnai Yissaschar*. On Shabbat Nachamu our *avodah* is to integrate all that we have experienced and learned in the Three Weeks into our daily lives. In this way, we begin to prepare ourselves for the *teshuvah* of Elul and the *Yamim Hanoraim*.

PARSHAT *VE'ETCHANAN*

Finding Comfort

The Ari points out that the numerical equivalent of the name *Ve'etchanan* equals that of *tefillah*, prayer. This hints at Moshe's numerous prayers to enter the Land of Israel. Rav Leibele Eiger writes that Moshe desired to enter Israel in order to achieve an even higher level of spiritual wisdom. In this he was successful, and even though such wisdom is not usually attainable outside Israel, Moshe was rewarded with it.

Parshat Ve'etchanan is always read on *Shabbat Nachamu,* the Shabbat of Comfort. For Rav Leibele, this is a parallel to prayer. We often pray, but are left with the uneasy feeling that our prayers have not been answered. Of course we need to remind ourselves that the main purpose of prayer is to get close to Hashem, not to "get something." Nonetheless, we all pray, hoping for an answer. Sometimes that answer is *no*. We need the spiritual maturity and perspective to realize that this is also a blessing, even if we can't see how at the time. Often many years pass before we realize how much better our lives turned out because we weren't able to do that which at the time seemed so important to us. Thus, our prayers in fact are answered, but often the answers are hidden from us, or the answers are actually very clear, but we are too obtuse to understand them.

This is also the case with the comfort on *Shabbat Nachamu.* Do we really feel comforted? Have all our problems and those of the Jewish People been solved? Have all the Jews returned to Israel? Is there a Temple? Has unity replaced divisiveness? In response to such questions, Rav Leibele writes, "But in truth, on the inner level, comfort and salvation appear every year on this Shabbat, and before Hashem the salvation is revealed." Although we want so much to see the salvation with our physical eyes, for the time being we need to look inward, to see it in our hearts. When we do so, we feel closer to Hashem. Of course we must do more to actualize these gains in external reality as well, but in the meantime we are comforted by the inner feeling that whatever happens is guided by Hashem's strong hand, the hand that also caresses and comforts us. Amid all of our sorrows, we can only pray that *Am Yisrael* feels this comfort.

PARSHAT EIKEV

God As Provider of All Our Needs

Parshat Eikev contains several crucial principles of our faith and divine service, including the verse, "And now Yisrael, what does the Lord your God ask from you? To fear … go in His ways and to love Him and serve … with all your heart and with all your soul." This verse is part of Moshe's final instructions to us before we enter the Promised Land. There, we are told, there is no river like the Nile to irrigate all the fields and to provide water. In Israel, rain is the barometer of our relationship with Hashem, and we need to pray for it. We are also reminded that even if we do merit material wealth in the Land, we should be careful to make sure that it does not blind us to the truth and pull us away from Hashem.

We are warned that we should not attribute our achievements solely to our own efforts by saying, "My own strength and power brought me this greatness." Rather, we should "remember that it is the Lord your God who gives you the strength to achieve greatness." The *Mai Hashiloach* develops this theme. He teaches us that the most important thing is to always remember who it is that provides for us. Furthermore, "God decreed that man could never be without food so that he would always be lacking and need much work and remember the One who influences. This is the greatness of Israel, who always remember the One who influences goodness and therefore they receive spiritual sustenance from their food."

This verse teaches us that it is a blessing to be in need. For this reason, the snake that tempted Adam and Eve received what appears to be a paradoxical punishment of crawling on the ground and eating the dust. It is explained that the snake's punishment was to always have access to food, and thus never feel lacking and the need to daven to Hashem. Similarly, the Egyptians, who had a constant water supply, are described as those who do not pray. When Moshe wished to daven, he actually left the city because it was a place that intrinsically stifled prayer. The *Mai Hashiloach* also tells us here that by recognizing that it is God who provides for our material needs we not only receive the physical benefits of His generosity, but spiritual ones as well. When we eat with this awareness, we engage in *avodah shebegashmiut*, serving God through corporeality.

The *Mai Hashiloach* also informs us that, "even in the words of Torah, if one doesn't remember who gave the Torah, his knowledge is worthless." We should always endeavor to make sure that in all of our actions, both physical and spiritual, we always remember to thank God, our ultimate provider.

PARSHAT RE'EH

The Hidden Goodness in Our Lives

Parshat Re'eh begins with the verse, "Behold, today I set before you a blessing and a curse. The blessing if you listen to God's mitzvot ... and the curse if you don't listen to the mitzvot." On the Shabbat before Elul, the month of *teshuvah,* the Torah sets out both of these alternatives in stark simplicity. In fact, the *Mai Hashiloach* informs us that if good things happen we know for sure that we have followed God's will, and if not, we suffer the consequences. However, our instinctive reactions are often quite different because although "everything is from Hashem, human nature is to complain when one suffers, 'what have You done to me?' However, when Hashem blesses a person with only goodness, he refuses to see that it is from Hashem and he says, 'I have achieved all of this with my strength and the power of my hands.'"

Yet things are not always as they appear. The *Mai Hashiloach* continues, "When Hashem gives goodness He dresses it in a way that makes it appear the opposite so that the person can clarify the good and bring it to light ... by the toil of his hands." Similarly, the *Beit Aharon* writes that there is both hidden good that is *tov,* good, and revealed good that is *chessed,* loving-kindness. In this way, "the righteous rejoice even in what does not appear to be good, for they rejoice in its hidden goodness."

We invariably find that the future is filled with uncertainty and trepidation. This parsha is generally read when the Jewish nation enters Elul, a time to renew our optimism and simultaneously undertake a serious and painful *cheshbon hanefesh,* reckoning of our deeds, as individuals, a community, and a nation. Every painful experience is an opportunity for growth, and without it growth is impossible. The seed must rot in the ground before a tree can sprout, and a woman in childbirth sits upon the *mashbar,* the birthing stool. The word *mashbar* also means "crisis," but it is a crisis that leads to a new birth. This is the revelation of the hidden good.

Midrash Tanchuma states that a woman giving birth cries out 100 times - 99 for death and once for life. The first 99 cries represent the time of uncertainty preceding any new birth or growth. The final cry is that of happiness, when the birth has occurred and a new life is revealed. When this happens, we see the past in a new light and realize that *Hashem hu HaElokim*, and that even the difficulties we have endured have also been for the good. This is the clarity that sustains us after we have been through difficult times, whether as individuals or as a people. It is what we experience during Elul and the High Holidays, as the previous year's sufferings and tribulations are washed away or elevated to a new level or understanding. It is our annual process of closure. We should pray that Hashem will grant us all the clarity to understand the deeper meaning of our own lives.

PARSHAT SHOFTIM

Elul – A Time of *Teshuvah* and Forgiveness

In *Avodat Yisrael*, the Kozhnitzer Maggid writes, "Behold, this parsha [*Shoftim*] is always read in the month of Elul, the time for everyone to do *teshuvah* and to be forgiven." What can we learn from this parsha regarding *teshuvah*? According to the *Mai Hashiloach*, the *shoftim* (judges) represent our own ability to judge for ourselves whether or not something is appropriate behavior, whereas the *shotrim* (policemen) symbolize our ability to abide by those decisions. Elsewhere, he writes that the word *shoftim* is an allusion to Halachah, Jewish law, while the term *shotrim* is a reference to *Aggadah*, narrative and philosophical literature. In other words, it is incumbent upon us to study Halachah so that we know the law, but at the same time we must strengthen ourselves through the study of *Aggadah*, including philosophy and Chassidut, which help motivate us to observe the law.

We are told to place judges and policemen in "all of your gates." According to Rashi, this means "in every city." The Kozhnitzer Maggid sees these gates as the eyes, ears, nostrils, and mouth, all of which are the gateways to the soul. At those places where we sensuously interact with the outside world we need extra caution. The *Sod Yesharim* points out that this is stated in singular language for, "Everyone has their own special gates in their service and behavior." Of course, every Jew has to observe the 613 mitzvot, but each of us also has a personal mission in this world for which we, and we alone, were created. In this personal matter our judging and guarding must be particularly exacting. One may ask, how am I to know what my personal task is in the world? According to the *Netivot Shalom*, whatever I find to be the most difficult is my special mission in the world.

From all of the above, it is clear that each of us has a lot of individual work to do, and if we take it seriously we won't have too much time left over to focus on other people. In this light, the *Mai Hashiloach* explains another mitzvah in this parsha, that of pursuing justice: "*Justice justice,* this means to be punctilious in observance, *pursue,* this refers to the person himself, but he should not get angry at his friend who is not so careful." This particular point, a prime example of *ahavat Yisrael,* reminds us that the *yahrzeit* of Rav Kook, who embodied *ahavat Yisrael,* falls on 3rd Elul, around the time when this parsha is usually read. In addition, the Piaseczner Rebbe tells the following story in *Derech Hamelech:* Rebbe Elimelech and his brother Rebbe Zusha were once walking during Elul when they heard a peasant woman screaming at her drunken husband, "These are days of work, how can you sleep?" Rebbe Elimelech and Rebbe Zusha understood that this was a message for the days of Elul, which are days of work, and we all need to wake up!

The month of Elul is a time to awaken from our spiritual slumber, to judge ourselves honestly and work upon the aspects of ourselves that need to be corrected before the *Yamim Hanoraim.*

PARSHAT *SHOFTIM*

True *Teshuvah*

The Kozhnitzer Maggid writes in *Avodat Yisrael* that *Parshat Shoftim* is always read in Elul because it is relevant to our *teshuvah* process. Judges are enjoined from taking bribes that cloud their ability to judge impartially. For the Maggid this is a warning to be wary of the bribes we are offered by our own *yetzer hara*. We allow ourselves to think, "True, I have transgressed, but if I do a mitzvah, or study some Torah, it will all even out." However, this is nothing more than our *yetzer hara* bribing us to continue to transgress by letting ourselves off the hook easily. In reality, says the Maggid, the reward for doing the mitzvah and the punishment we deserve for the sin are two separate issues. A transgression is only atoned for by true *teshuvah*, which prevents a person from repeating that particular action.

In *Hilchot Teshuvah*, the Rambam tells us that we all have a balance sheet of merits and sins. "One whose merits are greater than his sins is a tzaddik," he writes. "One whose sins are greater than his merits is an evil person. Half and half, he is in the middle ... if his sins are greater than his merits; he immediately dies in his evil." If that isn't frightening enough, the Rambam informs us that only God Himself is capable of "keeping score," as the balance is more qualitative than quantitative. For Rav Shagar, this is a message that we need to live lives of spiritual tension because we can never really know where we stand. (This is also a further reminder not to judge others, for we surely can't know where *they* stand!) This spiritual tension builds up in Elul, intensifies on Rosh Hashanah, and peaks on Yom Kippur.

The existential pain we experience when honestly evaluating our merits (often tainted by ulterior motives) and our transgressions (how often blessed with truly extenuating circumstances?) can be overwhelming. We must be on guard not to despair. Rebbe Nachman and all the holy Rebbes teach us that depression is the ultimate enemy of divine service. Therefore the Maggid ends his discussion as follows: "One should say to himself, 'As long as my Jewish soul is inside me I am sure that my *teshuvah* will be accepted. Even though I have done much evil in the eyes of Hashem, His loving-kindness and truth will not abandon me.'" This is of course only relevant when we really do *teshuvah* to the best of our ability. We can only aspire to that level, with the hope that our wrongdoing is forgiven and we can actually feel that God's mercy is with us.

PARSHAT KI TETZEI

Mercy and Compassion Within God and Ourselves

In this parsha, we read about the mitzvah of sending away the mother bird before taking her eggs. Already in Mishnaic times, this mitzvah stood at the center of the debate regarding finding reasons for the commandments. In *Mishna Brachot* 5:3 we read, "One who says that God's mercy reaches even a bird's nest ... should be silenced." The Gemara gives us two explanations for this expression. The first is that this statement may create jealousy within the animal kingdom. The second is that it creates the impression that the mitzvot are meant to be merciful, when they are simply decrees. It is in fact wrong for us to search for their rationale.

Although the Rambam quotes both of these explanations in different places, this is not the place to deal with this seeming contradiction. He does, however, state clearly in one place that the purpose of this mitzvah is to be merciful to the mother bird. Here, the Ramban strongly disagrees. Had the Torah wished to be merciful to the bird (or to the cow mentioned in the mitzvah not to slaughter an animal and its offspring on the same day), it would have prohibited meat altogether. Rather, this particular mitzvah comes to inculcate the quality of mercy *within us*, so that we will act with compassion toward other human beings. A similar approach to all of the mitzvot regarding eating is found in Rav Kook's *Vision of Vegetarianism and Peace*.

The Maharal disagrees with both the Rambam and the Ramban. The mitzvot were given, as *Chazal* state, "to refine the people." The actual reason behind the mitzvah is therefore not central, but rather its meticulous fulfillment as part of the acceptance of the "Yoke of Heaven" is the main point. By fulfilling the will of God, the Jew is brought closer to Him, purified and sanctified.

We can only hope to fulfill the mitzvot according to all of the interpretations, accepting upon ourselves the Yoke of Heaven, acting mercifully, and *being* merciful, so that we will in turn merit a compassionate judgment from Hashem.

PARSHAT *KI TETZEI*

Preparing for War Against the Evil Inclination

Parshat Ki Tetzei opens with the laws pertaining to warfare, with the words, "When you go out to wage war upon your enemies." In Chassidut, this homiletically refers to our ongoing battle with the *yetzer hara,* the evil inclination. Reb Simcha Bunim of Pshischah goes further, claiming that the *pshat,* the simple meaning of the verse, hints at the *yetzer hara,* while the war against human enemies is relegated to *drash,* homily. We are then immediately confronted with three seemingly strange halachot – the beautiful captive woman, the firstborn son of a hated wife, and the stubborn and rebellious son. *Chazal's drasha* on this subject is well known. There is, in fact, a process here. By giving into the *yetzer hara* and marrying the beautiful captive woman, one gives birth to a firstborn son who is not loved. This child eventually becomes rebellious and is ultimately executed.

It is also possible to view these laws as reflecting different circles of relationships that we all have. Firstly, we engage with the *ultimate other* (the enemy), secondly with our spouse, and thirdly with our children. Later we read of the precept of sending away the mother bird, addressing our relationship with animals and the environment.

Rav Shagar writes that among the components of *teshuvah* it is necessary for me to accept the *other* in his *otherness* in order to truly forgive. This is especially true regarding the *close other,* such as our parents, siblings, spouses, and children. It is sometimes easier to feel empathy for the starving African that we see on CNN than it is for us to accept our family members as they are. A person must accept the fact that they will never be exactly as *he* would want them to be (just as he will never be exactly the way that *they* would want him to be). We must judge those we love favorably, giving them the benefit of the doubt that they did not desire to cause us pain or suffering. Each of them is an entire universe, a complex being made up of many components including personal needs, and with "baggage," including pain, frustrations, and fears. By internalizing this concept, it is easier to let go of our anger and build relationships characterized by understanding, compassion, and love.

This is also the first step to an individual letting go of his anger at himself, deepening his relationship with Hashem. This is not passivity. We bear serious responsibility to help ourselves and those around us to meet our full potential. This needs to be done with love, with the good of the *other* as the paramount goal, and with the realization that everyone is different and has a unique role to play.

Later on in the parsha, we read of the holiness of the Jewish army camp. In addition to the *pshat*, that we must strive to make the IDF an absolutely holy army, we can learn an important message for any community, including our schools and synagogues. In every communal setting there exists a high level of communal responsibility, and each individual is largely dependent upon every other person.

The *Netivot Shalom (Mishmeret Harishona* 15*)* writes, "A Jew is uplifted only through the power of the community." According to his words every shul must be a *spiritual home*, where the atmosphere of holiness is all-pervasive. The community's success is largely dependent upon the concept of *sharing together in the yoke*. Here, we widen our circle of involvement to address the wider community that we need to strengthen. Public prayer is a central facet. Other examples of what we can do are to work harder to get to shul on time, and to pray with more concentration and intensity. A person should even sing and dance during prayer, although he should be authentic. On the one hand, he may lose himself in the fervor of his prayers, disregarding what others think as he communes with Hashem. On the other hand, we should always remember that we are part of a community. The people around us deserve respect. Respecting the space of the other members of the congregation, and being more cautious regarding conversations are prime examples of how we can create the communal davening experience that we yearn for.

By making a serious effort to strengthen all of our relationship circles, including family, friends, and community, and by sincerely judging others favorably, they will in turn judge us favorably as well. In this way, all of *Am Yisrael* will emerge innocent from our collective judgment on Rosh Hashanah.

PARSHAT KI TAVO

Hearing the Rhythm of the Soul

Ezra the Scribe decreed that we read *Parshat Ki Tavo* before Rosh Hashanah, "to end the year and its curses and begin the year and its blessings." Other than the blessings and curses in this parsha, what connection does it have with our preparations for the New Year?

The parsha begins with the verse, "And when you come into the land that the Lord your God gives you as an inheritance and you inherit and settle it." Moshe transmitted this parsha to *Am Yisrael* as we were poised to enter the *Holy Land*, and we read it as we are about to enter a *Holy Time*. To be a *Holy People* we need to know how to live in the different times of the year, for each one radiates its own special holiness. At the time of the year that *Ki Tavo* is read (Elul), we are working on our *teshuvah* to be worthy for another year of serving Hashem on Earth. We need to reaccept the *Yoke of Heaven* and the *Yoke of the mitzvot*. Sometimes, when we do so we feel the truth of the Baal Shem Tov's dictum, "the strongest feeling of Chassidut (piety) is at its beginning." Hashem gives us a gift as we start to come close. We feel His closeness, the warm embrace of His love, and the guidance of His Providence. But this feeling often dissipates, we feel let down, and we are again confused. We ask ourselves if what we felt was real or an illusion? The truth is that *now* I am experiencing the illusion of Hashem's distance.

What happens if even at the beginning of my service I feel a lack of inspiration? The *Mai Hashiloach* writes on the parsha, "When one arouses himself to divine service and to accept the yoke of Torah, he doesn't yet feel enjoyment, since Hashem isn't giving him clarity as he has not yet internalized it." Nonetheless we need to be persistent, for "once one feels enjoyment from divine service then he will never feel suffering from it, and it will be easy to serve Hashem and be a Holy People." The key to this persistence is *emunah*, faith, "that in the future it will be good."[3]

---

3. See also Rebbe Nachman's story, "The Bitter Herb." Each of us is an individual with different spiritual (as well as physical and emotional) rhythms. Part of the self-awareness necessary for spiritual growth is to be in touch with our deepest feelings. The Piaseczner Rebbe teaches that if we would write down everything that goes on in our soul we could write a thick book every day, but we are too busy, indifferent, or afraid to stop and listen. We should try to take some time to try to listen, and in the merit of these efforts Hashem will bless us with the ability to hear our inner voice and His.

PARSHAT KI TAVO

The Mitzvah of *Bikkurim*-
Implications for *Teshuvah*

Parshat Ki Tavo opens with the mitzvah of *bikkurim* – when farmers bring the first fruits to the Temple. This mitzvah has two parts – the actual bringing of the *bikkurim* to the kohen [priest], and the farmer's declaration, a speech that later assumed the central role in the Pesach Haggadah. This declaration essentially thanks Hashem for having brought us out of Egyptian slavery into *Eretz Yisrael*, and for giving us the ability to grow produce of intrinsic holiness by working the soil of the Holy Land.

In the *Mai Hashiloach*, Rav Mordechai Yosef of Ishbitz makes a startling observation. In biblical Hebrew there are several verbs meaning "to tell" or "to say," each with its own unique nuance. In verse 3, it says *higaddti hayom* – "I have said on this day." The *Mai Hashiloach* comments: "[The word] *Haggadah* [usually translated as "narrative"] hints at words of rebuke, for he speaks harsh words to the kohen, hinting to him that even though he (the kohen) serves in the Temple, while he (the farmer) toils in the field, nonetheless when a Jew reaches the Temple bringing the *bikkurim* it is clarified that in his own place he was in a state of holiness like the kohen serving (in the Temple)."

This statement encapsulates a major tenet of the Torah's worldview. *Kedushah*, holiness, is not something limited only to "ritual" or "religious" matters, but is primarily concerned with the elevation and sanctification of everyday life. As *Chazal* state in *Avot* 2:12, "All of your deeds should be *leshem Shamayim* – for the sake of heaven."

This concept can help us to elucidate an interesting *mishnah*. Chapter 3 of *Bikkurim* describes the procession of the farmers bringing the *bikkurim* to the Temple in Jerusalem. At the end of the third *mishnah* we read: "All of the craftsmen in Jerusalem stand up (in honor) of them greeting them: 'Our brethren from such and such a place - come in peace.'" The Bartenura questions this *mishnah* with another halachah: Even though it is obligatory to rise when a Torah scholar passes by, craftsmen do not have to stop their work to stand up for a *talmid chacham*, for this disrupts their work. Why then, asks the Bartenura, do they stand for those farmers bringing the *bikkurim*? His answer is that this constitutes a case of *chavivah mitzvah b'sha'ata*, a mitzvah that is beloved at its special time. In other words, this is a special event, like a funeral or a brit, when everyone also stands.

However, based on the *Mai Hashiloach*, we can perhaps glean an additional insight. If a craftsman was required to stand up for a passing Torah scholar, the result might have greater ramifications than a momentary delay in his work. It might also serve to reinforce an inferiority complex of sorts. The craftsman may feel that, "The *talmid chacham* (parallel to the kohen in the Temple) spends all his time engaged in the service of Hashem, studying and teaching Torah, while I am only a lowly shoemaker. When he goes by, I need to interrupt my work, which is really of little significance." When the craftsman, on the other hand, rises before the farmer bringing *bikkurim*, the opposite impact is achieved. Both are members of the working class, one a rural proletariat, the other an urban proletariat. Standing up for the farmer, while causing a momentary interruption in his work, is actually an act of spiritual "class solidarity," which should serve to instill new pride in the importance of his own work. Just as the farmer discovers the holiness of his own occupation as a means of sanctifying everyday life to the service of Hashem, so does the urban worker who rises to greet him.

The grandson of the *Mai Hashiloach*, Rav Gershon Chanoch Leiner, goes a step further. In *Sod Yesharim* he writes, regarding the same verse, "Since he has come from working in the field to the Temple, and has realized that the honor (of Hashem's) majesty is found also in physical matters, he is on a higher level than the kohen, who serves constantly in the Temple where (God's) light is very clear and refined." In other words, it's relatively easy to be holy and pure while in the Temple (or in today's yeshiva environment), but it's a much greater challenge to discover and maintain holiness while in the marketplace, at work, or in graduate school.

Rav Kook writes in *Orot Hateshuvah* 14:30 as follows: "Specifically from within true, pure *teshuvah* we must return to the world and to life, and with this we restore holiness to its proper foundation, and enthrone the Shechinah (divine Presence) in the world." It is not sufficient to be holy only in the realm of ritual. Chassidut stresses *avodah begashmiut*, corporeal service, through which we sanctify and elevate all of reality, infusing even the profane realm with holiness. This path is more demanding, and yet anything less is a dichotomized approach to reality which contradicts the holistic nature of divine service. Through our sincere *teshuvah*, we should gain the wisdom and strength to internalize the message of the *bikkurim*, sanctifying the entire world as Hashem's Kingdom.

PARSHAT NITZAVIM

A Time to Be Judged

Parshat Nitzavim is always read on the Shabbat before Rosh Hashanah because, as Rav Leibele Eiger points out, *Nitzavim* is the appropriate preparation for the Day of Judgment. We enter this day with more than a little trepidation. As the Piaseczner Rebbe states, only a madman or a drunkard could be unaware of his spiritual shortcomings. *Parshat Nitzavim* begins dramatically: All of us, from the greatest to the lowliest, even after all of the exilic sufferings described in *Ki Tavo* (and according to the Ramban this is a description of the exile after the Second Temple's destruction) stand again before Hashem. Is there not a similar trajectory each year? In Tishrei we feel close to Hashem, but then a whole year passes, with its ups and downs. Are we satisfied with our year? Did we reach our spiritual goals? Have we really improved our relationships? Do we perform the mitzvot with real happiness? All of a sudden it is Elul, and once again we feel inadequate to be judged.

Rav Soloveitchik writes that *Parshat Nitzavim* is the source of the personal covenant between Hashem and each individual Jew. But is that a comfort, or does it just drive home our depressing situation? Let us return to Rav Leibele, who states: "We read this parsha on the Shabbat before Rosh Hashanah to give ourselves strength and trust for this awesome day ... for all of us have a standing. In fact, the salvation comes in response to our broken heart ... for only out of darkness does light come. From the very brokenness of our heart we have trust that all of us will experience many types of salvation." Nonetheless, the feeling of a broken heart sometimes fills us with a sense of melancholy or at least uncertainty. Even the change in the weather has an impact upon our mood. This autumn feeling was captured by the poetess Leah Goldberg in *The Neighbors Have Already Packed:*

And someone came and said
the Days of Awe are approaching
the summer is over
the pear tree in the garden has lost its leaves
into the yellowing grass
...the summer was short
and shorter yet
was the spring
...in the city they await us for the Days of Awe.

With the fall comes a sense of uneasiness as we approach the unknown. A melancholy that Rav Shagar describes as "the death of time" fills the air. Nonetheless, there is a certain familiarity in the process, and in Rav Shagar's words, "new time can now be born." The summer sun has blinded us and now, with the fall, we know that we must go home. Although the leaves have fallen, the tree continues to grow. The nights grow longer, but the moon will shine brightly.

It is frightening to be judged, but it means that I am not alone, that I am worthy of being judged. The Kafkaesque tragedy of modernity is the inability to be judged, the total lack of certainty, of closure. How much worse is postmodernity, where we don't even know the rules by which one is judged? We, however, *can* be judged. We present ourselves in judgment before the throne of the Almighty, and announce in advance our readiness to accept the verdict, whatever it may be. We can go home. At the end of his story *The King and the Emperor*, Rebbe Nachman allegorically writes, "Addressing her true bridegroom, she then said, 'And you, royal prince, let us go home.' With that they both returned home. Blessed be God forever, Amen and Amen."

On Rosh Hashanah we will return home, into the realm of the Holy One. Amen.

PARSHAT NITZAVIM

The Circumcision of the Heart and the *Teshuvah* Process

Before Rosh Hashanah, we read the Torah portion of *Nitzavim*, one of the most difficult portions in the Torah. According to the Netziv, this is the "the portion of the redemption, a clear prophecy of the details and order of the future redemption." It is clear that there is a strong connection between redemption and *teshuvah*, as we see in the formulation of the Rambam, "The Jewish People are only redeemed through *teshuvah*." Rav Soloveitchik sees *Parshat Nitzavim* as the personal covenant between each individual Jew and the Creator, the source of each Jew's personal holiness. It therefore is crucial to analyze this parsha's vision of the redemption and its implications for the *teshuvah* process of the individual.

"When all these things befall you - the blessing and the curse that I have set before you - and you take them to heart amidst the various nations to which the Lord your God has banished you, and you return to the Lord your God, and you and your children heed His command with all your heart and soul, just as I enjoin you this day, then the Lord your God, in His compassion, will restore your fortunes. He will bring you together again from all the peoples where the Lord your God has scattered you. Even if your outcasts are at the ends of the world, from there the Lord your God will bring you to the land which your fathers occupied, and you shall occupy it; and He will make you more prosperous and more numerous than your fathers. Then the Lord your God will **circumcise your heart** and the hearts of your offspring to love the Lord your God with all your heart and with all your soul, in order that you may live."

According to the simple meaning of these verses, the people will repent after the exile and Hashem will bring them back to *Eretz Yisrael*. Afterwards, there is an even higher stage of *teshuvah*, that of the circumcised heart. This would appear to be the ideal *teshuvah* that we all yearn for. But what exactly does this mean?

According to the Ramban, it is a description of the spiritual revolution that will take place in the Messianic period. "From the time of the creation each person was given free choice to be a saint or an evildoer ... but in the Messianic period it will become natural to choose only good ... this is the circumcision mentioned here ... at that time people will become like Adam was before the sin ... this is the annulment of the Evil Inclination." The Evil Inclination will therefore be entirely eliminated during the Messianic era, and we will all be like Adam before his sin. This is in clear opposition to the position of the Rambam, that "there is no difference between this world and the Messianic era except for the subjugation of the nations over Israel." The Ramban, on the other hand, paints a picture of a spiritual utopia, in which, unlike our current existence, there is no battle between good and evil, between the spiritual and the physical. But is this truly what we desire?

Rav Kook writes in *Orot Hateshuvah* that, "*Teshuvah* preceded the creation of the world, and is therefore the foundation of the world ... from this perspective sin is necessary ... the cancellation of the very nature of life, so that a person will be by definition a 'non-sinner,' is in itself the greatest sin." What Rav Kook is telling us is something that we may have already intuited, that all of the glory of the human being, as opposed to animals on the one hand and angels on the other, lies in the fact that he does have an Evil Inclination, and therefore the possibility of sin and free will. As the Rabbis stated in *Bereishit Rabbah*, "'Behold it is good,' refers to the Good Inclination. 'Behold it is very good', refers to the Evil Inclination!" Do we really strive to turn into "robots," as the Ramban's words would seem to suggest, or is it preferable to spend our lives in the constant struggle for righteousness with all of the spiritual danger that this entails, and as Rav Kook seems to suggest? Perhaps ultimately Rav Kook disagrees with the Ramban, and perhaps they are speaking on completely different levels of reality. Let us attempt to build a bridge between them, not in the realm of theology, but rather in that of *Avodat Hashem*, of divine service. We will examine two possible models.

The *Meshech Chochma* asks about the commandment to believe in the words of Moshe, "How did God command us to always believe the words of Moshe, for everything is in the hands of Heaven except for the fear of Heaven, and perhaps Moshe might decide later to add (to the Torah) on his own? You must say that God took away Moshe's free will like the angels." The *Meshech Chochma* goes on to reject this position, for like Rav Kook he sees no value in Moshe's service without free will. He therefore concludes, "Moshe worked and struggled so much that he raised himself up to the highest possible human level. He therefore merited that his free will was annulled. This then is the essential goal, to purify one's physicality until his very flesh becomes spiritual."

The position of the *Meshech Chochma* can in theory agree both with the Ramban and with Rav Kook. We are happy to have been created with free will, the Evil Inclination, and the potential for sin. We know that human greatness is dependent completely on our struggle between good and evil, with all of the inherent danger that this entails. On the other hand we do not wish to remain forever bound in constant inner struggle. As we grow in Torah and in the fear of God, we develop spiritually so that our struggles revolve around more refined issues. Slowly, through a lifetime process, we edge ourselves closer to the Ramban's ideal. Not by means of a divine annulment of the Evil Inclination, but through constant and difficult inner work. We have no illusions that we will reach the level of Moshe, but each of us, on his or her level, strives for self-perfection and to annul their own freewill, so that ultimately the fulfillment of the Divine will becomes second nature.

Rav Yizchak Hutner, a student of Rav Kook, articulates a radically different vision in his *Pachad Yitzchak*. In his dialectical view, there exists an intrinsic contradiction in the world of divine service. "The attribute of the fear of sin pushes for the elimination of (spiritual) danger ... for contained within the fear of sin is the desire to annul the existence of sin. However, the annulment of sin is also the annulment of the power of free will. And since, when free will is annulled there exists no possibility of divine service, we find that the service of the fear of sin intrinsically contradicts itself. For the desire to be a servant of God includes within it the desire for the existence of free will which requires the existence of sin; whereas the desire of the fear of sin is for the annulment of the possibility of sin... This combination of service and the fear of sin can only be understood as an intense and powerful desire for the existence of sin, so that there exists the possibility to yearn for its annulment ... which is an aspect of the Kabbalistic concept of *ratzo veshov* (running and retreating) in our service of the Divine."

For Rav Hutner, unlike the *Meshech Chochma*, the goal is not to transform oneself into a person who has annulled one's own free will. For at that stage, life would become meaningless. Only the struggle inherent in service gives life its existential significance. Yet at the same time the true servant of God simultaneously desires to be freed of the shackles of the Evil Inclination, since he sincerely desires never to displease God. The nature of the divine service, and hence *teshuvah*, is pregnant with dialectical tension, and therefore with existential meaning.

On the eve of Rosh Hashanah, we review our year. Rav Shlomo Carlebach teaches that we need to transform the previous year into a vessel ready to contain all of the light of the coming year. May we merit to do so, and to live rich lives full of inner meaning, marked by the service, the fear, and the love of the Divine.

PARSHAT VAYELECH

The Meaning of *Hakhel*

In *Parshat Vayelech,* we read about the mitzvah of *Hakhel,* in which, on the Sukkot after *Shemittah* [the Sabbatical year], all of *Am Yisrael,* men, women, and children, gather in the Temple, where the king reads portions of the Torah to the public. All of the people reaccept the covenant in a ceremony that some commentators describe as a reenactment of the giving of the Torah. If this is the case, why is *Hakhel* held on Sukkot? Surely Shavuot would have been more appropriate.

The *Mai Hashiloach* gives a fascinating answer. At the end of the *Shemittah* year, during which everyone has dedicated themselves to spiritual pursuits, there may be a natural tendency to jump on the tractor, get to work in the field and ... forget what one learned during *Shemittah.* The Torah gives us the mitzvah of *Hakhel,* precisely when the demands of making a living may cause us to forget the spiritual lessons that took a year to learn. *Hakhel* reminds us that the work we are setting out to do must also be dedicated to heaven.

Similarly, says the *Mai Hashiloach,* we are accustomed to continue *seudah shlishit* [the third Shabbat meal] into the night after Shabbat ends, in case we rush immediately into our weekday activities and forget the spiritual lessons we internalized during Shabbat. For the same reason, the Psalm of the day on Sunday includes the words, "The earth and all of its fullness belong to Hashem." When we recite this psalm we are reminded that while we do make Havdalah and separate between Shabbat and the week, our weekdays must also be days of holiness. Rav Soloveitchik wrote in *Al Hateshuvah* that while there are plenty of Jews who are *shomer Shabbos,* there are not enough Jews that are *shomer erev Shabbos!*

This important message, of bringing the holiness of Shabbat into the week through *seudah shlishit,* and bringing the holiness of the *Yamim Noraim* into Sukkot, the Time of our Rejoicing, and the entire year through the mitzvah of *Hakhel* needs to be internalized, giving meaning to our daily lives.

PARSHAT HAAZINU

Spiritual Preparations for Sukkot

The Netziv writes in *Parshat Vayelech* that, "near his death the light of Moshe's level began to dim." In a similar vein, the *Kedushat Levi* writes that in *Parshat Haazinu*, the reason why the song of *Haazinu* is so difficult to understand is that unlike Moshe's earlier prophecies, which were transmitted in his usual manner of *the clear lens, Haazinu* was given close to his death, when much of his prophetic strength had already been given to Yehoshua, leaving Moshe to prophesy in the *unclear lens* manner of the other prophets.

We usually read *Parshat Haazinu* on the Shabbat between Yom Kippur and Sukkot, which marks a break in our busy preparations. What is the nature of this four-day period? Is it a continuation of the Ten Days of Repentance, or something different? Rebbe Nachman writes that these four days are parallel to the four white garments that the High Priest wears on Yom Kippur, reflecting the purity that we drew down from Yom Kippur into these days. Therefore, sins are not counted at this time and we throw ourselves into the building of the sukkah. Returning to the *Kedushat Levi,* he contrasts these days with those of repentance that were characterized by *teshuvah m'yirah,* repentance from fear. In contrast, during the four days before Sukkot, "everyone is busy with the mitzvot of the sukkah, the *lulav,* and the Four Species, giving charity to the best of their ability and serving God with happiness and a good heart. This is *teshuvah m'ahavah,* repentance from love," the highest level of repentance.

The prophecies of *Haazinu* may not be clear, but other, more material aspects of our preparations are very much in evidence. We need to build a sukkah, prepare a lulav and etrog, and cook for the holiday. As we scurry about busily from mitzvah to mitzvah, it is important to feel the love and happiness that is in the air and in ourselves. Our sins are in the past, and now we can truly serve Hashem with love. Then we will be ready to enter the sacred space of the sukkah, the *zela d'mihemnuta*, the shade of faith.

Once inside, together with the *Ushpizin*, the holy guests of Sukkot, and with our earthly guests, we are enveloped in the holiness of the Shechinah, the Divine Presence, which is also a manifestation of the unity of *Am Yisrael*. As the Sages teach us, all of Israel can dwell in one sukkah. The unity of the sukkah combines with the unity of the *arba minim*, the Four Species, which represent all types of Jews bound together. The Chassidic custom is to bless the *arba minim* in the sukkah, thus bringing together all of the unities. As the numerical equivalent of *sukkah* is equal to that of the divine names of Hashem and A-donai combined, Sukkot emphasizes the concept of unity, of the Jews with each other, with Hashem, and with the entire cosmos.

PARSHAT VEZOT HABRACHA

Like a Bride and Groom

When Moshe begins to bless *Am Yisrael* before his death, he states the famous verse, *Torah tzivah lanu Moshe morashah kehillat Yaakov*, "Moshe commanded the Torah to us, an inheritance of the community of Yaakov." This verse is such a crucial element of our faith that the Rambam tells us that this is the first verse to teach our children when they begin to talk, followed by *Shema Yisrael*, and the rest of the Torah. Rav Saadya Gaon explains that this verse teaches us that God gave us the Torah, via the transmission of Moshe. Rashi writes that the significance of an inheritance is that we hold on to it and don't abandon it. The Ramban adds that the "community of Yaakov" not only includes all of Yaakov's physical descendants, but also all of the converts that would join *Am Yisrael* throughout the generations.

Chazal use an interesting play on words to express our deeper connection with the Torah. They reread *morashah* (inheritance) as *maurasa* (betrothal). This exchange expresses the intimate, sensual nature of the relationship between *Am Yisrael* and the Torah, which is similar to that of a groom with his bride. This is an exclusive relationship and explains the Rabbinic adage that "a gentile who engages in Torah study is deserving of death." In this, the Torah is similar to Shabbat, also the subject of a sensual, intimate relationship with *Am Yisrael*, about which it says, "a gentile who observes Shabbat is deserving of death." (It should be noted, however, that neither case is a literal death penalty, but is rather a hyperbole to emphasize the point.)

The Netziv sees this verse as describing a certain aspect of Torah study, *pilpul*, the in-depth study of Halachah, which is so powerful that it cements the relationship of the student to his material. The *Mai Hashiloach* explains both the original word and the Rabbinic substitution. *Morashah*, inheritance, refers to the innate bond that every Jew has with the Torah, which is passed down from the Patriarchs, and is a connection that cannot be marred. *Maurasa*, betrothal, on the other hand, is the connection that each individual must make for himself, and that he or she expresses through their own *chiddushei Torah*, novel Torah interpretations. (These two categories are similar to Rav Kook's distinction between *segula* and *bechira*, and Rav Soloveitchik's between *brit Avot* and *brit Sinai*. The concepts of *segula* and *brit avot* refer to the essential inherited aspect of our relationship with the Torah. *Bechira* and *brit Sinai*, on the other hand, symbolize the relationship with Torah born of free will and our decision to accept the obligations upon ourselves.) We should strive to merit both aspects of the relationship with Hashem's holy Torah.

THE FESTIVALS

ROSH HASHANAH

The Signs of Rosh Hashanah

Much symbolism is utilized on the night of Rosh Hashanah, as discussed in the *Shulchan Aruch*. Despite our misconceptions, *simana milta*, a sign, is in fact a real thing. The signs and symbols that we experience on Rosh Hashanah consist of eating special foods and reciting special prayers regarding the significance of their names. These signs vary from community to community, but often include the head of a fish or a sheep to symbolize leadership, apples in honey for a sweet New Year, pomegranates for many merits, a new fruit, and other, similar symbols. The *Bnei Yissaschar* (*Tishrei* 2:11) writes that these signs are eaten only on the first night, for, "The first night is Leah, and the second night is Rachel, and Rachel transmitted the signs to Leah." This is of course a reference to the Biblical story where Leah took Rachel's place on the night of her marriage to Yaakov. According to Rashi, Rachel gave Leah certain signs, so that she would be able to fool Yaakov regarding her true identity. Although most people are accustomed to eating the signs on both nights, the *Bnei Yissaschar's* statement at first seems very strange and requires elucidation. What is the significance of this connection between Rachel and Leah and Rosh Hashanah?

It is widely discussed in Chassidic literature that Leah represents the *alma ditkasia*, the hidden world. This is congruent with her biblical character, who has weak eyes, stays inside most of the time, and is very unworldly. Rachel, on the other hand, the worldly shepherdess, is considered to represent *alma d'itgalia*, the revealed world. The holy Ari writes that the first day of Rosh Hashanah represents the interior (*pnimi*) correction of reality, while the second is focused on fixing the exterior (*chitzoni*) manifestation. Based upon this concept, the Kozhnitzer Maggid advises us to pray on the first day of Rosh Hashanah for our spiritual needs, and for our physical ones on the second.

According to the holy *Zohar* in *Terumah,* Leah equals the divine manifestation (*sefirah*) of *Binah,* understanding, while Rachel is equated with the *sefirah* of *Malchut,* God's Kingdom in the world, also known as the Shechinah, the Divine Presence. Yaakov equals the *sefirah* of *Tiferet,* beauty and truth. By marrying both Leah and Rachel, he unites *Binah* with *Malchut,* bringing down the influx of divine influence from *Binah,* in the hidden upper realms, into *Malchut,* the revealed reality in our world.

The *Baal Hatanya* writes in *Igeret Hateshuvah* that *Binah,* associated with the first letter *hey* in the four-letter name of Hashem, is the world of Higher *Teshuvah. Malchut,* the second *hey,* is the world of Lower *Teshuvah.* The letter *vav,* which includes *Tiferet,* is the conduit which unites the two, and through which the Divine influx flows.

The holy Ari writes that on Rosh Hashanah, the world was conceived, its birth being in the month of Nisan. According to the *Bnai Yissaschar,* we can explain that on the first night of Rosh Hashanah, Yaakov unites with Leah (unknowingly, in a union orchestrated by Heaven). This is the union of *Tiferet* with *Binah* (the Higher Shechinah), in other words, the Higher *Teshuvah* of the Hidden World. Only after this has been achieved is it possible for Yaakov on the next night, to unite with Rachel, knowingly.[4] This is the unity of *Tiferet* and *Malchut,* the Lower *Teshuvah* of the Revealed World, and the coronation of Hashem as King, as the Lower Shechinah reveals Herself.

The signs that we perform are, according to the *Bnei Yissaschar,* equal to the union of Yaakov and Leah. Leah needed these signs to seduce Yaakov on their wedding night, in order to create a cosmic rectification of the highest magnitude. Similarly we must

---

[4] We refer of course to the supernal union on the second night of Rosh Hashanah. The actual marriage of Yaakov and Rachel took place a week after his marriage to Leah.

245

"seduce" Hashem[5] with our signs. This higher, hidden *Teshuvah* paves the way for the next night. Rachel needs no signs to unite with Yaakov, and nor do we, in order to "unite" with Hashem. Now this can be actualized in a lower, revealed way in our world. By perfecting the spiritual world on the first day of Rosh Hashanah, we are able to perfect the physical world on the second.

----

[5] The idea of "seducing" Hashem on Rosh Hashanah, based on the Midrash, is discussed by Rav Tzaddok Hakohen of Lublin. See Rav Shagar, *Sichot leYemei HaTeshuva*, Efrat, 5763, pp.18-19.

ROSH HASHANAH

Blending the Spiritual with the Physical

On the night of Rosh Hashanah we are accustomed to eat special foods as signs for the New Year. In this context the *Magen Avraham* states that the Maharshal would not eat fish on Rosh Hashanah because he enjoyed it so much, and he wanted to lessen his physical enjoyment. The *Maor V'shemesh* explains that the signs are spiritual activities, used to activate the upper spheres, bringing down blessing into the world. If one eats them for their taste, they accomplish nothing. For this reason, the Maharshal would not eat fish on this night.

However, this explanation does not make sense in light of our eating the most famous sign, the apple and honey, for a sweet year. We must distinguish between the apple, eaten for its taste, and the other signs, eaten because of their names. One could eat the other foods, concentrating on the significance of their names, without enjoying their taste. However, when we eat the apple and honey, and pray for a sweet year, we must also taste the sweetness in our mouths.[6]

On Rosh Hashanah we blend various spiritual activities, such as *tefillah* and *Tekiat Shofar*, with physical activities, such as our holiday meals. The Ari writes that the first day of Rosh Hashanah is focused upon our spiritual needs, and the second upon the physical. Clearly we believe that no true *Avodat Hashem* is possible without this holistic approach.

On Rosh Hashanah, we pray that Hashem will help us to perfect all aspects of our spiritual and physical lives. We also hope that we and all of *Am Yisrael* will be blessed with a sweet year of

---

[6] Thanks to my wife Julie for this distinction.

247

happiness, health, livelihood, peace, good relationships, and most importantly, a powerful relationship with Hashem.

ROSH HASHANAH

The Rebirth of Rosh Hashanah

"I was also there at the time, and I was still an infant. I spoke up and said to them, "I remember all these events, and I remember absolutely nothing."... He is higher than all the rest, since he remembered even what was before the *nefesh*, the *ruach*, and the *neshamah*. This is the concept of nothingness."

Rebbe Nachman, *The Seven Beggars*

The Talmud, in *Rosh Hashanah* 34a, records a doubt regarding the definition of the *Teruah*, the broken shofar blast. According to some it is *yelalah*, hysterical crying, while others state that it is *anachah*, groaning. A third opinion is that it is *anachah* followed by *yelalah*, groaning which turns into hysterical crying. Rabbi Abahu therefore decreed that in order to fulfill all of the possibilities, we blow the shofar in all of the above ways, with our *Teruah* representing the hysterical cry, our *Shevarim* representing groaning, and the *Shevarim-Teruah*, representing the combination. Each "set" of shofar blasts also has a simple sound, the *Tekiah*, before and after it. All of this is codified by the Rambam in *Hilchot Shofar* 3:2. What is totally clear is that according to all of the views, the shofar blasts represent various types of crying. Why is crying the motif of the shofar, the central mitzvah of Rosh Hashanah?

The celebration of Rosh Hashanah is fraught with tension. On the one hand it is a *chag*, and the mitzvah of holiday happiness is applicable. On the other hand it is the Day of Judgment, and as such, the Jew is filled with awe, and even some fear. This point is aptly expressed in numerous *midrashim*, where, for example, the question of wearing nice clothing on Rosh Hashanah is discussed. Interestingly, even in Halachah there is a strong trend toward fasting on Rosh Hashanah. The *Tur* (O.H. 597) quotes Rav Netronoi Gaon, who favors fasting on Rosh Hashanah. Ultimately this position is rejected (*Shulchan Aruch* 597:1), partly due to a famous statement from the book of *Nechemia*, "And he said to them, 'go and eat good foods and drink sweet drinks, and send food to those who don't have, for this is a holy day to the Lord. Don't be sad, for the happiness of the Lord is your strength.'" Nonetheless, the position of fasting is not totally rejected, and for example, one who decides to fast on Rosh Hashanah must annul his vow, which is not the case on any other holiday. We also find other curiosities regarding eating on Rosh Hashanah. For example, we have the special foods we eat as "signs" at the evening meal, and according to the Vilna Gaon one should not eat grapes. Why?

Another halachic curiosity has to do with marital relations. The *Mishna Berurah* (240:7) informs us that the mitzvah of marital relations that applies on Shabbat also applies on the nights of holidays, due to their holiness, but that it is advisable not to have relations on Rosh Hashanah. (Note: This is a Kabbalistic custom, which does not have full halachic force, and there are exceptions to it as well.) Why is Rosh Hashanah an exception to the general holiday rule in this area as well?

Before attempting to suggest a conceptual framework within which to understand the above questions and the deeper meaning of Rosh Hashanah, we need to examine one more source. In *Rosh Hashanah* 10b, we learn of a fascinating dispute. While according to Rabbi Eliezer the world was created at the end of Elul, with the creation of man on Rosh Hashanah, the sixth Day, Rabbi Yehoshua holds that the world was created in Nisan, i.e. at the end of Adar, with the creation of man on Rosh Chodesh Nisan. According to Rabbi Yehoshua, what we call Rosh Hashanah is not the beginning of the year at all, but actually the very middle, the first day of the seventh month. If so, how can we understand all of the prayers we recite marking Rosh Hashanah as the day of creation?

Let us return to the very beginning. When man was created, God breathed the breath of life, which is the Divine soul, into his nostrils (*Bereishit* 2:7). According to the Aramaic translation by Onkelos, this transformed man into a "speaker," giving him his qualitative edge over the animals. Rashi adds to this motif, stating that man possesses "knowledge and speech." In other words, the human being is unique in his ability to verbally communicate his innermost thoughts, which are also directed toward abstract concepts, including the most abstract of all, the nature of God. In the words of the holy *Zohar*, "He can speak before the King, which is not true of the other creations."

When Adam and Chava sinned by eating from the Tree of Knowledge, they created several problems that have become embedded within human nature ever since. Our whole lives are dedicated to *Tikkun Chait Adam Harishon*, the rectification of Adam's sin, in order to perfect ourselves, humanity, and the cosmos, thus paving the way for the Ultimate Redemption. It is important to remember that this first sin, and the subsequent judgment, took place on Rosh Hashanah, and for this reason Rosh Hashanah remains the annual Day of Judgment for all of humanity. The ultimate problem relating to the sin was *Pgam Hada'at*, the tainting of knowledge, which was also the root cause of the transgression.

We can discern three negative results of Adam and Chava's sin. Firstly, there was *Pgam Hadibbur*, the tainting of speech. The snake misused the power of speech he then had by enticing Chava to eat. She did the same in relation to Adam. Adam misused his speech to blame the whole episode on Chava. Let us remember that speech is the essence of the human being. When one violates this by, for example, speaking slander, gossip, or profanity, he lowers himself to a level far below that of the animals. Secondly, there was *Pgam Haachilah*, the tainting of eating. By violating the commandment not to eat, the desire for food became a major aspect of human nature, which affects us to this day. For example, there are so many people who cannot stick to a healthy diet. Thirdly, we have a case of *Pgam Habrit*, the tainting of sexuality. Before the sin, Adam and Chava were naked. They had no self-consciousness, and therefore no embarrassment. After the sin, they became self-aware, and sexuality went from being natural to being desirous, and they were ashamed, needing clothing. Throughout history, the way in which we deal with human sexuality and morality has been one of the major issues every human being must contend with.

While we are constantly trying to perfect ourselves in these areas, certain times are more propitious, and Rosh Hashanah, the anniversary of this event, is foremost among them. The way we do this is to rectify those areas that were negatively affected by the sin. Therefore we work on our eating by consuming the special signs, and by eating in a holy manner. The custom not to eat grapes on Rosh Hashanah, according to Rav Soloveitchik, is based upon the opinion that grapes were the forbidden fruit. This is also, according to Rav Tzaddok Hakohen, the basis for the opinions that one should fast on Rosh Hashanah. Regarding the perfection of sexuality, this is perhaps the reason that we are urged to abstain on Rosh Hashanah. While eating is perfected through an action of eating, and not through fasting, sexuality is more inherently bound up in ego, desire, and physical pleasure, and therefore too potent to be perfected (on this occasion) through its fulfillment.

Before turning to the issue of the perfection of speech, let us reexamine the dispute regarding the date of creation. According to Rabbanu Tam in the *Tosafot*, both opinions quoted above are true, for God decided to create the world in Tishrei (Rosh Hashanah), and this creation was actualized in Nisan. Based upon this, the holy Ari explains that Rosh Hashanah is the day that the pregnancy of the world began, and the world was born in Nisan. (All of this is of course solely from our limited human perception. God exists completely beyond time, which is part of the creation. It is therefore ultimately meaningless to state that an event happened a certain amount of time before creation, for there was no time. This is, however, beyond our comprehension, and we must speak in human language.) On Rosh Hashanah, then, we actually return, not to the moment of the *birth* of humanity, but to its very *conception*! Since the person's genetic makeup is determined at the moment of conception, we return to engage in "spiritual genetic engineering," recreating ourselves at the moment of our own conception, and therefore correcting all of the results of Adam's sin by fixing their root, before they can occur. This is achieved through our special eating, and through sexual abstinence. In what way do we, however, deal with the crucial issue of speech?

According to Rebbe Nachman, the shofar represents the highest manifestation of speech, the "silence that is higher than speech." The shofar is simply a *kol*, a voice, not yet manifested in individual words. This is of course related to the fact that the blasts of the shofar are actually crying, as we have learned. Crying is a primal expression of deep emotion, more basic and powerful than that which can be expressed in words. By blowing the shofar, we also return to the state of a newborn baby, who cries, incapable of speech. While according to Halachah, 30 shofar blasts are sufficient, we are accustomed to blow 100 times. Various explanations have been offered, and I would propose another. The *Midrash Tanchuma*, (*Tazria* 4), states that during a birth a woman cries 100 times, 99 for death, and once for life. The uncertainties associated with birth create existential crises expressed by crying. As the baby actually emerges, there is a cry of joy, signifying the relief and knowledge that new life has emerged, after all of the uncertainty.

In the same way, as we hear the first 99 blasts of the shofar on Rosh Hashanah we experience our own conception, pregnancy, and labor, ultimately being born. Additionally, we experience our entire lives, all of our fears, pain, sinning, confusion, and frustration. This is our *Teshuvah*. Finally, with the 100th blast, the *Tekiah Gedolah*, we are reborn, and this is the cry of life. This also explains the simple *Tekiah* before and after the *Teruot*. Rebbe Nachman and others see this as the intrinsic goodness with which we are born. This is followed by all of the struggles of our lives, and our *Teshuvah*. Ultimately we come home to ourselves, signified by the simple *Tekiah* closing each set.

Rav Soloveitchik writes of two types of *Teshuvah* - intellectual and emotional. Rav Kook sees the different types of *Teruot*, of crying, as the embodiment of this idea. The groaning of the *Shevarim* represents the intellectual analysis of one's situation. The hysterical crying of the *Teruah* is the powerful emotional response to the awareness of sin. We do both together, (*Shevarim-Teruah*), for in this way *Teshuvah* is most effective.

On Rosh Hashanah, our breath into the shofar, which, according to the *Pachad Yitzchak*, is the same breath that Hashem

253

breathes into our nostrils at Creation, should help transport us back to that very nothingness before our own conception. When we reach the level of "remembering absolutely nothing," we will then be in a position to recreate ourselves as more perfect beings.

ROSH HASHANAH

Kavanot on Not Blowing the Shofar

On Rosh Hashanah, humanity was created, i.e. was born. *Chazal* explain that man and woman were created *du-partzufim*, like Siamese twins, attached back-to-back. Afterwards, Hashem separated them through the process known as the *nisira*, so that they could face each other and fulfill the role of being an *ezer-kenegdo*, helpmate. The Ramban explains that the relationship of those fated to be permanently attached is meaningless, for only a relationship born of choice has significance. This is especially true when we consider that the former state precludes the ability for one half of the couple to gaze into the face of the other, whereas the latter is predicated upon the possibility of just such a gaze. According to the Ramchal, this description is a microcosm of the Creation itself, when we were separated by Hashem from the *Ein Sof*, the divine reality, and became part of a seemingly independent world, where we have the responsibility to reestablish a meaningful relationship with the Shechinah, the Divine Presence.

In the Torah, Rosh Hashanah is only one day, and the shofar is blown. The Rabbis later decreed that there should be two days of Rosh Hashanah, and that the shofar would not be blown on Shabbat. Rosh Hashanah never falls out on Friday, but it does fall, and not infrequently, on Shabbat, creating a situation in which the shofar is not blown on the first day, Shabbat, but only on the second. It is quoted in the name of the holy Ari that that the first day of Rosh Hashanah is the day for perfecting *pnimiut*, the interior dimension, whereas the second day corrects *chitzoniut*, the exterior.

Before the *nisira* of the creation, we were all enveloped in the *Ein Sof*, the Infinite. This was not, however, a meaningful relationship, and could be described by the Kabbalistic concept of *achor*, of "facing the back." Paradoxically, only after the separation of creation, of *nisira*, are we able to reach *panim*, the meaningful face-to-face relationship with the Shechinah. When Hashem created Adam, He blew into his nostrils the breath of life, the divine soul, thus separating from him, birthing him, giving him the power of independent breathing, and therefore of life. This can be compared to the cutting of the umbilical cord in a human birth, when the baby ceases to receive oxygen directly from the mother and begins to breathe and hence live independently, while deepening the relationship through the face-to-face activity of nursing.

The *Pachad Yitzchak* writes that the blowing into the shofar on Rosh Hashanah (the only mitzvah done through breathing) is the same breath that Hashem breathed into the nostrils of Adam on Rosh Hashanah, the day of his creation, the breath that instilled within him the divine soul. The Kozhnitzer Maggid writes, "The ultimate fixing on Rosh Hashanah is to perform the *nisira* (separation) through the blowing of the shofar." Based on the above, we can say that on the second day, which is not Shabbat, the day of exterior correction, the blowing of the shofar is the aspect of the divine breath, which is the *nisira*, like the cutting of the umbilical cord, an act, which while necessary, is also somewhat violent. This reflects the aspect of the shofar, described by the prophet Amos as, "Can the shofar be blown in a city without causing the inhabitants to tremble?"

What happens, however, when the first day of Rosh Hashanah, the day of interior correction, falls on Shabbat and we refrain from blowing the shofar? Chassidut teaches that Shabbat itself achieves everything that is generally achieved through the blowing of the shofar. This is appropriate to the "interior" nature of the first day. However, if there is no divine breath, no *nisira*, no cutting of the cord, what is our status? We are still attached; we cannot live or even breathe independently. What kind of significant relationship can we hope to build with the Shechinah, with our divine Mother, if we are still attached by our umbilical cord?

One of the principles of natural childbirth is to delay the cutting of the umbilical cord for as long as possible, to avoid the violent act of complete separation. This is the moment that the mother takes her new baby, still attached to her by the cord, into her arms, face-to-face, and nurses her. This is a pure moment of an interior and intimate relationship, *panim*, while still attached, nourished both from within and without simultaneously. At this point, the pain of separation has not yet been experienced. All is softness, *chessed*, envelopment, and complete peace. This is what we experience when Rosh Hashanah falls on Shabbat. The Shechinah, our supernal Mother, nurses us, while we are still attached, still physically connected to the Infinite. In such a state, we are "born but yet not born." When a baby nurses from its mother, the milk, the influence that he receives, flows according to the intensity of the sucking. In the same way, divine influence flows to the extent that we yearn for it, we cry out for it, and open ourselves to receive it. Our *itoruta deletata* stimulates Hashem's *itoruta deleala*.

By showing Hashem that we yearn for the Divine influence, we can also connect with the Shechinah, who nurses us with mercy, love, light, and warmth. On Rosh Hashanah, when it falls on Shabbat, we not only recognize Hashem as the King who rules over us, but also the Shechinah as Queen. We are therefore able to connect with all aspects of Divinity and feel God's kingdom within every aspect of our lives.

SHABBAT SHUVAH

The First Act of *Teshuvah*

While we tend to think of *Shabbat Shuvah* as the Shabbat that *happens* to fall out during the Ten Days of *Teshuvah*, in fact the opposite is true. Based upon the Midrash in *Bereishit Rabbah*, the *Pri Tzaddik* explains that Adam and Chava were created on Friday (Rosh Hashanah). On that very day they also violated the Divine commandment not to eat from the Tree of Knowledge and were judged, the sentence being banishment from the Garden of Eden. Nonetheless, they were allowed to spend Shabbat in the Garden of Eden, and were only banished after Shabbat. Why? The Midrash continues that the moment Shabbat began, Adam first grasped the concept of *Teshuvah* and repented. Hashem knew that Adam would not dare to eat from the Tree of Life on Shabbat, for there is a halachic concept (*Aimat HaShabbat*) that people are afraid to do the wrong thing on Shabbat.

Every Shabbat has the power to help us do *Teshuvah*, and we know that even the two words *Shabbat* and *Teshuvah* are made up of the same letters. This is a major theme in the *Netivot Shalom* of the late Slonimer Rebbe.

Shabbat Shuvah, the first Shabbat in the year (i.e. the first of creation), has the greatest power, since on it the first act of *Teshuvah* in history was performed. Its influence is so great that it lights up the days before and after it, transforming them into the Ten Days of *Teshuvah*!

We must aspire to reach perfect *Teshuvah* out of love for Hashem on this holy Day. This will ensure that each of us, together with everyone in our community and all of *Am Yisrael* will be sealed in the Book of Life for the coming year.

SHABBAT SHUVAH

To Write the Book of *Teshuva*h

Rav Shagar tells the following story: Once, at the time of the High Holidays Reb Aryeh Levine, *zt"l*, had a conversation with Professor Hugo Bergman of the Hebrew University. Professor Bergman complained to Reb Aryeh that he didn't know what to do with himself at that time of the year. "For you religious people it's easy. You just open up the Rambam and the *Shulchan Aruch*, and do what is written. We secularists, on the other hand, don't have any similar instructions." Reb Aryeh replied, "Yes, and for exactly that reason you have a chance of doing real *teshuvah*."

I once read an article in which a "religious" person recounted the following incident: "I was sitting behind two 'secular' men on the bus. One turned to his friend and asked, 'Do you believe in God?' The latter replied, 'Yes of course I do.'" The author raised the following seemingly bizarre question: perhaps today's 'secular' Jews should be identified with the Chassidic concept of the *Simple Jew*. For, he pointed out, when a "religious" Jew is asked that question, he has to give the correct answer, or else by definition he ceases to be "religious." The "secular" Jew, on the other hand, has real freedom to answer honestly, as he has no ideological stake in giving this or that answer. While this hardly qualifies one as a *Simple Jew* (which is essentially a very high spiritual level), the question raised in both of these stories is worthy of our consideration.

How authentic are we, or our *teshuvah*? Are we not locked into pre-conceived patterns that define us so much that we have little chance of actualizing our freedom? Those of us that actually made the radical switch from a secular to a religious lifestyle are often incapable of persevering in the smallest improvements to which we have committed ourselves. Perhaps part of our problem is that we rely too much on books written by others. Maybe we need to work harder to write our own book each year. As Rav Kook writes, "The inner pain of *teshuvah* is great material for the

poets of sadness to awaken their violins, and for the tragic paint-
ers to reveal their talents." Of course it is easier to read another's
poems, to hear his music, to view his art. But is it authentic? Is it
really me? This year, in addition to finishing the Rambam's *Hilchot
Teshuvah,* let's begin to write our own.

SHABBAT SHUVAH

Removing the Impurity of Our Transgressions

In *Al Hateshuvah*, Rav Soloveitchik writes that any transgression carries with it two negative repercussions – liability and impurity. Although the sinner is obviously liable to punishment, the more serious issue is the *tumah*, the impurity that has resulted from the sin. This is not in the technical halachic sense, but rather refers to the metaphysical aspect of the spiritual uncleanness that distances us from Hashem. Consequently, explains the Rav, Yom Kippur has two results, *kapparah*, atonement, and *taharah*, purity. Each of these is the antidote for one of the results of sin. Rabbi Yehudah Hanasi held that Yom Kippur provides atonement even if the individual does not repent. While this opinion is not accepted, it nonetheless needs to be understood.

For this reason, Rav Soloveitchik writes, "There is atonement without repentance, but there can be no purity without repentance." In other words, just as the sin has a technical ramification in the realm of punishment, so too can the special holiness of Yom Kippur together with its potent sacrifices technically remove the liability for punishment. But can this properly correct a damaged relationship? Does this relieve us of our personal need to appease Hashem? In this situation, does it give us the status of *baal teshuvah*, penitent, so beloved before God? Obviously not! That can only be achieved through sincere *teshuvah* with a broken heart!

In the Mishnah, Rabbi Akiva dramatically declares, "You are happy, O Israel! Before whom are you purified, and who purifies you? Your Father in heaven ... just as the mikvah purifies the impure, so God purifies Israel!" The Rav points out that this statement was made not long after the destruction of the Second Temple. The Jews at that time were despondent. With no Temple, High Priest, incense offering, or scapegoat, how could they possibly achieve atonement? They felt doomed to lead eternal lives of spiritual *tumah*, with no chance of repairing their misdeeds and coming close to Hashem. Against this backdrop comes Rabbi Akiva, the eternal optimist, to remind *Am Yisrael* that ultimately there is only one source of forgiveness, atonement, and purity – Hashem Himself! Even a mikvah is only a mikvah because God has decreed it to be so. Since we no longer have a Temple, the answer is sincere repentance, which brings with it both atonement and purity. For this reason, Rav Soloveitchik concludes his discussion with an idea found in the Maharal and other sources, and takes the comparison between God and the mikvah quite literally. "We must enter into God, into the holiness of Yom Kippur like we enter a mikvah, with no foreign item interposing between our body and the water, with no part of our body remaining outside of the water." As long as we are holding back, as long as we aren't ready to jump in and completely immerse ourselves in *Elokut,* we cannot really be purified.

The Slonimer Rebbe writes in *Netivot Shalom* that the three forces that can purify the Jew are the mikvah, *Am Yisrael,* and Hashem Himself. He then quotes the *Beit Avraham* that, "just as the mikvah only purifies if there is no interposition whatsoever, so too *Am Yisrael* can only purify if there is no interposition between one Jew and his fellow." This is, of course, another explanation for the halachically mandated need to appease anyone whom we may have offended before Yom Kippur, and to forgive whole-heartedly anyone who has offended us, even if they did not ask. The *Netivot Shalom* ultimately sees us going through a process in which the mikvah purifies the body (and one must immerse on the eve of Yom Kippur). The connection with *Am Yisrael* purifies the lower portions of the soul, and finally, Hashem purifies the higher levels of our souls. This is reminiscent of the Piaseczner Rebbe, who writes that to achieve spiritual unity we must first integrate our own personalities, and only then achieve Jewish unity. After that, all of *Am Yisrael* can finally unite with Hashem.

On Shabbat Shuvah we enter into high gear preparing for Yom Kippur, which is just a few days away. As we have learned from Rav Tzaddok Hakohen, the Shabbat before any holiday contains that holiday's essence, and in this case that is most certainly true. On Shabbat Shuvah, we can already feel the awe and joy of Yom Kippur, its holiness and beauty. Now is the time to plunge into all of the mikvaot: those of water, *Am Yisrael,* and ultimately that of Hashem Himself. Wash carefully; remove all particles that stand in the way. Nullify yourself to the purifying powers that surround you. Then you will be ready for a Yom Kippur that provides you not only with atonement, but with purity as well.

YOM KIPPUR

Before Kol Nidrei

The Rambam has a famous position that only those Jews who live in *Eretz Yisrael* are referred to as the *tzibbur*, the public community. This fact invests the Jews living in Israel with a serious responsibility for our brethren who are still in the Diaspora. The Maharil, in his *Laws of Yom Kippur*, quotes Mahari Segel, who asks why we have longer *piyutim*, liturgical prayers, regarding the goat that was offered in the Temple than we do about the scapegoat, whose power of atonement was far greater? One of the answers given is particularly interesting. The goat offered in the Temple atones for violations of the Temple's purity and holiness. Since the Temple's holiness is still in effect even when the building is destroyed, and entering the Temple Mount in a state of ritual impurity is a grievous sin, the Jews of the Diaspora ask Hashem to forgive the Jews of Israel who may have been remiss in this area. This reflects the principle that all Jews are responsible for each other. As a proof, the Maharil cites the confessional liturgy in which every Jew asks forgiveness, in the plural, for a long list of sins he may never have committed, since in fact, each of us is asking for forgiveness for every Jew. Let us take a deeper look at the mutual responsibility that every Jew has for each other.

In *Chovat Hatalmidim*, the Piaseczner Rebbe describes the states of *yichud ilaah v'yichud tata*, upper and lower unification. Lower unification takes place within *Malchut*, the collective body of *Am Yisrael*. After all of the Jews have united (lower unification), then they can collectively unite with the upper *sefirot*, i.e. with Hashem Himself, reaching the state of upper unification and rectifying all of reality. The Rebbe uses this idea to explain the statement made before we perform many mitzvot, "for the sake of the unity of *Kudsha Brich Hu* (Hashem) and the Shechinah (represented by the collective Jewish People) ... in the name of all of Israel."

The Rebbe explains that this process actually has three stages. Firstly, each one of us must work to make ourselves into an integrated personality, in which the body, brain, and soul all work together to serve Hashem. We all know that when we are feeling personally "not put together" we are not in a state in which we can maintain proper relationships with other people. Secondly, each one of us must work to unite ourselves with all of *Am Yisrael*. Unfortunately this is easier said than done, but we must never cease in our efforts to bring authentic unity to the Jewish People. Only after these two aspects have been perfected are we, *Am Yisrael*, as represented by the Shechinah, able to unite with Hashem. Thus the prayer formula which discusses uniting Hashem and the Shechinah ends "in the name of all of Israel," since the higher unity of God and the Shechinah is absolutely dependent upon the prior unification of all of Israel.

The Piaseczner Rebbe further writes in *Zav v'Ziruz*, that if we want to make spiritual progress, we should set ourselves an annual goal. Where do I want to be one year from now? What kind of person do I want to be by next Yom Kippur? Then, throughout the year, I should measure myself by the standards of the "new person" and check periodically if I am succeeding in closing the gap between the old and the new. If at the end of the year, I am no closer than I was a year ago, then in a sense I have wasted a year of my life, God forbid. Every year we should make it our goal to work on unity, including the personal, national, and cosmic levels. If we all sincerely make this our top priority, we can, with Hashem's help, really change ourselves and the world.

YOM KIPPUR

To Forgive, But Not to Forget

It is not possible to begin Yom Kippur without first forgiving all of *Am Yisrael* from the depths of our hearts. This is not always an easy task, and in some circumstances it seems nearly impossible. One prime example in contemporary times is after the events of the summer of 5765/2005, when the brave Jewish residents of the Gush Katif bloc were cruelly ejected from their homes as part of Israeli government policy. These shocking events left all of us deeply wounded and in pain. For months afterwards, these unfortunate evictees were left homeless and jobless. Everything was taken away from them – for nothing. This issue was so explosive that it threatened to divide Israeli society.

Such a serious, divisive issue raises the question of how we can forgive in such circumstances, where both the victims and the perpetrators were in fact Jews. In such a situation, we still need to find the strength and ability to forgive, otherwise it only weighs us down and prevents us from moving forward. After all, none of us is perfect, and certainly not in terms of interpersonal relations. All of us often offend and hurt others. Yet, we then desperately want them to forgive us, and for Hashem to forgive us. In the same way, we also must forgive those who have hurt us.

Shortly after the disengagement, there was a popular bumper sticker bearing the slogan, *lo nishkach velo nishlach*, "we won't forget and we won't forgive." The message of this sticker is deeply disturbing. Of course it is absolutely forbidden to forget, because in such a situation we must continue to help the refugees and to work intensively on every level to ensure that nothing of this sort ever happens again. And of course we do not stand in the place of those who were uprooted. We certainly have no right to "forgive" the government for the tremendous debt, both moral and financial, that it incurred. Yet it just doesn't seem Jewish to announce that we won't forgive other Jews. It is also incorrect to state that we never forgive someone who doesn't ask for forgiveness, because that is exactly what we do every year before Kol Nidre.

In the case of the disengagement, we have to find a place in our hearts to forgive the simple soldiers and policemen who took part in the expulsion. Even though there were calls for them to disobey their immoral orders and most of them failed the test, these young men and women underwent months of brainwashing and every kind of pressure beforehand. Some of them were following the religious directives of their own Rabbis, which whom we disagreed. In a way, they too were victims of the violent disengagement policy.

Regarding those who gave the orders, it is much more difficult. Although those of us who were not expelled from our homes are not in the place of those who were directly affected, we too feel we have been attacked, that our values have been trampled, and our deepest sensitivities violated. On the other hand, as a nation we are collectively responsible because had we been worthy Hashem would have spared us these horrible events.

In such circumstances, we may not feel ready to forgive, but we need to begin the process. At the very least we need to be able to pray with a full heart, "no Jew should be punished on my account." We should endeavor, even under the most extreme circumstances, to avoid being burdened with too much anger. By moving forward toward forgiveness (while at the same time never forgetting) *Am Yisrael* should merit living in peace throughout *Eretz Yisrael.*

YOM KIPPUR

Keeping Ourselves Out of the Mud

When I was a yeshiva student it was very popular to augment the regular Yom Kippur *machzor* with an additional booklet that elucidates the words of the *vidui*, the verbal confession that stands at the center of the liturgy of the Day of Atonement. In these booklets many additional transgressions were added "between the lines" of the acrostic confessions. They would be either linked conceptually to the general topic heading, or simply added alphabetically. The feeling we internalized was that it was insufficient to merely recite the words of the confession as it appeared in the *machzor*, for to do so was to fall into the trap of praying by rote without sincere regret for our transgressions. Prayer without intention is bad enough; in fact, confession without intention is in itself a sin we confess on Yom Kippur!

I continued in this way for years, confessing very slowly and reciting endless lists of sins that I had not committed (and some that I had never even thought of). Often I found this to be a depressing experience. It didn't seem to help me focus on the sins that *I* really needed to be working on, and was even a diversion. By reading such long lists of transgressions I was also able to lapse into the dangerous feeling of pride regarding my "seriousness." But ultimately the feeling evoked was that of melancholy, for if there are so many transgressions out there, how can we ever really do *teshuvah*? How can we get closer to Hashem?

A couple of years ago a friend showed me an amazing statement of the *Chiddushei Harim*, which profoundly affected the way I relate to Yom Kippur:

"If one has sinned, God forbid, and is busy trying to move away from his evil by contemplating it, he is thinking about evil, and in the place where one's thoughts are, that is where he is found. He is thus within the evil and can't do *teshuvah*, for his brain has become physical, his heart is covered, and he may fall into depression, God forbid ... and when he thinks about the 'mud,' he wallows in mud and will remain in the mud. Either he sinned or he didn't; what does God get out of all of this? While he is thinking about sin he could be 'stringing pearls' and making something for Heaven's honor. So leave evil, remove yourself from evil. Don't think about evil. Do good, and if you committed many sins, do many mitzvot in their stead... we have to feel that we have left sin behind, calmly, from the heart... with resolve for the future and in happiness. Say the confession quickly and don't sink into it."

The Rebbe's advice here is similar to that of the Piasezcner Rebbe, "Leave evil by doing good." It is similarly stated in many Chassidic works that our main *teshuvah* must be focused on the future. We need to avoid getting bogged down in the past, which can lead to depression and despair. None of this is meant to mitigate against a serious confession of one's sins, as is legislated in Halachah, but rather to put it in a constructive overall *teshuvah* framework. I need to focus on the good and strengthen it, rather than getting bogged down in the swamp of sin. Furthermore, Rav Shagar has recently written that the confession we recite on Yom Kippur is of a decidedly communal nature, and it may be that while private confession is a crucial part of the process, it should be done on "one's own time," and not when we are in the midst of our communal *teshuvah*. In addition, *vidui* is meant to be an intimate experience of our closeness with Hashem. Reading through someone else's lists will likely take me to places that I don't really need to go to at this unique and crucial time. If anything, we should be writing our own list, as I heard from Rav Mendel Blachman.

On Yom Kippur, we should all merit to fully repent with sincerity and happiness and to feel the purification of Yom Kippur as we annul ourselves within the reality of the Divine.

YOM KIPPUR

Before Neila

When we are on the threshold of reciting the Neila prayer, it is an opportune time to briefly take stock of exactly where we stand. What exactly is being closed? What is the gate we are davening about, and most importantly, where are we? What side are we standing on, and can we still go in? Do we even want to go in? Paradoxically, a look at secular literature can help to put our special existential place into perspective.

Academic Kabbalah scholars love to speculate about the famous Czech-Jewish author Franz Kafka. Was he a "secular kabbalist" or not? In *Before the Law*, Kafka begins: "Before the Law stands a doorkeeper. To this doorkeeper there comes a man from the country and prays for admittance to the Law. But the door-keeper says that he cannot grant admittance at the moment. The man thinks it over and asks if he will be allowed in later. 'It is possible ... but not at the moment.'" The story continues as the years go by and every time that the man asks for admittance he is rebuffed, even though the gate always remains open. When the man is finally old and dying he asks the doorkeeper his final question: "Everyone strives to reach the Law ... so how does it happen that for all these many years no one but myself has ever begged for admittance?" As the man is about to die he receives his answer: "No one else could ever be admitted here, since this gate was made only for you. I am now going to shut it." The tragedy of modern man is that he always remains outside, even though he could enter at will. When he finally realizes the truth, it is too late for him. How much more is this true for post modern man, who would have trouble even identifying the gate, and if he did, would be unable to decide if he even wants to enter?

From this perspective, we can conclude that Kafka, while interested in Kabbalah, was himself no mystic. He is far too pessimistic, and the complete alienation and failure to attain redemption expressed in the story is radically different from the

Kabbalistic descriptions of the interior of reality and the open invitation it extends to us to enter. In the holy *Zohar* there is a marvelous parable in which a beautiful maiden stands inside a luxurious palace, constantly encouraging a young man to enter and to unite with her. The meaning of this parable is simple. The maiden represents the Torah, and the young man is every Jew. The Torah is beautiful and enticing, calling to each and every one of us. Instead of always holding back we simply need to relax and do that which is natural, to allow ourselves to be seduced by her beauty and her truth. The door is open, and we *can* walk in, at any time. Unlike Kafka's anti-hero, we can unite with the Torah and achieve personal salvation. During Neila we pray, "Open the gate for us at the time of the shutting of the gate." We stand at the threshold, Hashem is waiting for us inside, and all we need to do is to step through the doorway. For the Lubavitcher Rebbe, Neila is post-redemptory. We are already inside, and now the door is locked behind us. This is the moment when we stand face to face with God. It is just I; there is no one else to hide behind. This is the moment of *yechidut*, the private audience that I have been working towards during the Ten Days of *Teshuvah*, even since the beginning of Elul, or even Tu B'Av. Now the moment of truth has arrived, don't squander it! Let us not be afraid! It is time to go in and unite with Hashem! The beautiful maiden beckons us to enter the palace, so we should close our eyes and step inside.

SUKKOT

From Yom Kippur to Sukkot

Having just "landed" from the intense spiritual high of Yom Kippur, we plunge right into our preparations for Sukkot. How are these two *chaggim* related, and what is the nature of this transitional period?

Yom Kippur is the ultimate day of *teshuvah*. (Rambam, *Teshuvah* 2:6). Sukkot, on the other hand, is described by Rambam at the end of *Hilchot Lulav* as the holiday of *simcha yitara*, extra happiness. In this context he describes the celebrations of the *Simchat Beit Hashoevah*, which took place in the Temple on Sukkot. (*Zman Simchatanu*). Here we may ask how these two festivals interface.

Rav Hutner (*Pachad Yitzchak, Yom Kippur* 8:1) describes Sukkot as serving a dual function. It is one of the three pilgrimage festivals, and simultaneously caps the cycle of the *Yamim Hanora'im*. The latter point is based on the Midrash, which sees the Four *Minim* of Sukkot as a divine gift, bestowed upon *Am Yisrael* to testify to their innocence after Yom Kippur. But is there a deeper connection?

The Gemara in *Sukkah* 53a describes the songs that were sung during the *Simchat Beit Hashoevah*: "Our Rabbis taught: Some say, 'Happy is our youth that did not embarrass our old age'– these are the pious ones. ... Some say 'Happy is our old age, which has atoned for our youth'– these are the penitents. And both say, 'Happy is he who has not sinned, and he who has sinned should do *teshuvah* and be forgiven.'" This clearly indicates the strong sense of *teshuvah* that pervades Sukkot. It is also a well-known idea that Yom Kippur, the day of our closest relationship with Hashem, is also the day of our greatest joy.

Yet, if both *chagim* include elements of joy and *teshuvah*, their observance could hardly be more different. On Yom Kippur all physical pleasures, such as eating, drinking, and marital relations are severely prohibited (*Mishnah Yoma* 8:1). On Sukkot we are required to live in the sukkah in the way that we normally live in our homes. The *Shulchan Aruch* (*O.H.* 639:1) explicitly mentions eating, drinking, and sleeping. The *Biur Halachah* goes so far as to call for marital relations in the sukkah (modesty permitting). Paradoxically, the sukkah, which represents the *Ananay HaKavod* (Clouds of divine Glory), an extremely holy place, is a place for the fulfillment of normal physical pleasures – seemingly the opposite of the holiness of Yom Kippur. How can the sukkah be so "spiritual" and so "physical" at the same time?

Rav Hutner (*Pachad Yitzchak, Yom Kippur* 8:8) quotes the Vilna Gaon to the effect that the *Ananay Hakavod* of Sukkot are not just "ordinary" *Ananay Hakavod*. When we built the Golden Calf, the enveloping clouds departed from *Am Yisrael*, to return only after the Jews had been forgiven on Yom Kippur. Thus the sukkah actually symbolizes the *teshuvah* of *Am Yisrael* and Hashem's subsequent forgiveness.

How are we to truly actualize this *teshuvah*? Rav Kook writes in *Orot Hateshuvah* 14:30: "From pure, true *teshuvah* we must return to the world and to living. Thus we restore holiness to its proper place and crown the Shechinah in the world." This is the purpose of the sukkah after Yom Kippur. Rebbe Nachman is paraphrased in *Likkutei Halachot (Rosh Hashanah* 4:7) as saying: "Whoever wants to do *teshuvah* ... is the concept of *Ratzo V'Shov* (running toward the Divine and subsequently retreating - a basic Chassidic concept) ... and this is the concept of the mitzvah of the sukkah after the Ten Days of Repentance, as the Torah states: 'leave your permanent house and dwell in your temporary house.'"

Real *teshuvah* involves the incorporation of *kedushah* within our everyday lives. It cannot remain only in the *beit midrash*, but must be brought into the "real world" as well, giving Hashem a *dirah batachtonim*, a dwelling in the lower world, a major reason for the Creation. The experience of non-physical holiness on Yom Kippur is a once-a-year phenomenon that cannot be constantly maintained. How do we actualize it, bringing it with us into the world, for the New Year, and into our everyday lives? Sukkot is the transitional experience that empowers us in this regard.

And thus writes the *Meshech Chochma (Vayikra,* 23:43*)* regarding dwelling in the sukkah: "The mitzvah is to enter with your entire physicality - eating, drinking, sleeping, etc. ... Thus all of the physicality of *Am Yisrael* becomes sanctified ...This is why (*Am Yisrael*) merited to have clouds of glory envelop them in all of their physicality, with Hashem's clouds by day, and His fire by night."

In summary, we could say that on Yom Kippur, in emulation of the angels, we attempt to rise above the physical world in order to "meet Hashem." On Sukkot, Hashem "comes down" to meet us where we are in *Olam Hazeh.*

The *Kedushat Levi* writes in *Haazinu* that the *Aseret Yemei Teshuvah* are days of *teshuvah m'yirah,* repentance through fear. The days between Yom Kippur and Sukkot are days of *teshuvah m'ahavah,* repentance through love – a higher level. May we merit internalizing the *kedushah* of Yom Kippur and actualizing it as we dwell in our holy sukkot.

SHEMINI ATZERET - SIMCHAT TORAH

Prayers for Rain

In Israel, Shemini Atzeret and Simchat Torah fall on the same day. This day is therefore marked by both the *hakafot* of dancing with the Torah and by the prayers for *geshem*, rain. The *Baal Hatechelet* is quoted in *Dor Yesharim* as having made the following strange statement: "Let the ignorant rejoice on Simchat Torah for finishing the Torah. We will rejoice on Shavuot for beginning the Torah!" Nonetheless, *Am Yisrael* tends to follow the approach of the Piaseczner Rebbe, who writes in *Derech Hamelech*, "We do not dance with the Torah, She dances with us. The real *baal simcha* is the Torah, She dances with us, and we feel Her joy!" It is worth noting that once at a *Hachnasat Sefer Torah*, the Piaseczner Rebbe was so happy that he turned somersaults in the street.

Regarding Simchat Torah, the *Mishnah Berurah* states, "One should work hard to dance and sing in honor of the Torah, as it says about King David ... and it is also brought in the name of the Ari that the spiritual levels he achieved were due to his *simcha shel mitzvah*, joy at performing mitzvot. The Gra would also dance before the Torah with all of his energy." The *Pachad Yitzchak* writes that even though the *Mishnah Berurah* normally defines only the Halachah, not "higher levels of service," he goes out of his way here to encourage great joy on Simchat Torah. May we also merit dancing, singing, and rejoicing in the Torah, on Simchat Torah, and all year long!

In Mussaf on Shemini Atzeret we begin to mention God's power of rain (*gevurot geshamim*). When we think of the whole holiday season, beginning with *slichot*, continuing with Rosh Hashanah and the shofar, the Ten Days of Repentance, Yom Kippur, Sukkot, Hoshanah Rabbah, and ending with the *hakafot* on Simchat Torah, it is striking that *geshem* is essentially the end of the entire process. Rebbe Kalonymos Kalman HaLevi Epstein of Krakow explains in his *Maor V'shemesh* that Hashem has been patiently waiting (implied by the word *atzeret*) for *Am Yisrael* to

275

undergo the process of the holidays and to be ready to unite with Him. Finally we are prepared and God bestows rain, which symbolizes divine beneficence, upon us.

After the longing between Hashem and the Jewish People during the Three Weeks before Tisha B'Av, courtship was renewed on Tu B'Av and accelerated during Elul, the month of love between God and the Jewish People. On Rosh Hashanah, we court Hashem with the special foods we eat on the first night. These foods are *simanim*, signs, like those that Leah used with Yaakov on their wedding night (*Bnai Yissaschar*). In the morning the relationship intensifies with the sounding of the Shofar. Next come the Ten Days of Repentance and Yom Kippur. On Sukkot we add new elements to the relationship as we enter the sukkah and shake the *lulav*, representing the masculine aspect of *Yesod*, foundation, and the *etrog*, the feminine *Malchut*, royalty. Finally, we dance on Simchat Torah. The *Pachad Yitzchak* points out that dancing is found in two places, on Sukkot and at a wedding, and our wedding with Hashem takes place on Sukkot. (For the *Sfat Emet*, the sukkah represents the *chuppah*). The culmination is when we recite *geshem*, the rain blessing, and then the divine influx, symbolized by rain, flows into the world.

On Simchat Torah we hope that our *hakafot*, dancing, and prayers for rain will be answered by a very rainy winter and great revelations of Hashem's holy Torah.

SIMCHAT TORAH –
SHABBAT BEREISHIT

From *Bereishit* to Simchat Torah,
And Back Again

One principle often mentioned in Chassidic commentary is *Noetz Sofo Bethechilato*, connecting the ending with the beginning. Nowhere is this felt more strongly than on Simchat Torah, when we read the very end of the Torah, and then immediately read the beginning again. If we think about the normal year's progression, from *Bereishit* at the beginning until *Vezot Habracha* at the end, we can discover a fascinating development.

In Rashi's famous first comment on the Torah, he quotes R. Yitzchak's question of why the Torah begins with the Creation, and not with Rosh Chodesh, the first mitzvah given to *Am Yisrael*. Rashi answers that if the nations of the world were to accuse *Am Yisrael* of stealing *Eretz Yisrael*, we could cite the Creation story as proof that, "The entire world belongs to Hashem. He created it, and He distributes it to whomever He pleases."

In the last Rashi on the Torah, regarding the verse, "And in all that mighty hand, and in all that great terror which Moshe performed in the sight of all *Yisrael*," he comments, "that Moshe took heart to shatter the tablets before their eyes ... and Hashem agreed with him."

What we can discern here is a powerful progression. The Torah opens by stressing Hashem's absolute power. He created the world, He alone rules the world, and therefore He alone decides to whom the various lands will be distributed. There is no room whatsoever for human action or initiative, and certainly no expression of human power. Yet the end of the Torah tells an entirely different story. By this time human beings, represented here by the highest spiritual leadership, that of Moshe Rabbeinu, have received the Torah. It is already "no longer in Heaven." This is so much the case, that Moshe can make the radical decision to

277

shatter the Divinely revealed Tablets, and Hashem retroactively agrees. According to the Gemara upon which this Rashi is based, Hashem even praises him for it.

From here, we can see a clear message that is especially appropriate at the beginning of each year. Hashem does not expect us to sit around passively waiting for others, even for Him, to do the work for us. Rather, we are all enjoined to engage in *Tikkun Olam*. On all levels, including the personal, the familial, the communal, and the national, we are expected to show initiative, think and act creatively, and to follow the dictates of the Torah in our constant struggle for spiritual and physical perfection. "It is not incumbent upon us to finish the work, but neither are we free to desist from it."

If we all fulfill our capabilities, in all spheres of our endeavors, we will all be blessed with lives of peace, health, happiness, and a rich and fulfilling relationship with Hashem.

CHANUKAH

The Merits of the Maccabees

Parshat Vayechi contains a number of allusions to the festival of Chanukah, which always falls around the time that this parsha is read. In this parsha, Yaakov blesses all of his sons before dying. He tells Yehudah, "the scepter shall not depart from Yehudah, or the ruler's staff from between his feet, until Shilo comes." Rashi explains that this is the prophecy of monarchy and rule that Yehudah receives. It begins with the Davidic dynasty, branches into the religious/political leadership of the Jews in Israel and Babylonia, and ultimately concludes with the Messiah, also a descendant of Yehudah, via David.

The Rambam's great praise of the Maccabees is well known. There is, however, also dissent. According to a Rabbinic tradition, all of their descendants were ultimately wiped out, and in our parsha, the Ramban gives the following explanation for this shocking idea: "In my opinion, the kings from other tribes that ruled after David violated God's will and removed the inheritance ... this was the reason for the punishment of the Maccabees, who took power during the Second Temple era. Even though they were very pious, and if it weren't for them Torah and mitzvot would have been forgotten, nonetheless they received a great punishment ... that their entire line was destroyed because of this sin." Similarly, some claim that the reason why there is no Talmudic tractate about Chanukah is that Rabbi Yehudah Hanasi, the editor of the Mishnah, was from the Davidic line, and was personally offended by the impudence of the Maccabees in usurping the throne.

This theory, however, bothers Rav Tzaddok Hakohen, who writes in *Resisei Leila* that the Maccabees were responsible for transmitting the holiness of the Jewish People to future generations. In his opinion, the Ramban went too far in attacking them. While it is true that those who actually became kings deserved to be punished, this does not justify the wiping out of all of their descendants.

Much in Jewish history is not black or white. We often feel more comfortable when we can clearly label something (or someone) as having been good or bad. Yet many historical phenomena and personalities are not so clear-cut. The Maccabees are a good example. Although they may not have been perfect, without them the Jewish nation would have all assimilated into Hellenistic culture. As the Ramban admitted, they saved Judaism as well as the Temple, and thus paved the way for the Messianic redemption, when the true light will finally shine, and forever. We need to be clear-sighted and honest enough to criticize that which is wrong, while still praising and giving thanks for that which was good. Perhaps this is yet another message we can learn from the Chanukah story.

CHANUKAH

A Precious Mitzvah

The Rambam goes out of his way to describe the mitzvah of lighting Chanukah candles as "a very beloved mitzvah." It is interesting to note that even though it is a Rabbinic precept, all of the Jewish People fulfill this particular commandment in the manner of *Mehadrin min Hamehadrin,* the strictest possible position in the Talmud. In the Rambam's view, our love for the Chanukah lights stems from the publicizing of the miracle inherent in the candles. In addition, we can point out that much practical advice on how to serve Hashem can be learned from this seemingly "little" mitzvah.

Rebbe Nachman of Breslov is quoted in *Likkutei Halachot* as stating that the candles symbolize "one's initiation into the service of the Divine." Within this mitzvah there are three stages. Firstly, before we can light a candle it is necessary to shatter our "power of illusion" (also identified with the *Evil Inclination*), and to bring ourselves to a state of spiritual clarity. This is parallel to the war that was fought by the Maccabees against the Greeks before the Menorah [Candelabra] could be rekindled in the Temple. We are now ready for stage two, lighting the first candle. This is the crucial candle, for it is the one that dispels the darkness, transforming it into light, and with it, evil into goodness. Since "all beginnings are difficult," this candle signifies our victory in transforming ourselves from pleasure-seeking individuals to those who seek holiness. In the third stage, we continue to light more candles each day, for we must constantly grow in the service of God. It is forbidden to become complacent, and one who stands still will likely fall backwards. Therefore we daily add candles and grow in holiness, according to the opinion of the School of Hillel. During this entire process we not only add candles, but we continue to light the "old" ones as well. Why? Since the beginning was so difficult, it gives great spiritual energy for the continuation of the process. We therefore "take the beginning" with us as we grow each night.

Rebbe Nachman points out that in addition to the Chanukah candles, we also recite the *Hallel* prayers each morning in order to praise Hashem and reveal His presence in the world. Interestingly, the Rambam chose to include the laws of *Hallel* together with the laws of Chanukah, the holiday of "praising and thanking God." So on Chanukah we perform two seemingly small mitzvot, candles at night and *Hallel* in the morning, and in between we are meant to go about our business as usual. This framework, publicizing the miracle each evening and praising Hashem each morning, gives us a real opportunity to rededicate ourselves to divine service and to see everything we do in a new light, the light of God.

May Hashem grant us the wisdom to internalize the message of Chanukah, and to illuminate both the entire universe and ourselves.

CHANUKAH

Appreciating the Miracles

Chanukah is clearly the holiday of miracles. The commentaries even debate which was more important: the military victory, or the miracle of the oil. Before discussing the relationship between these two miracles, it is worthwhile examining the nature of miracles in general, although we are only scratching the surface of this immense topic.

The Maharal of Prague (in the Second Introduction to *Gevurot Hashem*) writes that just as there is an order in the laws of nature, so too is there an order in the way miracles happen. This is especially true regarding miracles done for the Jewish People who, through their relationship with the Divine, exist on a supernatural plane. The *Sfat Emet* (*Parshat Hachodesh*) takes this a step further. In his view the "normal" state of affairs is what is miraculous, whereas the laws of nature actually represent the deviation.

The Ramban (at the end of *Parshat Bo*) states that the purpose of revealed miracles is to sensitize us to the existence of hidden miracles. In other words, without occasionally witnessing a grandiose change in the laws of nature, we stand in danger of becoming oblivious to the fact that everything that happens is essentially miraculous. For if we stop to think about it, the fact that the sun rises in the East is no less amazing than if it were to rise in the West. What we call "nature" is no more than the same miracle repeating itself at certain set intervals to the extent that we have become accustomed to it. In the Ramban's estimation, miracles are the basis of the entire Torah, and one who does not believe in them is essentially placing himself outside of the Torah's orbit.

A beautiful description of the nature of miracles is found in the *Pachad Yitzchak* (Chanukah, *Reshimah* 4). In his words, the Primordial Light, hidden at the time of Creation, actually still exists, but it is blocked from our perception by nature, as though behind a screen. All of nature is, as we have stated, actually a series of hidden miracles. And what constitutes a "revealed" miracle? This occurs when a tiny pinprick in the "screen" of nature allows a ray of primordial light to shine into our seemingly natural world, illuminating our existence. When this occurs we are reminded anew that everything is truly miraculous, as we have learned from the Ramban.

The Maharal at the end of *Ner Mitzvah* raises the question of the relationship between the two Chanukah miracles. His answer is truly startling. The most important miracle was that of the military victory. The miracle of the oil was halachically unnecessary for a variety of reasons that we will not address here. Why, then, did God bother with this second miracle? The Maharal tells us that the people were unaware that the military victory had been a miracle. They were convinced that they had won through their own guerilla warfare tactics and nothing more. God then made the revealed miracle of the oil in order to illuminate the hidden miracle of the victory, and awaken everyone to the fact that it too had been miraculous. Chanukah is therefore an application of the Ramban's principle that through the revealed miracles we can come to appreciate the hidden ones.

We should hope that Hashem will continue to illuminate our reality with continuous miracles, and give us the spiritual sensitivity to appreciate them.

THE TENTH OF TEVET

The Source of our Suffering

The Fast of the Tenth of Tevet commemorates the beginning of the Babylonian siege of Jerusalem before the destruction of the First Temple. According to the *Avudraham* (quoted by the *Beit Yosef*), if this fast were to fall on Shabbat we would still need to abstain from eating, even though when Tisha B'Av (which marks the Temple's actual destruction) falls on Shabbat the fast is deferred until Sunday. Although this never actually happens, the Fast of Tevet is the only fast that we would theoretically observe on Shabbat, and is actually the only fast we celebrate on Friday, *erev Shabbat*. Rav Soloveitchik was of the opinion that this *Avudraham* is spurious, but with all due respect, it is widely quoted in Rabbinic literature. The question then remains, why is the fast of the Tenth of Tevet so severe?

This siege is mentioned in both *Kings II* and *Jeremiah*. In *Ezekiel* (24:2) we read the following prophecy, "Write down the name of this day, **this very day** the king of Babylonia connected to Jerusalem, on **this very day**." The expression "this very day" (used here twice) is the source for the *Avudraham's* position, for it is identical to the language of Yom Kippur, which overrides Shabbat. But what is its deeper meaning? The *Chatam Sofer* suggests that the siege actually began on Shabbat in response to the wanton desecration of Shabbat during the First Temple period, which was a contributing factor to the destruction. Therefore, he argues, we should fast on the Fast of Tevet even if it falls on Shabbat.

The *Chatam Sofer* also mentions another idea, that "the beginning of the tragedy (the Fast of Tevet) is worse than its culmination (Tisha B'Av) for then the redemption begins." This idea is also discussed by the *Bnai Yissaschar*, who connects it with the rule *itchalta d'puranuta adifa*, ("the beginning of suffering is greater"), which is why we fast on the Tisha B'Av (when the Temple began burning) and not on Tenth (when most of it was destroyed). He also points out that in *Sefer Yetzirah* the month of Tevet is connected with the letter *Samech*, which is shaped like a circle and alludes to the siege (because of the encompassing nature of a siege, when the Romans encircled Jerusalem). *Samech* is also the Hebrew word in *Ezekiel* that means "connected," in the context of the beginning of the siege.

When we contemplate the month of Tevet, we find numerous events connected with the processes of exile. On the First, there was the exile of King Yochniyahu. News of the destruction of the Temple reached the Jews in Babylonia on the Fifth. On the Eighth, the *Septuagint* (Greek translation of the Bible) was completed, which, according to *Masechet Sofrim,* was tantamount to building the Golden Calf, and according to *Megillat Taanit* brought three days of darkness to the world (similar to the plague of darkness). The Ninth of Tevet is the anniversary of the deaths of both Ezra and Nechemia, the leaders of the return from Babylonia. On the 23rd of Tevet the Jews of Portugal were expelled. Rebbe Nachman also points out that Esther was kidnapped and brought to Achashverosh's court during the month of Tevet.

All of the above are signs of *Am Yisrael*'s weakness when in exile. The source of all of these disasters is the Tenth of Tevet, "this very day," and "the beginning of the tragedy." It is therefore not surprising that the Israeli Chief Rabbinate proclaimed the Tenth of Tevet as *Yom Kaddish Klalli,* the memorial day for Holocaust victims whose *yahrzeit* is unknown. On a deeper level the Ramban points out that the journey of Yaakov's family to Egypt, which occurs in the *parshiyot* that are always read at this time of year, is the prototype for all future exilic sufferings.

The *Mishnah Berurah* emphasizes that the purpose of a fast day is to promote *teshuvah*. In the merit of our actions on this day, we will ultimately witness the fulfillment of the prophecy of Zechariah: "...and the fast of the tenth month will be for the house of Yehudah a day of joy and happiness and a holiday."

TU BISHVAT

Rosh Hashanah of the Trees

After crossing the sea, the Jewish People began to receive the sustenance of the manna, the spiritual food that the Rabbis teach was a prerequisite for receiving the Torah, stating that, "the Torah was only given to those who eat the manna." The manna is first mentioned in *Parshat Beshallach*, which is usually read around the time when we celebrate Tu Bishvat, the New Year of the Trees. Is there a connection?

The Mishnah in Rosh Hashanah explains that there are four Rosh Hashanahs, meaning four yearly halachic cycles (mostly agricultural), that begin annually on a day which is designated as Rosh Hashanah. Obviously, one is also "our" Rosh Hashanah, the Day of Judgment for the entire world. Regarding Shvat, there is a disagreement; Beit Shammai designates Rosh Chodesh Shvat as the New Year of the Trees, while Beit Hillel says that this New Year falls on the 15th of Shvat, in the middle of the month. On the surface Beit Shammai appears to be correct, as all the other Rosh Hashanahs fall on Rosh Chodesh. What, then, is Beit Hillel's reasoning?

The Gemara describes the New Year of the Trees as the day when most of the annual rainfall has already fallen. Rashi adds that since the moisture has been absorbed into the ground the sap goes up into the trees and the new fruits begin to bud. By free association we can make some interesting connections. The description of the rain falling, the sap rising, and the fruits budding sounds like a description of *itoruta d'liayla* and *itoruta d'litata*, arousal from above and arousal from below. One example would be that God gave us the Written Torah, and our response was the (divinely inspired) Oral Torah, which gives forth fruits of deeper understanding and additional mitzvot. Similarly, when it rains very hard we make a special blessing. Raining very hard is when the drops appear to bounce up from the ground to meet those descending, "like the meeting of the bride and groom." There is a similar principle regarding mikvaot, stating that, for every measure of rainwater that falls, two measures of spring water go up to meet it. Remember that water always symbolizes Torah, and all of this fits together very beautifully.

The *Bnai Yissaschar* explains that Beit Hillel and Beit Shammai here follow their usual approaches (such as in their famous dispute about lighting Chanukah candles). Beit Shammai represents *gevurah* and therefore places the New Year on the first day of the month, when there is just a sliver of the moon, a drop of pure light. Beit Hillel, symbolizing *chessed,* disregards the usual pattern and insists upon the middle of the month, when there is a full moon, like many other holidays, such as Purim, Pesach, and Sukkot. The *chiddush* here is that unlike other Rosh Hashanahs, Tu Bishvat is the Rosh Hashanah of *Chessed,* the Day of Judgment of Mercy. When we remember that the Torah compares people to trees (our fruits are our children and our good deeds), this becomes even more significant.

There is a tradition from the Ari to make a *Seder Tu Bishvat* and eat all of the various fruits of *Eretz Yisrael* and more in order to correct the sin of Adam and Chava, who, by eating fruit, brought evil into the world. At this time we also recite passages from the Torah and *Zohar* regarding the fruits that we eat. The *Bnai Yissaschar* also mentions the famous custom to pray on Tu Bishvat for our etrog for next Sukkot. As this is the day when the fruits begin to bud, it is the right time for some spiritual genetic engineering.

For the *Pri Tzaddik,* Tu Bishvat is the beginning of a process of *tikkun ha'achilah,* rectifying our eating, in which we train ourselves to eat in a holy manner, thus atoning for Adam's sin. This process advances with our feast on Purim and culminates with the Pesach Seder.

The parallel seems clear. Our spiritual consumption of fruit on Tu Bishvat helps us to elevate ourselves and get closer to Hashem. Similarly, the manna we were fed in the desert was the preparation to receive the Torah on Mount Sinai. Once our eating becomes holy, we can then absorb all of the Divine influence.

TU BISHVAT

Treating our Land with Respect

Rav Kook, *zt"l*, writing in 1912, described the month of Shvat in a poem:

Orchards of fruit trees on holy soil
Sprout the hopes of generations

With these words, Rav Kook was expressing the actualization of Rashi's words on *Sanhedrin* 98a: "When the Land of Israel gives abundant fruit ... this is the most open sign of the redemption." Rav Uzi Kalcheim elaborated as follows, "The land's wisdom, revealed in the giving of fruit, is the awakening after the slumber of the exile. The first blossoms express the beginning of the period of rebirth of the dry bones."

The produce of Israel is primarily a response to our presence here, and to our proper behavior toward our Holy Land. The *Sefer Chareidim* writes, "every Jew must love the land and come to it from the corners of the world with great yearning, like a son comes to his mother's bosom." As children, we are enjoined to treat our mother with both awe and respect. An additional point is raised in the *Shnai Luchot Habrit*, " This is the reason that the Holy Land retains the name 'Canaan'... for Canaan is a slave and Canaan is the language of submission (*hachna'ah*), and this is the sustenance of the land that we are slaves to God ... the main sustenance of the land is our being submissive and slaves to Him."

On the one hand, the land is ours to fulfill the commandments of conquest and settlement. We should also plant trees, as in the Vilna Gaon's prayer,

May Hashem give me merit,
To plant trees with my own hands
In the environs of Jerusalem
Fulfilling, 'when you come into the land and plant'
In the mystery of the most open sign.

On the other hand, the land is our mother. In the words of *Sefer Chareidim* above, and in the words of *Aim Habanim Semachah*, the land rejoices when her children return to her, just as a mother rejoices upon her own child's return from exile. The land also demands submission - submission to God and to the Torah, and to the punctilious observance of the commandments in the palace of the King. But there is also submission to the land itself. It is forbidden to relate to the land with impudence or contempt. When one speaks of "concessions," as though the land is his own private property, that is chutzpah, impudence. But air and water pollution are also contempt for the land. When trees are cut down in an irresponsible manner, that is impudence, as is the littering of forests. One does not behave in such a careless manner at home, and one certainly doesn't behave that way toward his mother!

Tu Bishvat is a time to reflect upon the holiness of our land and internalize the submission needed to live here. We should protect our land from all forms of chutzpah, and witness the open sign of redemption becoming the complete redemption.

SHABBAT SHEKALIM

To Be Complete

There are four special Torah readings that surround Purim: *Shekalim, Zachor, Parah,* and *Hachodesh,* illustrating an interesting fusion between time and space. Rebbe Nachman teaches us that just as in space the desert camp was divided into twelve tribal camps, so too, in time the year is divided into twelve months. In the realm of space Amalek attacked the tribe of Dan, positioned at the end of the camp. In terms of time, his power peaks at the end of the year, and Esther was therefore abducted to the royal palace in Tevet, the tenth month, while Haman's decree to destroy the Jews fell in Adar, the last month.

This process repeats itself on the spiritual plane every year, and we need a strategy to defeat the forces of cosmic evil and to strengthen Hashem's kingdom. Before the month of Adar, we begin with *Shekalim,* which discusses the giving of the half-shekel for the *Mishkan.* In the merit of this *tzedakah,* we are able to fight against Amalek, who was the ancestor of Haman. We next read *Zachor,* which teaches us the mitzvah to remember and destroy Amalek right before Purim, as the final preparation for battle. After Purim we have conquered evil, but have also been defiled by our contact with it, so we read *Parah,* regarding the purification process of the red heifer. The cycle ends with *Hachodesh* as we prepare to enter the month of Nisan and renew ourselves at Pesach.

On *Shabbat Shekalim,* we remember the half-shekel, which served both as a census and to raise money for the upkeep of the *Mishkan* and its sacrifices. The Chassidic commentaries ask why we are commanded to give only a half-shekel and not a whole one. The *Beit Aharon* writes that each half of the shekel represents one world. One half is *Olam Haba,* created with the letter *yud* of God's Name, and the other is *Olam Hazeh,* created with the letter *heh* of His Name. On the level of our own divine service, the *Sod Yesharim* teaches us that the half-shekel indicates that Yisrael

understands clearly that on their own they are not complete
without Hashem. And Hashem also states that there is (so to
speak) no completeness for the honor of Heaven without the
service of Yisrael. Thus, the combination of God's will and the
service of Yisrael equal a complete shekel.

When we read *Shekalim*, we try to feel that yearning which
comes from the knowledge of being incomplete. As we yearn for
Hashem, we remember that this very longing is most precious to
Him. And it is this knowledge that brings us to the true and
intense joy of Adar.

SHABBAT ZACHOR

The Sin of Amalek

On *Shabbat Zachor*, we fulfill our obligation to obliterate the memory of our perennial enemy Amalek. According to Rebbe Nachman, Amalek's evil power peaks every year preceding Purim, and on *Shabbat Zachor* we focus our energy on preparing for the decisive battle.

In order to prepare for this spiritually, it is necessary for us to first define the evil of Amalek and its influence upon us. Rav Tzaddok Hakohen states that whenever *Am Yisrael* engages in the type of evil behavior that typifies a certain nation, that nation becomes empowered over Israel. Amalek is the descendant and spiritual heir of Esav, who sells his birthright for a bowl of soup saying, "Behold I am going to die, why do I need a birthright?" The Gemara (*Baba Batra* 16b) interprets Esav's statement as one of heresy – denial of Hashem and the resurrection. Esav (Amalek) believes only in what he can see – the here and now, in this case the reality of his hunger, without faith in a transcendent reality.

Let us examine the first encounter between Israel and Amalek in *Parshat Beshallach*. *Am Yisrael* has just experienced the great miracles of the Exodus, the splitting of the sea, and the giving of the manna. Now, they bitterly confront Moshe regarding a lack of water, asking, "Is Hashem in our midst or not?" This occurs in Refidim, a name explained by *Chazal* to mean: *Sherafu atzmam m'divrei Torah* – "they loosened themselves from the Torah" (*Sanhedrin* 106a). In the next verse we read: "And Amalek came and fought with Israel in Refidim."

Two questions should puzzle us: Why do the people experience a loss of faith after witnessing such great miracles, and why does Amalek attack at precisely this time? Rav Y.M. Poupko has explained that, paradoxically, the exposure to dramatic miracles actually weakens faith! At the first crisis unaccompanied by miraculous salvation, doubt sets in. Amalek, representing doubt in Hashem's presence in the world, was thus empowered over *Am Yisrael*, in application of Rav Tzaddok's rule.

293

The Purim victory of the Jews over Haman, the descendant of Amalek, represents the "fixing" of this lack of faith. The ability to see Hashem's Hand in history during a period of *Hester Panim*, when God "hides His Face," and to recognize miracles that are clothed in natural occurrences, is the unique message of Purim (*Pachad Yitzchak:* Purim 34). The now mature *Am Yisrael* is no longer dependent upon miracles, is able to maintain faith even in times of divine concealment, and can overcome Amalek (Rav Poupko).

According to Rabbinic historiography, the Roman Empire (Edom) and Christian culture represent the continuation of Esav in the world (*Pachad Yitzchak:* Purim 35). In Christianity we find the spiritual ideal of flight from the physicality of this world in asceticism and monasticism. The physicality of our lives is perceived as essentially irredeemable, and therefore should be abandoned. It would seem that this philosophy is ultimately based on the same lack of faith as found in Esav's worldview. Faith is based upon miracles alone, God's presence is not perceived within the world, and therefore one who wishes an encounter with the Divine must flee the world and all that it entails.

In *Parshat Tetzaveh*, we read about the Priestly garments. Among them we find the *me'il*, the robe of the High Priest, which has bells suspended from it in order that, "its voice will be heard when he comes into the Sanctuary... and he will not die." What is the function of these bells, and how do they save the High Priest's life? According to the *Beit Yaakov*, "the High Priest, because of his great love of Hashem, may wish to remain there ... and not return to this world." The bells ring in order to remind him that, " he needs to return again to this world in order to serve Hashem again ... he should know that this world also belongs to Hashem, and that Hashem desires the experience of the body just as He desires the experience of the soul."

The Torah's view of spirituality is therefore diametrically opposed to that of Esav. Healthy service of God is based upon the proper balance of the body and the soul, and the ability to sanctify the world by elevating all of its components to be for the sake of heaven. According to Rav Tzaddok and Rav Kook, this is the meaning of the mitzvah of drunkenness on Purim – to show that for the Jew even bodily matters such as eating and drinking can be sanctified, and that "on Purim the physical is not opposed to the spiritual."

It is only by acquiring deeper faith and carrying out our divine service properly at all times that we will obliterate the Amalek both inside and outside ourselves.

SHABBAT ZACHOR

Remembering Amalek's Crimes Against Us

On *Shabbat Zachor*, we fulfill our Torah obligation to remember what Amalek did to us when we left Egypt. For the *Sefer
Hachinuch*, this prepares us to do battle against him. Others see this
mitzvah on a more metaphysical plane, which we shall explore
below.

Amalek, representing cosmic evil, attacked us when we were
"on the way." The "way" is not only geographical, but also
spiritual. The *Sod Yesharim* writes, "Amalek always appears to find
[*Am*] *Yisrael* when we are on the way ... at the time of no clarity,
before we have internalized the words of the Torah." In other
words, as we approach a new spiritual level Amalek tries to stop
us. According to *Midrash Tanchuma*, this occurred during the
generations of Moshe, Shmuel, and Esther, and the final battle will
be waged at the time of *Mashiach*. Rav Tzaddok explains that in
the time of Moshe we were attacked before receiving the Torah.
During Esther's lifetime, Haman tried to prevent us from accepting the Oral Law, and we can anticipate a similar battle before the
revelation of the Messianic Torah. The generation of Shmuel was
unique in that we fought an offensive war against Amalek. Having
entered the Land, we were now enjoined to fulfill the commandment to destroy Amalek, for only when one has a firm base is it
possible to go out against evil. When "on the way" all we can
hope for is to hold our own.

Other sources add to this list. For example, on *Shabbat
Zachor* in Jerusalem during the Holocaust, Rav Zalman Sorotzkin
spoke of the first battle as that of Esav's guardian angel, who
attacked Yaakov to try to prevent him from entering *Eretz Yisrael*.
Rav Sorotzkin viewed the Nazis as the Amalek of his time,
responding to the messianic return of the Jewish People to their
Land. Rav Soloveitchik took this idea so seriously that he actually
prohibited accepting reparations money from Germany on the
grounds that this fell under the prohibition of benefiting from the

property of Amalek. His statement that any nation seeking to destroy the Jewish People has the status of Amalek, including the Arab nation (although not each individual Arab) is well known.

The *Pachad Yitzchak* sees the division of Purim into two days as reflecting the two types of war against Amalek. Purim is the defensive war, in the same way that the Jews in Persia fought to save themselves. Shushan Purim is the offensive war, similar to when Esther asked the king for one more day to go on the offensive. Shushan Purim is celebrated in Jerusalem and other cities that had walls from the time of Yehoshua, for it was he that brought us into the Land where we became obligated to destroy Amalek.

The Piaseczner Rebbe, writing in the Warsaw Ghetto, points out that we are enjoined to fight against "the seed of Amalek." This refers to the seeds that Amalek plants within us. As Rav Sorotzkin pointed out, the battle against Amalek is always fought on two levels, the physical and the spiritual. Each and every one of us needs to serve as the Chief of Staff in our personal battles against our inner Amalek, the Evil Inclination. When *Am Yisrael* is truly ready we will merit freedom from all manifestations of evil, both internal and external.

PURIM

The Joy of Purim

The intense joy of Purim seems obvious. With costumes, drinking, and *graggers*, we celebrate our victory over our arch-foe, Amalek. But of course there is a deeper meaning. After the victory, the Megillah tells us *L'Yehudim hiyta ora v'smicha v'sason v'yikar*, "the Jews had light and happiness, joy and glory." *Chazal* explain that they renewed their commitment to Torah (especially the Oral Law), Yom Tov, Brit Milah, and Tefillin. Rav Tzaddok explains that these four things represent Jewish identity and particularism, overturning the assimilationism that was rampant before the crisis.

The ultimate joy is that of fulfilling God's will as we do when we observe Purim, a holiday found in the Writings, therefore having the status of *Divrei Kabbalah*, the highest type of Rabbinical mitzvah. How do the specific laws of Purim help us to achieve true spiritual joy? Regarding the mitzvah of *Matanot L'Evyonim*, giving gifts to the poor, the Rambam writes that in general regarding holidays, t*zedakah* is a central mitzvah because by giving it we enable others, less fortunate than ourselves, to also be able to celebrate and enjoy. "But one who locks his doors eating and drinking with his family but doesn't feed the poor and downtrodden, this is not the joy of mitzvah, but rather the joy of his stomach." Similarly, the *Mishnah Berurah* writes that we should spend more money on Purim gifts to the poor than we do on our *seudah* (festive meal) and *mishloach manot,* since there is no greater joy than making poor and unfortunate people happy.

Regarding *mishloach manot,* the *Sfat Emet* writes that the entire purpose of this mitzvah is to promote unity and *ahavat Yisrael,* the love of the Jewish People. This is crucial, because we learn in the Megillah that Haman's power over the Jews was due to their lack of unity, and Mordechai's first job was to unite them. Only then were they able to save themselves and win a decisive victory. The *seudah* on Purim is obligatory (unlike on Chanukah) as is explained by the *Levush*. Since Haman decreed the physical killing of the Jews, we must celebrate with our bodies as well, to experience the kind of pleasure that he wished to rob us of. The *Mishnah Berurah* urges us to join with family and friends, "since it's impossible to celebrate properly when you are alone." Part of the rejoicing should include words of Torah, "for the laws of Hashem cause the heart to rejoice." Drinking to a degree beyond the norm is possible on Purim, explains Rav Kook, since on this unique day the physical and spiritual are in complete agreement.

Of course the main event of the day is reading *Megillat Esther* both at night and during the day. The *Beit Aharon* explains that the word *megillah* comes from the word *legalot*, to reveal. Far more than anything else, the Megillah, in which God appears to be hidden, comes to show the hand of Hashem within apparent hiddenness, teaching us true belief, the greatest joy of all.

In short, everything about Purim, both law and custom, exist to teach us numerous ways of proper spiritual rejoicing. In a world unfortunately all too filled with *simcha shel hollolot*, frivolous joy, the very fact that Purim enables us to experience pure *simcha shel mitzvah*, the joy of performing mitzvot, is in itself a great and joyous experience.

PURIM

A Time for Love and Unity

As is well known, the Jewish People are nearly invincible when united, but conversely they are very vulnerable when they are divided. In *Megillat Esther*, this message is all too apparent.

The *Sfat Emet* quotes a *midrash* that states that the name *Mordechai haYehudi* implies *haYichidi* (the only one), for he had the ability to unify the Jews. "For when *Am Yisrael* forms one entity, Amalek has no control over them .... Therefore Haman described the Jews (to Achashverosh), as 'a spread-out and divided nation.'" Haman-Amalek is all too aware of our internal cohesion – or lack thereof. Therefore Esther urges Mordechai to "go, and gather all of the Jews together." By uniting all of the Jews, Amalek can be overcome. Even our celebration of Purim is indicative of this idea. The principle of *Berov Am Hadrat Melech*, which enjoins us to read the Megillah with as many people as possible, perhaps reflects, in addition to *Pirsumai Nisa*, publicizing the miracle, the importance of unity as well. The other mitzvot of the day, *mishloach manot* and *matanot l'evyonim*, explains the *Sfat Emet*, are clearly meant to foster *ahavat Yisrael*.

Similarly, Rav Charlop writes about remembering Amalek: "The definition of the mitzvah is to love [the nation of] Yisrael with a natural love, to sense and feel what Amalek did to us, and through this to hate him with a natural hate ... and through our natural love for Yisrael we erase Amalek from the world." This is a beautiful and novel idea – the key to destroying Amalek is through *ahavat Yisrael.* Purim is the ideal time to rededicate ourselves to this ideal in order to ultimately witness the erasing of Amalek and his power from the world.

PURIM

Purim Meshulash:
When Purim Falls on Friday

When Purim falls on a Friday, most of the world makes an early *seudah* and tries to sober up enough to make Shabbos on time. But for people in Jerusalem, Hebron, Tzefat, and other special places, Purim actually falls on Shabbat and is celebrated as *Purim Meshulash* (Triple Purim), with festivities from Friday through Sunday.

For the *Netivot Shalom,* this special combination of Purim and Shabbat is a unique and powerful time of spiritual energy with the tremendous potential to get closer to Hashem. The *Tikkunei Zohar* compares Yom Kippur to Purim (*Yom ki-Purim*), and in Chassidut, Purim is seen in some ways as being even higher than Yom Kippur. Usually there is only one day on which to achieve the holiness of Purim, but *Purim Meshulash* provides us with three. It is therefore crucial to use this precious opportunity wisely. The Halachah on Purim is that any poor person who holds out his hand must be given something. All of us are somewhat impoverished in our divine service, and if we hold out our hand to Heaven on this holy day we certainly will not go away empty-handed.

The Rizhiner Rebbe tells the story of a prince exiled by his father among simple farmers. Eventually, the king sends his minister to visit the prince to see what he needs. When he finds the prince, the minister asks him what request he has of his father, the king. The prince replies, "If it would please His Majesty the king, with all of my labor, my boots have torn. I would be so grateful if the king would supply me with a new pair of boots." The minister weeps profusely, for the prince has apparently deteriorated so much that he doesn't even dream of returning home. At his moment of grace his greatest aspiration is for a mere pair of boots.

Hashem gives every Jew many moments of grace, every Shabbat and Yom Tov. At such auspicious times, we need to

301

know exactly what to ask for and it should not be for simple trivialities. We should do our best not to waste such precious moments on mere foolishness. Purim is the day in which "all was reversed and the Jews ruled over their enemies." This is the day in which we can overcome our internal enemy and return home to Hashem.

The peak of the process for the *Netivot Shalom* is at *seudah shlishit*. Always seen as *rava d'ravin*, the ultimate moment of grace, this moment is even more powerful as the holiness of Shabbat combines with the holiness of Purim. On *seudah shlishit* of *Purim Meshulash* we have one last chance to turn toward Hashem and seek spiritual enlightenment. This is the most propitious moment to get close to Hashem, and it is catastrophic if we waste it. So we must think carefully about what to ask for - and it had better not be a pair of boots...

SHABBAT HAGADOL

The Great Shabbat

The *Shulchan Aruch* states that, "The Shabbat before Pesach is called *Shabbat Hagadol* (the Great Shabbat) because of the miracle that occurred on it." The *Aruch Hashulchan* explains that in that year Shabbat was the tenth of Nisan and the Jews took the sheep, destined to be slaughtered as the *korban Pesach* four days later, and tied them up. Although the Egyptians saw the Jews getting ready to sacrifice their god, they did nothing to stop them. This is the main explanation of the miracle that occurred on *Shabbat Hagadol.* The Midrash, however, also explains that on that day the firstborn of Egypt, realizing their fate, began a civil war against Pharaoh and his henchmen. The holiday is always marked on Shabbat and not on the tenth, as that day was also Miriam's *yahrzeit.* Additionally, the Jews were later to cross the Jordan River on the tenth and there could have been confusion regarding which miracle was paramount.

The *Aruch Hashulchan* further points out that this miracle was intrinsically tied up with Shabbat, as the Egyptians saw that the Jews were tying, an activity that is prohibited on Shabbat. This led them to ask for an explanation, and even though they were informed that their gods were to be slaughtered in a few days, no pogrom ensued. We also know that Shabbat and Pesach are intricately related in many ways. Shabbat represents God's creation of the world and His intervention in nature, while Pesach stands for His intervention in history to save the Jewish People. These are the universal and particularistic aspects of our faith. The Torah even refers to Pesach as "Shabbat."

Rav Tzaddok Hakohen writes that the Shabbat preceding any holiday includes the holiness of that holiday within it. We know that God created the holiness of Shabbat at the time of Creation. How and when did the holiness of the *chagim* come to be? The *Mai Hashiloach* explains that the holiness of *Shabbat Hagadol* was so powerful that it actually overflowed into the weekdays afterwards and provided the basis for the holiday of Pesach to take place and to become part of sanctified time. His grandson, in *Sod Yesharim*, quotes the *Zohar* to the effect that the tenth of Nisan is like Yom Kippur. What's the connection? We know that Pesach and Sukkot are related and that *Chazal* draw a clear parallel between Seder night and the first night of Sukkot. Rav Charlap writes in *Mai Marom* that the four days between the Tenth of Nisan and Pesach are like the four days between Yom Kippur and Sukkot, (which, as Rebbe Nachman explains, are also parallel to the four white garments the High Priest wears on Yom Kippur). Both are days of preparation for fulfilling mitzvot, and in the same way that Yom Kippur is the preparation for Sukkot, *Shabbat Hagadol* is the preparation for Pesach.

It is also interesting to note that in the *Yovel* (Jubilee Year) the shofar is sounded on Yom Kippur to herald the freedom of the slaves, another parallel to *Shabbat Hagadol*, which essentially marks the final stage of freedom from the Egyptian bondage.

Rav Leibele Eiger notes that the Shabbat before *Shabbat Hagadol* is called *Shabbat Penuyah*, the free (bachelor) Shabbat that precedes the marriage, which takes place on Pesach. He adds that Pesach is also the *Brit* between Hashem and *Am Yisrael*. It emerges from his words that *Shabbat Hagadol* has the combined qualities of an *aufruf* and a *Shalom Zachor* all rolled into one, making it a Shabbat of great holiness.

On *Shabbat Hagadol* it is customary for the Rav to give a long *drasha* and explain the laws of Pesach. Some even see in this great *drasha* the source for the name *Shabbat Hagadol*. The Rema mentions the Ashkenazi custom to recite part of the *Haggadah* on *Shabbat Hagadol*. Rav Tzaddok explains that this particular custom is a preparation for the *Tikkun Hadibbur* (rectification of speech) that we undergo at the Seder. The *Kaf Hachaim* notes the Sefardi custom of reciting a special blessing on this Shabbat, *Shabbat Hagadol mevorach*, "Blessed Shabbat Hagadol."

From here, we see that *Shabbat Hagadol* is much more than merely the Shabbat that happens to come before Pesach. It is a crucial stage in our spiritual preparations for the liberation that we are to undergo. When we recite the Haggadah on *Shabbat Hagadol*, we should try to enter into a state of mind that will carry us through the next four days on our journey to Pesach and to freedom.

SHABBAT HAGADOL

The Seasons of Our Lives

The Piaseczner Rebbe writes in *Derech Hamelech* that every Shabbat before a *chag* is a *Shabbat Hagadol*, a Great Shabbat. However, the Shabbat immediately before Pesach, the first *chag*, is the greatest of them all, and is therefore named *Shabbat Hagadol*. In the *Maor V'shemesh*, we find that *Shabbat Hagadol* is connected to the *sefirah* of *Binah*, which is the world of higher *Teshuvah*. He interprets the statement that if the Jews would observe two Shabbatot properly they would be redeemed as referring to *Shabbat Hagadol* and the Shabbat that precedes it.

Reb Leibele Eiger gives several interpretations to *Shabbat Hagadol* in his *Torat Emet*. When we put them all together, there emerges a startling and refreshing, all-inclusive view of our lives encapsulated within one potent day. Firstly, *Shabbat Hagadol* is like the *Shalom Zachor* held on the Friday night before a brit. This is because Pesach is the time of the covenant between *Am Yisrael* and Hashem, because all the Jews were circumcised as a prelude to the exodus. Secondly, *Shabbat Hagadol* is similar to a bar mitzvah, since at this time in Egypt we began to receive mitzvot from Hashem, such as the *Korban Pesach* and circumcision. Previously, we were like children, not yet commanded. We then reached adulthood as we accepted the yoke of commandments, like a boy at his bar mitzvah. In this way, we became *gedolim*, adults, and the day is called *Shabbat Hagadol*. Lastly, since Pesach is the time of our marriage with Hashem, the Shabbat before it has the quality of an *aufruf* or a *Shabbat Kallah* that precedes a wedding.

From here we see how *Shabbat Hagadol* contains within it all of the crucial stages of our lives; birth, bar mitzvah, and marriage. All of this is connected with the one crucial Shabbat in which we prepare to leave Egypt, to leave all of the constricting places that hold us back from fulfilling our potential in life. Perhaps we should meditate on our lives, traveling back in time to our earliest memories, through our childhood, becoming an adult, and if we have merited, starting our families. How have I gotten to where I am today? Where, in fact, am I today, and where do I want to go from here? What is the nature of my personal slavery and how do I envision myself as a truly free human being? Thus prepared, we can enter Pesach and leave the negative aspects of our past behind us, actually moving forward towards a more meaningful and positive life of divine service and love for others.

The Kozhnitzer Maggid teaches that every holiday has an aspect of masculinity (influencing) and femininity (receiving), like the relationship of the groom (Hashem) and the bride (*Am Yisrael*). Therefore, "the more that the bride – *Knesset Yisrael* – makes herself beautiful, the more the groom-Hashem brings Himself closer to her." Today is our *Shabbat Kallah*; it is time to make ourselves ever so beautiful for our *Chatan*!

We return to the words of the *Maor V'shemesh*, that *Shabbat Hagadol* is related to *Binah* and upper *Teshuvah*. We are *Binah*, the higher wife, and we now unite with the masculine *Chochmah*, so that on Pesach there will be the revelation of *Da'at*, which had also been in exile in Egypt. This is the *teshuvah* of *Shabbat Hagadol*, the *teshuvah* that transforms and elevates our entire lives, preparing us for the highest unification with our Creator as we leave Egypt behind us forever.

PESACH

Drawing the Holiness of Pesach into the Year

The Piaseczner Rebbe writes about our preparations for Pesach in *Chovat Hatalmidim*, including the following short excerpts:

"As Pesach approaches, a Jew who has prepared himself spiritually during the year begins the preparations. His soul begins to heat up from the light appearing in the distance. ... Pesach expresses the quality of divine love. ... A Jew will not need to reason to understand the connection. He feels the commandments of Pesach ... as a child hearing the loving words of his father who, from the midst of an embrace, coaxes him to do a task. ...Out of love for his Father in heaven ... he searches for *chametz* everywhere...he wishes he could enter every little crack and hole to search ... for his heart is full of longing that will not be calmed.

"It is difficult to talk of anything but Pesach; all his thoughts and words concern the preparations. ... He is completely immersed in Pesach. He learns the laws and their spiritual meanings and that of the Seder. He is quick to lie down at night and rise in the morning to burn the *chametz*. Greatest of all is to bake the matzah for the mitzvah. He bakes his own even though he already has matzah, even *shemurah matzah* at home. ... Just as we once did, we sing Hallel to Him.

"On Pesach one knows he is a Jew. One Hallel is not enough, one song will not quiet his soul ... he cannot hold himself back until the Seder. Right away, during Maariv, he must recite Hallel. He sits down to the Seder, makes Kiddush, recites the Haggadah and sets the table for the feast, which is like the feast of the world-to-come. ... How great is the Jew who can draw the spirit of this night into the whole year, and live continuously immersed in purity and holiness."

The *Mai Hashiloach* writes that the Shabbat before Pesach is *Shabbat Hagadol,* for its holiness overflows into the week, creating sacred time beyond Shabbat. When *Shabbat Hagadol* immediately precedes Pesach, we combine part of the Haggadah with the order of the *Korban Pesach,* flowing directly from the holiness of Shabbat to that of Pesach. As we perform our Pesach preparations, we should hope to fulfill the Rebbe's holy words, "drawing the spirit of this night into the whole year, and living continuously in purity and holiness."

PESACH

The Seder as *Tikkun*

When Adam and Eve ate from the *Eitz Hada'at* (tree of knowledge), several problems resulted, plaguing humanity ever since. All of our *Avodat Hashem* is designed to "correct" (*Tikkun*) this primordial sin, rectifying creation and preparing the way for the final redemption.

Firstly, this sin caused *Pgam Hada'at* – the corruption of consciousness. The curiosity that caused Adam and Eve to opt for *Da'at* instead of relying on *Emunah* (faith), damaged our ability to relate properly to *Hashem*, *Da'at* being the knowledge implied in the deepest relationship (as illustrated by the verse, *V'HaAdam Yada Et Chava Ishto*, "And the man knew Chava, his wife.").

Secondly, the misuse of language on the part of the snake to tempt Eve, by Eve to tempt Adam, and by Adam to make excuses for himself caused *Pgam Hadibbur*- the corruption of language. This is especially grave in light of the fact that language distinguishes humanity from animals, as a human being is referred to as a *Midaber*, "the speaker." Thus the corruption of language is a severe lack of human integrity. One of the manifestations is our difficulty in avoiding prohibited speech, such as *Lashon Hara* (*Shem MiShmuel*).

Thirdly, of course, is the *Pgam Ha'achilah*- the corruption of eating, caused by the sin itself. Next time you are tempted to cheat on your diet, realize that the temptation to eat is a very deeply engrained human trait, dating back to the beginning of history.

(This is not an excuse. If anything, it should spur you on to further self-control – the cosmos depends on it!)[7]

According to many Chassidic sources (Rebbe Nachman and Rav Tzaddok Hakohen), the Egyptian exile and redemption are part of the process of rectifying this primordial sin in all of its manifestations. And since every year, we as individuals and as the Jewish People reexperience this spiritual journey, our Pesach experience, and especially that of the Seder, helps us to work on these three areas, *Da'at* (consciousness), *Dibbur* (speech), and *Achilah* (eating).

In *Likkutei Aytzot* (*Mo'adei Hashem, Pesach* 3) Rebbe Nachman is quoted as saying that by reciting the Haggadah out loud, we arouse our *Da'at*, for speech is an external manifestation of consciousness. Through this process we merit the revelation of Hashem's *Da'at*, which is the essence of the redemption. This is predicated upon the understanding that the physical exile and redemption are external manifestations of a deeper spiritual process.

The fixing of *Dibbur* (speech) occurs through the recital of the Haggadah. The *Sod Yesharim* (*Pesach* 23) points out that according to Rabban Gamliel it is not sufficient to perform the mitzvot, we must also discuss them. Rav Tzaddok (*Pri Tzaddik, Pesach* 2) goes a step further. It is not enough to discuss – we must do so in the manner of questions and answers, for only through the process of questioning can we internalize the feeling of the lack of understanding, for which the story of the Exodus provides the answers. Through this process we experience *Geulat Hadibbur*, the redemption of speech, as did our ancestors upon leaving Egypt.

Our eating and drinking are perfected through the mitzvot of *Matzah, Maror*, the drinking of the Four Cups and ideally, the

---

[7] There is actually a fourth problem; *Pgam HaBrit*-the corruption of sexuality, as Adam and Chava became more self-aware and desirous after the sin. Rectifying this aspect of human nature is also a very significant part of our lives and, according to Rebbe Nachman, is also hinted at in the Seder.

Passover sacrifice. The centrality of eating at the Seder is so crucial that this is the only time of the year that we make *Birchot Hamitzvah* (*Asher Kiddishanu BaMitzvotav Vitzeivanu*) on eating. (Rav Tzaddok, *Pri Tzaddik, Pesach* 1). Even the custom of the *Karpas*, a vegetable, reminds us that Adam was cursed to eat from the ground instead of from the fruit of the trees. All of this eating, says Rav Tzaddok, is to correct the primordial sin in general, and *Pgam Ha'achilah* in particular.

The *Mai Hashiloach* (part two, *Parshat Bo*) sums it up beautifully: "'So that the Torah of Hashem will be in your mouth;' On the first night of Pesach, Hashem commands man to refine his mouth. Indeed, the powers of the mouth are eating, drinking, and speech. Hashem commanded the eating of matzah and the drinking of the cups of wine, and through this one refines one's eating and drinking of the entire year. ... Regarding the power of speech, Hashem commands the telling of the story of the Exodus, and this protects us all year long from speaking prohibited language. This explains the verse 'so that the Torah of Hashem will be in your mouth,' that all of the powers of the mouth will be completely perfected and filled with the words of the Torah."

May it be Hashem's will that we fulfill all of the mitzvot of the Seder night properly, according to Halachah and with the deepest intentions. Then we may merit completely rectifying the primordial sin and witnessing the complete redemption during *Chodesh Nisan*, the month of Israel's redemption.

SHEVI'I SHEL PESACH

Stages of Redemption

The *Netivot Shalom* identifies three stages in our redemption from Egypt: the Exodus itself, the splitting of the sea, and the receiving of the Torah at Mount Sinai. The middle stage of this process, the splitting of the sea, occurred on the seventh and last day of Pesach. Among the Biblical holidays, *Shevi'i shel Pesach* is unique in that we do not make the *Shehechiyanu* blessing when lighting candles or reciting Kiddush. As *Chazal* explained, it is not a separate festival (unlike Shemini Atzeret, which falls at the end of Sukkot, when we do recite *Shehechiyanu*), but is rather a continuation of the holiday that began on the first night of Pesach, when we left Egypt. What is the nature of this day? Is it a mere culmination, with nothing new to offer, or does it retain a unique spiritual message despite its seemingly "pareve" nature?

On the Shabbat of Pesach we read *Shir Hashirim*, the *Song of Songs*. The song begins with the passionate verse of, "Let him kiss me with the kisses of his mouth; for your love is better than wine." *Shir Hashirim* is fitting for Pesach with its spring imagery and its theme of the love between Hashem and *Am Yisrael*, expressed most potently when we were redeemed from Egypt despite our almost complete lack of merits, as an expression of divine love. In the hermeneutical tradition of the Vilna Gaon (followed by Rav Soloveitchik), *Shir Hashirim* also tells of the future redemption, which, according to tradition, will occur in the month of Nisan, just as the first, Egyptian, prototype redemption did. The splitting of the sea is also an image associated with matchmaking and weddings. As the Gemara states in *Sotah* 2a, "matchmaking is as difficult as splitting the sea." One popular explanation of this seemingly strange statement is that while splitting the sea is the separation of that which is one, matchmaking is the forging together of two disparate units, the inverse parallel. The Gemara contrasts its initial statement with the idea that matches are predestined in Heaven and concludes that it is specifically *zivug sheni,* second marriages, that are as difficult as splitting the sea.

The *Shnai Luchot Habrit* brings the idea that the days of counting the Omer, from the second night of Pesach until Shavuot, are like the seven "clean days" that a woman counts before she immerses in the mikvah and reunites with her husband, reenacting their wedding night every month. During the Omer, *Am Yisrael* does not spend seven days, but seven weeks, preparing to meet Hashem at the wedding of Mount Sinai. As Rav Simcha Bunim of Pshischah stated, Pesach is like the first meeting between the bride (*Am Yisrael*) and the groom (Hashem), and Shavuot is the wedding. The Baal Shem Tov was known to quote the statement of the *Rokeach,* that Chassidut is strongest at the beginning. In other words, when we first enter the realm of divine service, we are filled with tremendous enthusiasm, which afterwards tends to wane, before growing again. This process is also felt in relationships, and especially in marriage (the microcosm of Hashem's relationship with us), where the initial "falling in love" often gives way to a more subtle connection, sometimes interspersed with various temporary "crises," and even deeper love.

Regarding the process enacted during the holiday of Pesach, Rav Hutner writes in *Pachad Yitzchak:*

"At midnight on the 15th of Nissan ... all of the Jewish People beheld their entire future ... that all evil would eventually be eradicated, and that the world would be filled with divine wisdom and that death would disappear for eternity ... what would occur in the End of Days. But instantly that light was hidden as Pharaoh began to chase after them ... constituting the hiding of the light of the night of the 15th. The subsequent drowning of Pharaoh in the sea is the rerevelation of that hidden light which takes form as a holiday ... The special holiness of *Shevi'i shel Pesach* is the **secret of the rerevelation of the hidden**. This explains the custom of holy people throughout the generations, who refer to the meal of *Shevi'i shel Pesach* as the *Seudat HaMashiach*[8]. This is also a manifestation of the secret of the rerevelation of the hidden."

What Rav Hutner is telling us is that *Shevi'i shel Pesach* is both a continuation of the beginning of Pesach and a significant new stage as well. When the Egyptians pursued the Jews, it appeared as if their initial deliverance had been annulled. This illusion was dispelled when the sea was split and Pharaoh drowned. This day is therefore a replay of the first, but contains more permanence. Similarly, in the course of history, the initial redemption of life in *Gan Eden*, disrupted by a history of sin and exile, will reach its final climax when *Mashiach* finally arrives. That too, however, will not be a new reality, but also a rerevelation of the hidden.

The splitting of the sea is as difficult as matchmaking the second time around. But, as we have learned, before birth we were all one with our soul mates, like Siamese twins. Separated at birth, we spend years searching for our other half, striving to come home. This means that every match is in a sense a second match, as difficult as the splitting of the sea. Both splitting the sea and achieving a successful marriage are difficult because they represent the rerevelation of the hidden light, on the national and personal levels. These are also redemptions, thus foreshadowing the final redemption of the universe.

Shir Hashirim begins with the verse, "Let him kiss me with the kisses of his mouth; for your love is better than wine." Rashi explains, "for there are places where they kiss on the back of the hand or on the shoulder, but I yearn and desire to be with him as we were initially, like the bride and groom, kissing mouth to

---

[8] Rav Hutner refers to the Chassidic custom of making a *seudah shlishit* on *Shevi'i shel Pesach*. This custom was begun by the Baal Shem Tov himself, who was miraculously saved from pirates on that day when he attempted to travel to *Eretz Yisrael*. The custom reflects the messianism inherent both in Pesach and in Chassidut.

mouth." This too represents the redemptive process of the rerevelation of the hidden light, of coming home.

On all of the holidays we feel radical newness, which we express when blessing *Shehechiyanu*. But on *Shevi'i shel Pesach* we come home. Yes, it has been a long journey and we didn't always feel that we would make it. And yet, when we walk through the familiar door and sit down on the old sofa, we know that we are home again, in a familiar setting. The sense of déjà vu is palpable. After a few minutes it is though we had never left. We are home, so there is no need for *Shehechiyanu*.

SEFIRAT HAOMER

Sefirat Haomer and the Month of Iyar

In the commandment to count the Omer, the Torah tells us, *temimot tihiyena,* "they should be perfect." What spiritual message can we learn from this expression? The Lubavitcher Rebbe explained that the original days of the Omer, between the exodus and *Matan Torah,* were days of preparation marked by a terrific yearning for God. He points out the vast difference between the low spiritual level of the Jews upon leaving Egypt and the extraordinary level they reached in order to receive the Torah. This dramatic change was neither a gift nor a magical jump, but rather the result of constant and difficult spiritual work and striving.

Rebbe Nachman uses two allegories to describe the transition of *Am Yisrael* from the exodus until they received the Torah. The first is that of a progression from the level of an animal to that of a human being. This is symbolized by the fact that on Pesach we offer the Omer offering, consisting of barley, which was then primarily animal feed. On Shavuot we offer the two breads, made from wheat, the ultimate human food. This also reflects a progression from the speechless animal to the *midaber,* "the speaker," which characterizes the human being.

Secondly, Rebbe Nachman teaches us that when we left Egypt we were like babies, but we reached Mount Sinai as fully mature adults. In this context he quotes a famous allegory of the Baal Shem Tov. When a baby is learning to walk, the parent holds her hand and walks backwards, leading her step by step. At a certain stage the parent lets go and moves back, so that the baby can learn to walk on her own. At first the child feels abandoned, but of course that is an illusion, the parent's intent is for her own good, that she should learn to walk, and approach the parent on her own. In the same way, when we left Egypt, we were like children, unable to walk on our own, and God took us out and across the Reed Sea, even though we did not deserve it. At the sea we experienced great and profound revelations, but then everything disappeared and we were left asking, "Is God in our midst or not?" Ultimately, we had to go through *Sefirat Haomer* to learn how to walk on our own, to approach Hashem as mature adults ready to receive the Torah.

The Lubavitcher Rebbe additionally points out that, unlike Nisan and Sivan, which are both partially within *Sefirat Haomer*, the month of Iyar is completely within the *Sefirah*. The Rebbe points out that Iyar is also known as *Chodesh Ziv*, "the Month of Splendor," which implies that it is actually filled with light. It is also a month with special healing qualities, as Iyar is also an acrostic for *Ani Hashem Rofechah*, "I, Hashem, heal you." The basis for our service during this month is our emulation of the patriarchs and the matriarchs, for Iyar is also an acrostic for *Avraham, Yitzchak, Yaakov,* and *Rachel.*

In modern times, the holidays of Iyar, Pesach Sheni, and Lag B'Omer, have been augmented by *Yom Ha'atzmaut* and *Yom Yerushalayim.* These days of thanksgiving for the redemption of the modern period continue the theme of redemption begun at Pesach, and bring the theme of Nisan, the month of redemption, into Iyar as well. Thus *Sefirat Haomer* is coming closer to its original joyous vision, which the Ramban described as a lengthy *Chol Hamo'ed* connecting Pesach and Shavuot into one long holiday.

It is important to strive to use the month of Iyar wisely. It contains tremendous spiritual potential in several realms, including healing and deliverance. The key to everything is our yearning for Hashem and His holy Torah. Through this yearning we can grow from spiritual infancy to adulthood, and from a mute animal-like existence to become articulate human beings. We will then be ready to stand in the presence of Hashem, speaking words of Torah and prayer. If we do so, our days of counting will truly be *temimot*, perfect, and so will our service of Hashem.

YOM HASHOAH

Yom Hashoah - The Meaning of Suffering

In *Parshat Shemini* (always read around the time of *Yom Hashoah*) we find one of the most enigmatic stories in the Chumash. Aharon's sons, Nadav and Avihu, bring an incense offering described as *aish zarah* (strange fire). Fire immediately descends from heaven, consuming them in language identical to the Divine consumption of the sacrifice in the preceding verse. Moshe, comforting Aharon, describes them as *krovei*, those close to Hashem, through whom He is sanctified. Rashi states that Nadav and Avihu were actually greater than Moshe and Aharon themselves. The Torah tells us that Aharon's response to this event is silence, *Vayidom Aharon.*

All of the commentators wrestle with the numerous textual difficulties and with the central question that arises here – what exactly was their sin? If they were on such a high level – how could they have committed such a serious sin? And if it was not so serious, why were they killed? The myriad of definitions of this sin lead to fascinating insights in *pshat, hashkafah* and *avodat Hashem*, but ultimately we remain with a lack of clarity and must adopt the humble posture of Aharon – silent acceptance in the face of the overwhelming and bewildering expression of *Middat Hadin*, Hashem's justice.

Theodicy, the problem of evil, is a central theme in theology. From Avraham's pleading for the righteous of Sodom through Job, the seeming injustice of suffering has continued to plague both medieval and modern scholars alike. Nowhere does the problem reach its full magnitude as with the inexplicable horrors of the Holocaust.

Professor Shalom Rosenberg, in his book, *Tov V'rah Bihagut Hayehudit*, divides philosophers of the *Shoah* into two camps, those who feel that the *Shoah* can be explained and those who feel that it cannot. The former group includes Bruno Bettelheim, a survivor who analyzes the Holocaust in psychological terms, and Hannah Arendt,

319

who coined the phrase "the banality of evil" regarding the Nazi war criminal Eichmann (may his name and memory be blotted out) and sought sociological roots for the Holocaust.

The other group includes Eli Wiesel and Emil Fackenheim, for whom the Holocaust represents a "radical evil ... almost a mystical revelation ... of cosmic proportions" that cannot possibly be explained by any normal criteria. Rosenberg himself also leans to this position, describing the *Shoah* as "demonic and satanic."

Rav David Halivni, in *Al Hashoah v'Al Tefillatah*, sees things differently. Analysts of the *Shoah* are divided between those who view the Holocaust as some form of punishment, and those who radically reject this view as blasphemous, but are then left with no explanation at all. The former group, according to Rav Halivni, himself an Auschwitz survivor, include both the Satmar Rav, *zt"l*, also a survivor of the Holocaust, who wrote in *Vayoel Moshe* of the *Shoah* as the punishment for Zionism, and Rav Yissachar Teichtel, *Hy"d*, who wrote *Aim Habanim Smachah* in the Budapest ghetto before he was killed. According to the initially anti-Zionist Rav Teichtel, the *Shoah* is punishment for the Jews' love of the Diaspora and their refusal to leave for *Eretz Yisrael* when the opportunity presented itself. This is the diametrically opposite view from that presented by the Satmar Rav.

Basing himself on a variety of Biblical and Rabbinic sources, Rav Halivni dramatically rejects both positions, and proves that Hashem would not destroy *Am Yisrael* on such a massive scale as a punishment. But what then is the explanation?

Although Rav Halivni has previously written against any attempt to explain the *Shoah*, here he allows himself to speculate. The answer, rooted in Lurianic Kabbalah, has to do with the absolute importance of free will in human destiny and the need for cosmic balance between free will, born of *tzimtzum*, (divine self-limitation), and divine intervention in history. Ultimately the question becomes that of the Divine decision of nonintervention at the time of the *Shoah*, and at this stage Rav Halivni must admit that this is one of the mysteries of the Divine for which there is no human answer.

The deepest and most prolonged meditation on the *Shoah* is that of Rav Kalonymus Kalmish Shapira, the Piaseczner Rebbe, *Hy"d*, who was killed in 1943. In his Warsaw Ghetto *drashot*, *Aish*

Kodesh, the Rebbe creates a variety of theological constructs in an attempt to fathom the evil around him. After rejecting the notion that the *Shoah* could be a punishment, he comes to view the *Hester Panim* of the *Shoah* as an opportunity to grow closer to Hashem in the face of the absurdity of radical suffering and complete lack of understanding. Anyone who learns and internalizes *Aish Kodesh* will significantly strengthen his faith in situations of personal or national crisis.

The late Slonimer Rebbe writes in *Al Hahashmada v'haChurban* that the *Shoah* is one of the great mysteries of the creation. "A person's heart and brain are incapable of grasping what happened here. There is no expression for this, for natural human emotions are too inconsequential to feel pain of such breadth and horrible depth. Only mute silence, as it says, 'and Aharon was silent,' expresses our crushed hearts, better than any other expression, which is not appropriate or correct for such a matter."

Let us use our learning for the sake of the elevation of the souls of the holy martyrs. We should also remember that in times of suffering, Hashem comforts us like Aharon, so that even in a situation of complete lack of understanding, we are able to maintain perfect faith. In this way, our continued *avodat Hashem* serves as a living memorial to our brothers and sisters, the *krovim* of Hashem.

YOM HAZIKKARON

Fate and Destiny

In *Aish Kodesh*, the Piaseczner Rebbe quotes an ancient tradition regarding martyrdom: "We have a tradition that an individual who undergoes martyrdom to sanctify the name of God does not feel the pain of the torments inflicted upon him ... he is inflamed with a powerful yearning to surrender his life for the sake of the sanctity of His blessed Name, he raises up all his senses and his entire physical being...to the World of Thought ... his sensory awareness disappears, while his feeling and corporeality are stripped away so that he feels nothing but pleasure." These words were written in the Warsaw Ghetto and address the experience of the martyr himself. How are we, however, looking back and remembering, in this case Israel's fallen soldiers, supposed to feel?

The *Midrash Tanchuma* tells us that a woman in childbirth cries 99 cries for death and then one for life. Until the one hundredth cry the situation appears helpless, but ultimately it becomes clear that great goodness has been manifest through the prior suffering. The *Aish Kodesh* explains that this is the nature of *chevlei Mashiach*, the birth pangs of the Messiah, the suffering that must be endured for a new and greater reality to be created. This explains the difficult transition we undergo every year from *Yom Hazikkaron* to *Yom Ha'atzmaut*, from intense sadness to great joy. While some question this *smichat parshiyot*, a seeming non sequitur, it really couldn't be any other way. Any attempt to celebrate *Yom Ha'atzmaut* without being fully cognizant of the price that was paid for an independent state is a dangerous illusion. But *Yom Hazikkaron* is also part of another transition, as it follows *Yom Hashoah* by only one week. The timing for *Yom Hashoah* is very problematic, but that is not our topic. In reality, the two days, one week apart, seem superficially to share many similar characteristics, sirens, moments of silence, mourning the dead, endless ceremonies and speeches by people who don't really have anything meaningful to say.

Yet a deeper glance shows that beneath the superficial similarity, these two days, while both days of mourning, are radically different from each other. Rav Soloveitchik, in his classic essay, *Kol Dodi Dofek*, distinguishes between *goral*, fate, and *yeud*, destiny. Fate is characterized as a life lived passively under the force of others, as an object of outside forces. Destiny, on the other hand, is life lived as a subject, full of independent desire and self-direction. As Rav Soloveitchik writes, "A person is born as an object, and dies as an object, but he has the power to live as a subject ... the goal of a person in this world, according to Judaism, is to change fate to destiny."

In the Holocaust, we were the passive objects of fate, powerless to control our lives (and deaths) in the face of overwhelming power against us. In the State of Israel we can and must live a live of destiny. We are now the subjects of our own history and there is no longer any excuse for passivity. We are no longer powerless, and we now have great opportunities (and great responsibilities) for our collective lives and those of the peoples in our midst. The path from the Holocaust to an independent Israel, to *Yom Ha'atzmaut*, passes through *Yom Hazikkaron*.

During the Lebanon War in the early 1980s, the Gaon Harav Yisrael Gustman, *zt"l*, himself a Holocaust survivor from Vilna, paid a shivah call to a family whose young son had just fallen in battle. He wanted to comfort them by giving them perspective on the loss of their son. He told them that his own son had been dragged out of the house in the middle of the night and shot by the Gestapo. Although it was a snowy night he was not able to take his shoes. In the morning Rav Gustman traded his son's shoes for a carrot, gave half to the widow of Rav Chaim Ozer Grodinsky, *zt"l*, and ate half himself. In this way, he fulfilled the verse in the *tochachah* that parents would be forced to eat their own children. He contrasted this with the death of their son, who had fallen in battle as a soldier in the Jewish army of the independent Jewish State, and had died bravely defending the Land of Israel from its enemies. This is a perfect example of the difference between fate and destiny and enables us to clarify the difference between *Yom Hashoah* and *Yom Hazikkaron*. Both are sad days of mourning, excruciatingly difficult for those who have lost loved ones. Yet there is also a clear difference, and *Yom Hazikkaron* leads directly to *Yom Ha'atzmaut*, which is comforting, whereas in a sense *Yom Hashoah* stings with the existential pain of inexplicable absurdity.

Rav Soloveitchik continues, "Suffering comes in order to elevate man, to purify his spirit and to sanctify him ... in order to correct the imperfections in man's personality ... Suffering obligates one to do *teshuvah* ... and what is *teshuvah* if not the renewal and redemption of man?" The self-sacrifice of the martyred soldiers of Israel is intrinsically bound up in the national *teshuvah* of *Am Yisrael* in the modern era. While our mourning is very painful, we feel that it is not in vain. We embrace our friends who have lost their loved ones, and we daven to Hashem with all of our hearts that *Am Yisrael* will finally know real peace and tranquility, and that there will be no further sacrifices. May we all merit serving Hashem in *Eretz Yisrael*, ushering in the Final Redemption in our days.

YOM HA'ATZMAUT

Preparing for the Ultimate Redemption

Since the birth of the State of Israel, *Yom Ha'atzmaut* has been added to the calendar of our sacred holidays. The leading *poskim* of the previous generation, including Rav Goren, *zt"l,* and Rav Yisraeli, *zt"l,* wrote extensively about the halachic process of instituting a holiday. However, there are other spiritual insights that add to the meaningfulness of this day. For example, the *Shulchan Aruch Harav* writes that we begin to study the laws of Shavuot on the 5th of Iyar, since that is thirty days before Shavuot. From here we can discern that *Yom Ha'atzmaut* should be a significant stage in our preparation for receiving the Torah.

In *Numbers* 10:10, we read: "On the day of your rejoicing, your holidays and new months, you should blow trumpets over your sacrifices, and they should be for you days of memory before your God, I am the Lord your God." Ibn Ezra explains, "When you have returned from the land of your enemies, or defeated the enemy who has attacked you, you will set a day of rejoicing like Purim and Chanukah." On *Yom Ha'atzmaut,* we have both features, returning from the exile and victory over our enemies.

The *Sfat Emet,* in an amazing passage from 1880, teaches that each biblical holiday has a parallel Rabbinic one. Sukkot has Chanukah, and Shavuot has Purim. Regarding Pesach, he writes, "and for Pesach we hope that there will be a holiday, as it is written 'like the days when you left Egypt I will show you miracles'!" Sixty-eight years later, his prayer was answered. Another tzaddik whose prayer was fulfilled was Rav Yissaschar Teichtel, *Hy"d,* who named his work (published in the Budapest Ghetto in 1943, before he was killed) *Aim Habanim Smachah* (The Mother of Children Rejoices). The Land of Israel is the mother who mourns for her children in exile and who rejoices upon their return to her.

Rabbeinu Yonah writes in *Brachot* that when in the future Hashem will do great miracles for us, it will be a great mitzvah of

Kiddush Hashem for us to fully rejoice in order to publicize those miracles.

When *Yom Ha'atzmaut* falls out on Friday, however, we celebrate it on Thursday in order to avoid possible desecration of Shabbat. In the prayer for the welfare of the state, we refer to Israel as *raishit tzmichat geulatenu*, the "first flowering of our redemption." Shabbat is a day that represents the time of redemption, *yom shekulo Shabbat*. It would therefore appear that we should be able to celebrate *Yom Ha'atzmaut*, the day of the beginning of redemption, and flow directly into Shabbat, the day of redemption. The fact that we need to avoid this for fear of *chillul Shabbat* should send a sobering message to us all about how far we still have to go in order to fill *Medinat Yisrael* with true Torah content and values. Nonetheless, this *cheshbon hanefesh* should be done before the holiday. On the holy day itself, we should all be filled with *hakarat hatov*, gratitude to Hashem for all that He has done for us in our time. The shortcomings are our own. We need to take responsibility for them and work tirelessly to correct them, but our great *simchah* is still very real.

We should only hope and merit that the *reishit tzmichat geulatenu*, the first flowering of our redemption, will continue to blossom and grow into the *geulah shleimah*, the complete and ultimate redemption, speedily in our days. Then the State of Israel will fulfill its true mission, as Rav Kook wrote (long before there was a state) in *Orot HaKodesh*, "This state is our state, '*Medinat Yisral*,' the foundation of Hashem's throne in the world."

PESACH SHENI

The Holiday of the Second Chance

Pesach Sheni is a unique holiday. As recorded in *Parshat Be-haalot'cha*, it all began in the desert when people came to Moshe with an unusual complaint. They had been *temaim*, ritually impure, at the time of Pesach and were not able to offer the *korban Pesach*. They felt that they had missed out on something important and wanted to make amends. Moshe did not know how to answer, and he went to ask Hashem. (This is one of the incidents from which we learn that, unlike the other prophets, Moshe had constant access to Hashem.) God's response was no less than to create a new holiday – Pesach Sheni.

Pesach Sheni takes place on the 14th Iyar, exactly one month after the *korban Pesach* had been offered on the 14th Nisan. Anyone who had been *tamay* or far away, and was therefore unable to make it on time, was given a second chance to offer the sacrifice. This holiday was given in response to the desire of simple Jews to want to serve God. What makes this especially extraordinary is that those Jews who had been ritually impure or far away were actually under duress and *exempt* from the mitzvah, and had no need to make it up. Today, the custom is to eat matzah on Pesach Sheni. What are the deeper implications of this special day?

Pesach Sheni falls during *Sefirat Haomer*, the fifty days leading from the Exodus on Pesach to receiving the Torah on Shavuot. According to the *Zohar*, on Pesach Sheni special gates open up in the heavens to help us prepare for Shavuot. In addition, Pesach Sheni falls on the 29th day of the Omer, corresponding to the *sefirah* of *chessed she'hod*. *Hod* is the week associated with Aharon the Kohen, and it culminates four days later with Lag B'Omer, on *hod she'bhod*. Rav Tzaddok Hakohen explains in *Pri Tzaddik* that this is a special time of repentance, associated with the concept of the Oral Law, which is also connected with Aharon. When the Jews left Egypt they were accompanied by special lights and were nourished by the matzah they had brought with them. After thirty days passed, the light of the Exodus faded and the matzah was finished. It was now time for something new to happen. The manna replaced the matzah, and instead of divine inspiration *from above* the process began through which the Jews would inspire themselves *from below*. Why did these Jews feel so driven to do a mitzvah from which they were exempt? Rav Tzaddok explains that while one may have a good excuse for not performing a certain mitzvah, the holiness achieved by that mitzvah will still be lacking. A real servant of God is not satisfied just to be *yotzei*, to technically fulfill his obligation; he yearns to fulfill the mitzvot as a way of getting closer to Hashem.

The *Netivot Shalom* teaches that the two categories of impurity and distance represent the two major tests of our generation, which precedes the Final Redemption. Impurity is symbolic of *pgam habrit*, sexual immorality, and distance implies *pgam ha'emunah*, lack of faith in God. These two factors influence each other and are crucial to the definition of a proper Jewish state of being. On Pesach Sheni, as we move even closer to receiving the Torah on Shavuot, let us redouble our efforts in these two crucial areas and make ourselves truly worthy of epiphany.

LAG B'OMER

The Fires of Rashbi

On Lag B'Omer, the 33rd day between Pesach and Shavuot, weddings and haircuts are permitted, unlike during the rest of the Omer period, because the 24,000 students of Rabbi Akiva, who died from a plague due to internal dissent, ceased dying. In addition Lag B'Omer is celebrated as the *Hillulah d'Rashbi*, the *yahrzeit* of Rabbi Shimon bar Yochai (Rashbi), student of Rabbi Akiva and author of the *Zohar*, the foremost book of the *Kabbalah*. On this day, bonfires are lit throughout Israel, especially at Rabbi Shimon's grave in Meron, little boys have their first haircuts, and a great celebration is held.

According to the *Bnai Yissaschar* and Rav Tzaddok Hakohen, Rashbi not only died on Lag B'Omer, but he was also born on the same day. It is quoted in the name of the Ari that Rabbi Akiva ordained Rashbi and his colleagues on Lag B'Omer, thus ensuring the continuity of the Oral Law after the death of his earlier students. The Gemara (*Shabbat* 33b)[9] narrates how Rashbi and his son hid in a cave for twelve years after fleeing from the Roman decree of death. There, covered in sand, fed by a carob tree and drinking from a spring, the greatest secrets of the Torah were composed. Emerging from the cave, Rashbi perceived Jewish farmers working. Dismayed by their lack of Torah study, he "burned them up!" His shock is understandable in light of his position that Jews should only study Torah and not work. He is considered to be the only person whose Torah study is so great that he need not pray (although he did pray in the cave). Nonetheless Rashbi and his son were ordered to return to the cave for

---

[9] It is interesting to note that the story of Rashbi appears on the 33rd page of *Tractate Shabbat*, as his life is so bound up with the 33rd day of the Omer.

329

another year, after which a mellower Rashbi emerged, whose love for every simple Jew was all too apparent. This too, writes the *Aruch Hashulchan*, was on Lag B'Omer.

The *Zohar* relates how on the last day of his life, the sun stood still as Rashbi revealed the greatest secrets of the Torah. Dying happily, he encouraged his followers to make his *yahrzeit* a celebration. For this reason, the Ari, the *Ohr HaChaim* and other great Kabbalists would journey to Meron to celebrate on Lag B'Omer. We light bonfires, explains the *Bnai Yissaschar*, in honor of Rashbi, known as *Bozina Kadisha*, the Holy Candle, and in honor of the *Zohar*, the Book of Splendor. We also remember the great light of the day that the sun did not set, and mark the final stage of preparation for the giving of the Torah on Shavuot. On Lag B'Omer, seventeen days before the Torah is given, the light of the Torah begins to shine. Rav Baruch of Medzibuzh would finish studying the *Zohar* on Lag B'Omer, and in his *beit midrash* everyone would dance *hakafot* for the Simchat Torah of *Kabbalah*. Rav Tzaddok tells us that in the same way that the Rashbi continued the Oral Law of Rabbi Akiva, who was himself killed by the Romans, Lag B'Omer is a day when every Jew has the great potential for internalizing the Oral Law in all its manifestations. The reason for haircuts (as well as the ancient Sephardic custom of burning garments) may therefore be to symbolize our desire to throw off externalities (*chitzoniut*) and become connected with the deeper reality (*penimiyut*) that Rashbi teaches.

Parshat Bechukotai, which is usually read around this time, begins with the words, *Im Bechukotai Talachu*, "If you will walk in My statutes." The *Mai Hashiloach* uses play on words on the root *chok*, which, in addition to "statutes," means "to engrave." He writes, "so that My statutes will be engraved upon your heart." The Torah that flows from the heart is expressed when we reach the level of spiritual perfection that enables us to naturally flow with the mitzvot in all aspects of our lives. Rashbi is the greatest example of this aspect of the Torah. By appreciating the holiness of Lag B'Omer and internalizing Rashbi's message, we will merit that Hashem's statutes will be engraved upon our hearts.

YOM YERUSHALAYIM

Bamidbar and Jerusalem Day

Parshat Bamidbar is usually read between *Yom Yerushalayim* and Shavuot. How does it bridge between these two holy days? In *Bereishit Rabbah* we read, "Rabbi Shimon says ... 'And God separated between the light and the darkness – this is the book of *Bamidbar*, which separates between those who left Egypt and those who entered the Land.'" Based upon this *midrash*, the Netziv explains that that in the desert the Jewish People were guided in a miraculous, supernatural way, whereas in the Land of Israel they are led through natural means. *Bamidbar* is therefore also called "Numbers" because the book begins by counting those who left Egypt and lived a supernatural existence, and ends by counting those who entered Israel in a natural framework. All of the above seems very strange, for it posits that the desert was the place of light, whereas the Land of Israel is that of darkness.

The *Gemara* in *Yoma 29a* states, "Just as the dawn is the end of the night, so too Esther is the end of the miracles." Rav Tzaddok Hakohen points out in *Resisai Lilah* that it makes no sense to refer to the end of the miracles (when God is hidden) as the dawn, i.e. the light. He then resolves this issue by saying that during the time of open miracles our level of faith is immature and superficial, and so too is our relationship with Hashem. A deeper type of faith and relationship are possible only when natural living replaces open miracles, such as exist in Israel. This more mature and meaningful relationship is ultimately the real light that we are seeking.

The Ramban writes that the main topic of *Bamidbar* is the service in the *Mishkan* (Tabernacle), the forerunner of the Temple, and in this way as well *Bamidbar* serves as an introduction to our entering the land, where the Temple will eventually be built.

The prophet Shmuel died on the 28th Iyar, as recorded in the *Tur*. If we look at his career closely, we see that he was instrumental in fulfilling each of the three mitzvot that become incumbent upon us when we enter the land: fighting Amalek, appointing a king, and building the *Beit Hamikdash*. Shmuel was responsible for instituting the monarchy in Israel, anointing both Shaul and David as kings. He personally executed the Amalekite king Agag when Shaul failed in this duty. And it is recorded in *Zevachim 54b* (see Rashi) that he worked together with King David to determine the exact location of the Temple. According to *Sefer HaChezyonot*, Shmuel has been in continuous mourning since the Temple was destroyed. He truly deserves to be remembered as one of the greatest prophets and leaders who fought to establish and strengthen our connection with the Land of Israel and the Temple.

As we know, Jerusalem, or more specifically Mount Moriah, the Temple Mount, was the place from where the world was created and the place where humanity began. It is also the place where Avraham bound Yitzchak to the altar and where Yaakov dreamed of the ladder to Heaven where angels ascend and descend. It is truly the nexus where Heaven and earth meet, where our prayers and offerings ascend upward, and from where divine blessing and inspiration, both spiritual and material, descend to us. There, in the Temple, stood the Holy of Holies, where once a year, on Yom Kippur, the holiest day of the year, the High Priest, the holiest person in the world, entered the holiest space. This was a perfect fulfillment of the concept found in *Sefer Yetzirah*, of *Ashan, olam shana nefesh*, space, time and person, as these three elements came together.

The name *Yerushalayim* signifies two things, *yirah*, awe, and *shalem*, completeness. Isaiah refers to the city as the *kiryah nee-manah*, the city of faith. We therefore see that Jerusalem is a multifaceted center of religious ideals, to which David added the concept of monarchy, when he moved the capital city from Hebron to Yerushalayim. *Chazal* also teach us that Yerushalayim received nine tenths of the world's beauty. Another name for Jerusalem is *Zion*, which has the same grammatical equivalent as *Yosef*, whose physical beauty was actually an external manifestation of his inner holiness and purity, the ultimate beauty.

On the 28th Iyar, just over one hundred years ago, Rav Kook *zt"l*, arrived in *Eretz Yisrael*. On the 28th Iyar 5727/1967, we merited the liberation of Jerusalem, including the Temple Mount, followed by Hebron, Gush Etzion, and Bethlehem the next day. This is another connection with *Sefer Bamidbar*, the book "of those who enter the land," just as our generation has actually done.

Rav Neria, *zt"l*, was quoted as saying that Jerusalem could not be captured in 1948 because there were many different Jewish military groups. The city of completeness and unity needed to wait another 19 years until it could be redeemed from enemy hands by the IDF, a united force representing all of the Jewish People. Similar to Shavuot, in which *Matan Torah* was dependent upon our being "as one person with one heart," *Yom Yerushalayim* is also dependent upon our unity as a people. Only a united people can also unite with Hashem, receive Jerusalem, and receive the Torah.

We often ask why the Torah was given in the desert, and not in the Land of Israel. There are many answers, but here is one that is not so well-known. In *Midrash Tehillim* we read that at the time of *Matan Torah,* Mount Moriah was uprooted and came to Mount Sinai. This meant that in actual fact the Torah was given in both places simultaneously, creating another connection between Jerusalem (and Jerusalem Day) and Shavuot.

We hope that we will soon be granted to witness the fulfillment of the Ramban's interpretation of *Bamidbar*, the service of the Kohanim in the Temple. This would bring comfort to Shmuel and fulfillment of the vision of Rav Kook. May we be witness to Jerusalem's continued growth and spiritual strengthening. Just as *Am Yisrael* reaccepted the Torah after the miracle of Purim, we should also reaccept the Torah with love and joy on Shavuot.

Thanks to Rav Eliyahu Yedid for several sources on Jerusalem from his book, Mikra Kodesh.

SHAVUOT

The Choicest Holiday

Shavuot is, according to Rav Leibele Eiger, *Muvchar Hamoadim*, the "choicest holiday," so intense that it lasts for only one day, similar to Yom Kippur. Rav Leibele sees it as part of a set that includes *Shabbat Bereishit*, focusing on God the Influencer, Yom Kippur, centered upon humanity the receiver, and Shavuot, highlighting the Torah, intermediary between God and man. Shavuot and Yom Kippur are also unique among the holidays in that they deal with the present, not the past. For this reason, the Torah does not record a date for the giving of the Torah at Mount Sinai.

The *Netivot Shalom* quotes Rav Chaim Vital's statement that one's entire life is dependent upon the night of Shavuot. This night is so powerful that some of the Rebbes were unable to recite Torah, stating that, "The Torah from last year has been completed and the Torah of this year has yet to be revealed." For the *Netivot Shalom* the main *avodah* of the night of Shavuot is *bittul*, self-annulment, to Hashem and to the Jewish People.

In *Derech Hamelech*, the Piaseczner Rebbe agrees that the whole year is dependent upon this special night. The goal is to enable the holiness of this night to spread into the year with no interruption. We need to absorb some of the prophecy regarding Torah and the mitzvot and take it with us into the year. At Mount Sinai we all "saw voices." The Rebbe writes in *Aish Kodesh* that God teaches Torah to the Jewish People. When He taught us the Torah at Mount Sinai, it was the *Chumash*, the written Torah that is not to be spoken out loud without a written text. We were therefore shown the letters that we heard, floating through the sky, in order to provide a written backup for Hashem's oral teachings. As we know, the Rebbe places great emphasis upon the role of the community in Chassidic life. At *Matan Torah* we were "as one person with one heart." In order to receive the Torah on Shavuot we need to reaffirm our *bittul* to *Klal Yisrael*, as stated above by the *Netivot Shalom*. While prophecy is a highly individual spiritual experience, for the Jewish People its main application is in the communal setting. May we merit, as individuals and as a community, to reaccept the Torah as deeply as possible, taking the experience with us throughout the entire year.

SHABBAT CHAZON

Hearing God's Tears

Shabbat Chazon (the Shabbat of Vision), the Shabbat before Tisha B'Av, is a strange mixture of mourning and hope. One example of this is a dispute between various authorities regarding what clothes to wear on this day. According to the Rema, the mourning of the Nine Days outweighs the usual laws of honoring Shabbat and we should wear our regular weekday clothes. The Vilna Gaon disagrees, for the honor of Shabbat overrides mourning, and he requires us to change into our special Shabbat clothing. This latter opinion is the accepted *minhag*.

The Gemara in *Chagigah* 5b describes how, just as a king can only cry in his innermost chamber so as not to be seen, this is also the case with Hashem. We see a world of suffering and don't understand how it is that Hashem is not crying; yet in actual fact He is weeping with us. In the Warsaw Ghetto, the *Aish Kodesh* explained how the world could continue to exist despite the endless cries of Jewish children in the Holocaust. The reason he gives is that if God's cries were heard the world would revert to primordial chaos. Hashem therefore hides His tears, so as not to destroy the world. According to the Maharal in *Netzach Yisrael*, the outer room is our body and the inner room our soul. Our body is not aware of the destruction of the Temple, for physical life goes on. Our soul, however, hears the Divine weeping because it is acutely aware of all that has been lost.

The Kozhnitzer Maggid writes in *Avodat Yisrael* that we read *Parshat Devarim* at this time to remind us that, "even when we traveled from place to place Hashem was always with us, and even when we are *Bein Hametzarim* … God never abandons His people." In the *Tikkunei Zohar* the destruction and exile are compared to the unraveling of a family in which the angry father sends away his wife and children. Eventually, filled with loneliness and longing, he goes into self-imposed exile to seek his loved ones. The reconstitution of this cosmic family is the process of

336

rectification and redemption. A similar idea is expressed in Rebbe Nachman's beautiful story, *The Master of Prayer*.

Rav Levi Yitzchak of Berditchev writes that the Shabbat before Tisha B'Av is called *Shabbat Chazon* because on this day every Jew is shown a vision of the Third Temple. Perhaps we can only be conscious of this vision if we first train ourselves to hear the weeping of the Divine. And we will only hear the crying of the Divine if we first hear the weeping of our own souls. By crying together with God, we can help to reassemble the unraveled cosmic family, for all of us are Hashem's children. Only then will we be worthy not only of the vision of redemption, but to actually enter the Third Temple, the nexus of our connection with Hashem.

SHABBAT CHAZON

The Greatest Shabbat of the Year

Very often, Tisha B'Av either begins on *motzaei Shabbat Chazon* or falls on Shabbat itself, when the fast is delayed until Saturday night and is observed essentially in the same manner. Regarding this latter situation, the Apter Rav writes that *Shabbat Chazon* is the greatest Shabbat of the year, especially when it is coincides with Tisha B'Av.

The *Shulchan Aruch* codifies that when Tisha B'Av is observed on Saturday night there is no *seudah mafseket*, the mournful pre-fast meal. Instead, one eats meat and drinks wine ... and brings to the table as much food as King Solomon did. (The *Mishnah Berurah* points out here that there is no obligation to eat meat on Shabbat, but that is a different topic.) The Rema adds that, unlike other Shabbatot, we must end *seudah shlishit* before sunset, which is certainly the normative practice. However, the *Shaar Yissaschar* states that "the righteous students of the Baal Shem Tov continue this meal into the night like other Shabbatot," which does make sense in light of the sanctity of Shabbat. At the same time, there is a dispute about inviting friends to this meal. While the *Magen Avraham* calls for a somber meal without friends, others view this as public mourning that is prohibited on Shabbat, and encourage us to follow our regular *seudah shlishit* customs.

The Shabbat after Tisha B'Av is *Shabbat Nachamu*, the Shabbat of Comfort. In the last *drasha* in *Aish Kodesh*, the Piaseczner Rebbe states that, on the one hand, *Shabbat Chazon*, the Shabbat of Vision, which precedes Tisha B'Av, is so named due to the horrors of the **vision** of destruction. But perhaps even *Shabbat Chazon* can be comforting. The *Kedushat Levi* states that on *Shabbat Chazon* we are all shown a vision of the future Temple that, if we are meritorious, will be rebuilt speedily in our days. At the moment of the destruction, the *Kruvim* in the *Holy of Holies* were embracing, indicating the deep love between Hashem and the Jewish People even at the darkest moment. This foreshadows the

joy of Tu B'Av, when marriages, the microcosm of our relationship with God, are celebrated. Nothing is more comforting than a
holy *simcha*! On Tisha B'Av, even while we are mourning, we
should remain cognizant of the envelopment of Tisha B'Av
between *Shabbat Chazon* and *Shabbat Nachamu*. With this in mind,
we should seek comfort from Hashem.

SHABBAT CHAZON

A Divine Embrace Amid the Flames

According to *Midrash Bereishit Rabbah* 2:4, the verses of Creation hint to the future subjugation of *Am Yisrael* by the nations: "... Darkness is the Greek exile ... the face of the depths is the darkness of the evil kingdom (Rome) ... and the wind ... this is the spirit of *Mashiach*." Paradoxically, the light of *Mashiach* and *Geulah* shine forth from the depths of darkness and exile.

Chazal also tell us (*Yoma* 54b) that when the Roman general Titus burst into the *Kodesh Hakedoshim* while the *Beit Hamikdash* was being destroyed, the two *Kruvim* (Cherubim) on the Holy Ark were embracing each other. The Ritva, citing the Ri Migash, asks the following question: The Gemara, in *Baba Batra* 99a, states that the *Kruvim* served as an indicator of *Am Yisrael's* relationship with Hashem. If we fulfilled Hashem's will, they faced each other, and if not, they faced apart. Amazingly, at the moment the *Beit Hamikdash* was burning, the ultimate punishment for our sins, the *Kruvim* were not only facing each other, but they were actively embracing! Yet how could this be?

The Shabbat before Tisha B'Av is referred to as *Shabbat Chazon*, the Shabbat of Vision, after the beginning of the haftarah for *Parshat Devarim*, which is taken from Isaiah. Rav Tzaddok Hakohen (*Pri Tzaddik, Devarim* 13) asks why, and quotes a famous *midrash* on the Book of *Eichah*. According to this *midrash*, on Tisha B'Av, after the *Churban*, *Mashiach* is born. This is brought about through the merit of the *teshuvah* that *Am Yisrael* did (which unfortunately came too late) in response to the destruction. For this reason, the *Kruvim* were hugging each other, because at this moment of *teshuvah*, *Am Yisrael* were transformed from sinners into tzaddikim, doing the will of Hashem.

Rav Zvi Elimelech of Dinov, in *Bnei Yissaschar: Av* 3:1, quotes the Mezeritcher Maggid's startling response to the same question about the *Kruvim* hugging each other: "A man is obligated to be with his wife before departing upon a journey." This concept is also discussed in the laws of *Taharat Hamishpachah* (the laws of family purity). Since a couple, before an impending separation, feels great love and yearning for each other, there is a special obligation of *mitzvat onah*, marital relations. Here as well, as *Am Yisrael* and *Hashem* prepare to be separated by the journey of the exile, intense emotions of yearning and love overcome the prior negativity in their relationship, enabling the *Kruvim* to embrace amidst the flames of the *Churban*.

The Lubavitcher Rebbe explained this concept in *Likkutei Sichot*. In *chitzoniut* (external reality), we see flames, destruction, death, and exile. However, in *pnimiut* (internal reality), *galut* is no less than the first stage of the next *geulah*. Every step towards exile is actually one step closer to returning, bringing us one day closer to *Mashiach* and the Third Temple! This ultimately true inner reality is only really evident in the world's most "inner" place, inside the *Kodesh Hakedoshim*. Here, the *Kruvim* are embracing.

Tisha B'Av is the day of the most powerful expression of the yearning, longing, and desire between *Am Yisrael* and Hashem. Such love and passion is aroused, states the *Bnai Yissachar*, that it facilitates the birth of *Mashiach*, the world's "highest" soul. Only from the depths of destruction can there arrive a yearning that is powerful enough to lead us to full redemption.

This is a manifestation of the well-known Chassidic concept (very prevalent in Breslov Chassidut) of *Yeridah Tachlit Aliyah*, "in the very descent, ascent is already manifest." An important rule in each of our personal lives, this concept teaches us that *churban* and *galut* contain the sparks of *teshuvah* and *ahavat Hashem*, paving the way for *geulah* and *Mashiach*.

Why is this Shabbat called *Shabbat Chazon*? The *Pri Tzaddik* answers that since each Shabbat includes within it the *kedushah* of the following week, (a rule he employs frequently), this Shabbat therefore contains within it the vision of Tisha B'Av's future status as a *moed*, the holiday of redemption, which it is now only in potential. We hope that the vision that we experience on this Shabbat will become actualized speedily in our days, as the overriding experience of the holiday of Tisha B'Av that we all yearn and pray for.

TISHA B'AV

Should We Still Fast?

The question is often raised as to whether we need to continue to fast every year on Tisha B'Av and the other fast days. After all, these days were instituted in response to the destruction of the First and Second Temples, and the subsequent exiles. While it is true that the Third Temple has yet to be built, we have nonetheless been witness to the miraculous establishment of the State of Israel, and the Ingathering of the Exiles. Despite various setbacks, we have also seen tremendous progress in many areas of endeavor, including the tremendous growth of yeshiva learning and religious creativity that has taken place in the State of Israel. At what stage can we conclude that the Exile is indeed over, and that we no longer should have to torment ourselves with fasting?

Actually, this question is an ancient one, and it was first asked in a period somewhat parallel to our own. When the Jews began to return from the Babylonian exile, after the first destruction, they found themselves in *Eretz Yisrael*, seeming to reverse the process of destruction and exile. True, the Second Temple had not yet been rebuilt, but that was just a matter of time. How should they respond to their dramatic new situation? They addressed this question to the Prophet Zechariah, who in turned asked Hashem Himself. In Chapter Seven we read:

"In the fourth year of King Darius ... the word of the Lord came to Zechariah ... to address this inquiry ... 'Shall I weep and practice abstinence in the fifth month (Av – a reference to Tisha B'Av) as I have been doing all these years?' Thereupon the word of the Lord of Hosts came to me: 'When you fasted and lamented in the fifth and seventh (*Tishrei*, a reference to *Tzom Gedalia*) all these seventy years, did you fast for My benefit? And when you eat and drink, who but you does the eating, and who but you does the drinking?' Look, this is the message that the Lord proclaimed through the earlier prophets, when Jerusalem and the towns about her were populated and tranquil, when the Negev and the Plain were peopled."

The "answer" finally comes in Chapter Eight:

"And the word of the Lord of Hosts came to me saying ... The fast of the fourth month (The 17th Tammuz[10]), the fast of the fifth month, the fast of the seventh month, and the fast of the tenth month (*Asarah beTevet*) shall become occasions for joy and gladness, happy festivals for the House of Judah; but you must love truth and peace."

In other words, the answer is that someday the fasts will not only be cancelled, they will in fact become holidays. But when exactly that will come to be is not clear. And in the meantime, to fast or not to fast ... the answer is also not too clear. What we have are veiled references to the people's own fasting, to the earlier prophets, and to the importance of truth and peace. What we don't seem to have is an answer to our question.

The Gemara (*Rosh Hashanah* 18b) analyzes these verses: "These days are called fasts, but they are also called days of joy and gladness! When there is peace they are for joy and gladness, when not, they are fasts." The Gemara then arrives at the conclusion that not every situation is black or white; there are also gray areas: "When there is peace, they are for joy and gladness, when there is government persecution they are fasts, when there is neither government persecution nor peace, if [the Jews] desire they should fast, and if not, they should not fast." In other words, there are three situations. The optimal one of peace transforms the fasts into holidays, while times of persecution require continued fasting. The gray areas, times which are hard to define, leave the decision in the hands of the Jewish People. (It is important to

---

[10] Initially held on the Ninth of Tammuz following the destruction of the First Temple, it was changed to the seventeenth after the second destruction.

realize that this is a community decision, and not an individual one.)

The medieval commentators offer several interpretations of these various stages. The Ritva explains that they refer to the following realities:

Peace: We live in *Eretz Yisrael*, and the Temple has been built. The fasts are holidays.

Persecution: We are persecuted by other nations (i.e. we are not in *Eretz Yisrael*), and the Temple is destroyed. The fasts are obligatory fasts.

Neither Peace nor Persecution: We are not being persecuted, and are in *Eretz Yisrael*, but we don't have the Temple. The community is to decide.

The third category would seem to be parallel to our current reality. We live in *Eretz Yisrael* (and unlike those in the time of Zechariah, we have independence), but we do not yet have the Temple. To fast or not to fast … it's up to us!

By what criteria should we make such a weighty decision? I suggest we go back to the words of Zechariah for the answer. The medieval commentators (Rashi, Ibn Ezra, and Radak) all explain the answer in the following way: After the First Temple was destroyed, the Jewish People decided collectively to mark the event with a series of fast days. Upon returning from the Babylonian exile they asked Hashem if they should continue to fast. The answer, these commentators explain, is the following. God states simply, "I am the wrong address for the question!" For God never commanded the people to fast! (The only Torah-commanded fast day is Yom Kippur, which is entirely different). What did Hashem command? Well, the earlier Prophets, such as Yeshayahu, Yirmiyahu, and Amos, had preached against the evils prevalent during the first Temple period: idolatry, violence, immorality, and social injustice, especially the oppression of the poor and weak in society. These evils, as well as the violations of religious ritual, such as that of Shabbat, led to the destruction of the Temple. In the Second Temple period, these transgressions were largely replaced by a different evil – *sinat chinam*, baseless hatred between Jews.

Zechariah sums it up pretty clearly: we should love truth and peace. Then, and only then, can the fast days turn into holidays. For, as the *Mishnah Berurah* points out, fasting is meant as a vehicle for *teshuvah*. The fast in itself is an empty external act if it does not prompt sincere internal repentance as well. For this reason, Hashem tells the people very clearly, "don't ask me about fasting, for I don't really care if you fast or not! I do however care if you repent those sins that led to the destruction! If the fasting helps, fine, and if not, not, but it is not the main issue. That was your decision, and you will have to decide whether or not you are ready to stop!"

When we look at our society today and ask if we can stop fasting, we need to be honest with ourselves. Have we truly corrected all of the evils that led to the destruction and to the exile? Any honest person would have to say no. We are a society that is still torn by polarization and hatred. A huge percentage of Israel's population lives below the poverty line. To our shame, this country is apparently a "superpower" when it comes to "white slavery" and the exploitation of women, including young girls, for financial gain. We face growing amounts of domestic violence and child abuse. And our observance of Shabbat could use a lot of improvement as well.

In such a situation, we cannot honestly think that we "have made it." We have a long way to go to create the kind of just society that the Prophets demanded, and that is a precondition for the Shechinah to dwell in our midst. The purpose of a fast is to inspire us to do *teshuvah*. If we therefore all make a personal effort to do our best in *Mitzvot Bein Adam Lechaveiro* (interpersonal relations) and try to help the "Other," especially the poor and weak in out society, then with God's help we will merit not only to choose not to fast, but in fact celebrate Tisha B'Av as a joyous holiday.

TISHA B'AV

A Temple Visualization

(Note: This is a visualization meditation on the Temple, to make the idea of the Holy Temple and its destruction more real to the reader.)

You are walking through Jerusalem's Old City on Shavuot with your family, heading for the *Beit Hamikdash*. You are taking part in *Aliyah Laregel*, a pilgrimage to the Temple. As you get closer to the Temple Mount, more and more people appear, coming from all directions. There becomes a veritable stream, and then a great river of people, including all sorts of Jews from all over Israel, and even some from abroad. Here and there are also gentiles, on their way to witness the great holiness. You get closer and closer, finally going up one of the ramps, and through one of the gates. The beauty and splendor of the *Mikdash* are overwhelming. It is the most majestic place in the world, and the presence of the Shechinah is palpable. Thousands, tens of thousands of Jews davening to Hashem, now inside the courtyard, surround you. The Kohanim are doing the *Avodah*, the Temple Service, and the Levi'im are singing *Shir Hamaalot*, the songs of ascent. All would appear to be perfect.

Yet, deep inside you know that all is not well. There are too many divisions, too much factionalism, and even violence within the Jewish nation. *Am Yisrael* is divided into groups, each claiming that they follow the only true path to serving God. Even you sometimes catch yourself hating those with whom you differ. But why? After all, they are your fellow Jews, and they also believe in the Torah, keep the mitzvot, and serve Hashem. They are different, just different, that's all. If things continue this way, what will happen? Where is it all leading? It can't be a good thing...

After months of siege, you are tired, hungry, and depressed. Will it ever end? Will the Romans leave? Will we ever stop fighting among ourselves? The Roman battering rams and catapults incessantly bang and crash, and your head feels like it will explode from the noise. And then, Roman soldiers are actually in the city. They kill and destroy everything in their wake. You watch from the small window of your hiding place, terrified. Death is everywhere. Corpses litter the streets. The stench is overpowering.

Tisha B'Av arrives. You are well aware of its history. On this day, the Spies and *Am Yisrael* cried for no reason, disdaining *Eretz Yisrael*. On this day, some 600 years ago, Nebuchadnezzar destroyed the First Temple, and the Jews were exiled to Babylonia. What does this day hold in store for us now? Furtive glances toward the Temple Mount tell you that the *Mikdash* still stands. The enemy would surely not dare to touch it!

Toward afternoon, thick smoke fills the air. Glancing from your hidden window your worst fears are confirmed – the Temple is burning! Great flames fill the air and clouds of thick black smoke continue billowing upwards. Now all is truly lost, and you are filled with despair. Hashem must really hate us to allow such a thing to happen – to destroy His own house! Longing for the greatness that was once the *Mikdash*, for the beauty of *Aliyah Laregel*, you are filled with thoughts of *teshuvah*. But it is too late. What good can it do, now that the Temple is in flames?

Before long you are discovered, led outside into the courtyard, and bound with heavy chains. On top of everything else you will be led into exile and sold as a slave to the heathens in Rome. If only we had obeyed Hashem! If only we had loved each other! If only we had not hated! Now all is lost, our land, our Temple, and each other. Worst of all, it seems as though we have lost God Himself, lost the Shechinah! Never has She seemed so utterly remote, so inaccessible! The situation is completely hopeless, not only physically, but also spiritually. All of this is rushing through your brain as the endless march to Rome begins. ...

Although your perspective is limited to what your eyes can perceive, there is another, non-physical reality as well. As you continue the obliviousness of the march, your body aches, and yet paradoxically your mind is free, your *neshamah* is liberated from your body. At this stage you no longer feel your body, and your *neshamah* soars above, viewing that which is hidden to your eyes. Instinctively you fly back to Jerusalem, back to the *Mikdash*. The

347

city is completely devastated – nothing is standing! You fly up to the Temple Mount, and you find that all is in ruins. And yet, as you approach the place where the Temple once stood, your *neshamah* enters a different reality. You glide toward the Holy of Holies, filled with trepidation. There is no doubt that the *kruvim*, representing Hashem and *Am Yisrael*, will be facing away from each other, the final sign that we violated Hashem's will. This will be the final sign that Hashem no longer desires His once-Holy people. That will be the most terrible sight of all, the final confirmation that all is truly lost, that there is no hope.

You now enter through the *Parochet*. And what do you see? The two great *kruvim* still stand on top of the *Aron*, angelic, and yet human. One, in the form of a man, symbolizes Hashem. The other, a woman, symbolizes *Am Yisrael*, symbolizes you. They are not facing apart. They are facing each other. And yet, there are not only facing each other, they are touching each other. Filled with love, they caress each other; they embrace each other. Hashem and *Am Yisrael* still love each other. They desire and yearn for each other. You love Hashem, and you know, you actually feel, that Hashem loves you as well. You are now filled with warmth, with a feeling of contentment and well-being as you watch the sensuous embrace of the *kruvim*. Slowly, you make your way forward to the female *kruv*, to the *kruv* of *Am Yisrael*. You are part of that *kruv*, and you enter Her reality, you merge with Her. You are no longer watching the embrace; you are part of it. You can feel Hashem's actual presence that surrounds you, and feel His breath. Your *neshamah* is part of His breath. Your individuality melts away as you are subsumed in the Divine Presence. Hashem loves you. You feel His love enveloping you, protecting you. This is the true peace you have yearned for all your life. Now you can let go. Let go of all the hatred. Let go of all jealousy and competition. Let go of all the physical desires. There is only Hashem.

SHABBAT NACHAMU

Tu B'Av

The fast of Tisha B'Av is illuminated by the sparks of future redemption. It is therefore referred to in *Eichah* as a *moed*, a festival, and on that day *Tachanun* is not recited. In a similar vein, the *Sfat Emet* quotes the Ari, that when Aharon Hakohen made the Golden Calf and told the people *Chag Lashem Machar* (17th Tammuz), he was hinting at the verse in *Zechariah* that all the fast days will eventually be transformed into holidays. In the words of the Lubavitcher Rebbe (*Likkutei Sichot, Pinchas* 5749), "Not only are the *Bein Hameitzarim* and the exile for the purpose of going up, but the inner quality and truth of these days are the most exalted good ... therefore speedily in the future these days will be transformed into days of rejoicing ... since internally they are already days of the greatest love."

One obvious aspect of this process is the holiday of Tu B'Av. In the *Mishnah*, in *Taanit* 4:8 we find:

"Rabban Shimon ben Gamliel said, 'There were no holidays for Israel as the 15th Av and as Yom Kippur, for on them the daughters of Jerusalem go forth in borrowed white garments, so as not to embarrass whoever does not have; all the garments require immersion. And the daughters of Jerusalem go forth and dance in the vineyards. And what would they say? 'Young man, lift up your eyes and see, what you choose for yourself. Do not set your eyes on beauty, set your eyes on the family: 'Grace is deceitful, and beauty is vain, but a woman that fears the Lord, she shall be praised' (*Mishlei* 31:30), and it says, 'Give her the fruit of her hands, and let her works praise her in the gates' (*ibid*, v. 31)." And similarly it says, "Go forth, O you daughters of Zion, and gaze upon King Solomon, even upon the crown with which his mother has crowned him on his wedding day, and on the day of the gladness of his heart" (*Shir Hashirim* 3:11). "His wedding day" is the giving of the Torah, 'on the day of the gladness of his heart" is the building of the Temple, may it be built speedily in our days. Amen."

The Bartenura explains that on Tu B'Av those who had been decreed to die in the desert wanderings ceased dying, and those who were killed in the Roman conquest of Beitar were permitted to be buried. Both of these are clear rectifications of the sufferings that began on Tisha B'Av. From other sources, we know of other happy events on Tu B'Av. Several have to do with marriage, such as the decision to allow for intermarriage among the Twelve Tribes, and the decision to intermarry with the tribe of Binyamin after the incident of the *pilegish bagivah*. It is important that we bear in mind that every marriage is a microcosm of the relationship between Hashem and *Am Yisrael*.

The end of the *mishnah* speaks of two days: that of the wedding, which is the giving of the Torah, and that of the building of the Temple, ending with a prayer for its speedy rebuilding. On the simple level, we would have expected the giving of the Torah to be associated with Shavuot, leaving open the identification of the day of building the Temple. Alternatively, from a literary perspective, since the *mishnah* begins and ends with two days, it would be a very "neat" parallelism if it were referring both times to the same two days. Bartenura comments: "The day of giving the Torah: Yom Kippur, when the second tablets were given. Building the Temple: which was dedicated on *Yom Hakippurim*."

Rav Tzaddok Hakohen, in *Pri Tzaddik*, *Tu B'Av* 2, asks the following questions regarding the Bartenura's approach:

There is no parallel between the beginning and end of the *mishnah*. It begins with Tu B'Av and Yom Kippur, but ends with Yom Kippur. Why does Tu'B'Av disappear?

If the end of the *mishnah* is not parallel to the beginning, why not give the more obvious explanation for the day of giving the Torah - Shavuot?

Why is Yom Kippur identified as the day of building the Temple? This question already troubled the *Tosafot Yom Tov*. While Yom Kippur did fall out during the dedication week of the First Temple, this hardly qualifies it to be called *the* day of the building of the Temple."

If the end of the *mishnah* is referring only to the First Temple then the last lines appear to be no more than a vague prayer, lacking an intrinsic connection to the previous sentence.

Rav Tzaddok therefore offers an alternative interpretation of the *Mishnah*. Yom Kippur, not Shavuot, is the "real" day of *Matan Torah*. Since the First Tablets were broken, the first *Matan Torah* was in a sense annulled, or at least suspended. The *Matan Torah* that became permanent was the giving of the Second Tablets, which took place on Yom Kippur. Additionally, based on an inference in the *Midrash Pesikta*, Rav Tzaddok concludes that the Third Temple will be built on Tu B'Av. This is of course what we daven for at the end of the *mishnah*.

Thus, both Yom Kippur and Tu B'Av are symbolic of the "marriage" between *Am Yisrael* and Hashem. Yom Kippur, with the added dimension of the lasting *Matan Torah*, is the day in which the relationship is experienced in its most acutely intense form. Tu B'Av is the day on which the Third Temple will be built, because the Temple is the spatial nexus of this relationship. In the *Kodesh Hakedoshim*, known by *Chazal* as the *Cheder Hamittot*, the *Kruvim* serve to indicate the intense love and yearning between Hashem and His bride, the Jewish People. Thus, according to Rav Tzaddok's interpretation, all the questions are answered and a clear literary parallelism is maintained from the beginning of the *mishnah* until its end.

It is interesting to note, that previously in *Mishnah* 6, we find a discussion of the various tribulations that befell *Am Yisrael* on the 17th Tammuz, beginning with the breaking of the first Tablets, and of Tisha B'Av, culminating with the destruction of the Temples and the conquest of Beitar. Thus by viewing both *mishnayot* as a unified whole we are able to uncover a chiastic structure, since we have learned that Yom Kippur rectifies the 17th Tammuz, while Tisha B'Av is fixed on Tu B'Av, when the people of the desert cease dying, and the dead of Beitar could finally be buried:

A. 17th Tammuz (breaking of first Tablets)

B. Tisha B'Av (decree of death in the wilderness and conquest of Beitar)

B. 15th Av (end of death in the wilderness and burial
of the dead of Beitar)
A. Yom Kippur (Giving of the Second Tablets)

The *Kedushat Levi* writes that on *Shabbat Chazon*, every Jew is
shown a vision of the Third Temple. May Hashem comfort us on
Shabbat Nachamu with the fulfillment of that vision.

SHABBAT NACHAMU

Prayer and Hope

According to the Midrash, Moshe Rabbeinu prayed 515 times to be allowed to enter *Eretz Yisrael*. Rav Tzaddok Hakohen (*Pri Tzaddik* 3) states that we always read *Parshat Va'etchanan* on *Shabbat Nachamu* "in order to strengthen the souls of Israel who yearn for the redemption. They should not despair of Hashem's mercy!" One might, however, ask how this could be the case as in spite of his fervent prayers Moshe was still not permitted to enter the Land, to which Rav Tzaddok responds, "Because of the yearning that was expressed through his prayers, Moshe reached the spiritual reality of being in Israel even more than if he had physically entered."

We don't always see the "results" of our prayers, but they always accomplish a positive effect. We need to do our job, which is to daven, and let Hashem do His job of responding. Rav Tzaddok completes his words with the encouragement that also our prayers for the building of Jerusalem are working, even though we don't see the results, (although we could say that today we do see the results!).

Rebbe Nachman is quoted in *Likkutei Eitzot* as saying that we have no idea what impact our prayers actually have in Heaven. It sometimes just takes a long time to "complete the mission." The main thing is not to despair, but to keep davening.

In general, it is important to remember that prayer is not meant to be a "cash machine." The *Pachad Yitzchak* gives the allegory of two people who both requested something in their prayers, but neither received what they had requested. The first person responded, "No one is listening to me," while the second said, "When they hear my prayers, they turn away from me." While these two statements may sound similar, the *Pachad Yitzchak* states that the second, who acknowledges that his prayers have been heard (although seemingly rejected) is more of a "master of prayer" than the first, who imagines that his prayers are not even heard. "The feeling of closeness to God in a 'non-answered' prayer is no less than the feeling of closeness to God in an 'answered' prayer," concludes the *Pachad Yitzchak*.

We should therefore never give up hope when we pray, but should hope that in addition to seeing the results of our supplications; we will also experience prayers of feeling close to God. There is no greater comfort.

Printed in the United States
83211LV00003B/25-66/A